Android™ Tablets

FOR

DUMMIES®

A Wiley Brand

2nd Edition

by Dan Gookin

FOR

DUMMIES®

A Wiley Brand

Android™ Tablets For Dummies® 2nd Edition

Published by
John Wiley & Sons, Inc.
111 River Street
Hoboken, NJ 07030-5774

www.wiley.com

Contents at a Glance

Table of Contents

Introduction

. . . .

Somewhere filling the void between the smartphone and the computer lies the premiere device of the 21st century. It's probably something you've never used but will soon be unable to live without. It's the tablet — specifically, an Android tablet.

The Android tablet is a gizmo that could fully replace your computer, as well as several other pieces of electronics you may tote around. It's an all-in-one, lightweight, battery-powered, long-lasting, fully mobile, telecommunications, information, and entertainment gizmo.

Oh, but I do go on.

As an Android tablet owner, or someone who's interested in purchasing such a device, you obviously want to get the most from your technology. Perhaps you've attempted to educate yourself using that flimsy *Getting Started* leaflet that comes with the thing. Now you're turning to this book, a wise choice.

New technology can be intimidating. Frustrating. No matter what, your experience can be made better by leisurely reading this delightful, informative, and occasionally entertaining book.

About This Book

Please don't read this book from cover to cover. This book is a reference. It's designed to be used as you need it. Look up a topic in the table of contents or the index. Find something about your tablet that vexes you or something you're curious about. Look up the answer, and get on with your life.

The overall idea for this book is to show how things are done on the Android tablet and to help you enjoy the device without overwhelming you with information or intimidating you into despair.

Sample sections in this book include

- Locking the tablet
- Activating voice input
- Importing contacts from a computer
- Setting up an Email account
- Running Facebook on your tablet

> ✔ Talking and video chat
>
> ✔ Placing a Skype phone call
>
> ✔ Helping others find your location
>
> ✔ Flying with an Android tablet

You have nothing to memorize, no sacred utterances or animal sacrifices, and definitely no PowerPoint presentations. Instead, every section explains a topic as though it's the first thing you've read in this book. Nothing is assumed, and everything is cross-referenced. Technical terms and topics, when they come up, are neatly shoved to the side, where they're easily avoided. The idea here isn't to learn anything. My philosophy while writing this book was to help you look it up, figure it out, and get on with your life.

How to Use This Book

This book follows a few conventions for using an Android tablet. First of all, no matter what name your tablet has, whether it's a manufacturer's name or some cute name you've devised on your own, this book refers to your tablet as an *Android tablet* or, often, just *tablet.*

The way you interact with the Android tablet is by using its *touchscreen* — the glassy part of the device as it's facing you. The device also has some physical buttons, as well as some holes and connectors. All these items are described in Chapter 1.

The various ways to touch the screen are explained and named in Chapter 3.

Chapter 4 discusses text input on an Android tablet, which involves using an onscreen keyboard. You can also input text by speaking to the Android tablet, which is also covered in Chapter 4.

This book directs you to do things by following numbered steps. Each step involves a specific activity, such as touching something on the screen; for example:

>   **3. Touch the Apps icon.**

This step directs you to touch the graphical Apps icon on the screen. When a button is shown as text, the command reads:

>   **3. Touch the Download button.**

You might also be directed to *choose* an item, which means to touch it on the screen.

Various settings can be turned off or on, as indicated by a box with a mark in it, similar to the one shown in the margin. By touching the box on the screen, you add or remove the check mark. When the check mark appears, the option is on; otherwise, it's off.

Some settings feature a master control, which looks like an On–Off switch, as shown in the margin. Slide the button to the right to activate the switch, turning on a tablet feature. Slide the button to the left to disable the feature. Some tablets don't label the master control with the text *ON* or *OFF;* the control may change color instead.

Foolish Assumptions

Even though this book is written with the gentle handholding required by anyone who is just starting out, or who is easily intimidated, I've made a few assumptions. For example, I assume that you're a human being and not a colony creature from the planet Zontar.

My biggest assumption: You have an Android tablet — one that uses the Android operating system that's distributed by Google. Your tablet might be a cellular tablet (one that uses the mobile data network) or a Wi-Fi–only model. This book covers both.

Like Windows, Android has versions. The Android versions covered in this book include Kit Kat and Jelly Bean, which are also known by the famous numbers 4.4 and 4.3, respectively. You can confirm which Android version your tablet has by following these steps:

1. **At the Home screen, touch the Apps icon.**

   Refer to Chapter 3 for a description of the Apps icon.

2. **Open the Settings app.**

3. **Choose About Tablet.**

   This item might be named About Device. You might find this item by first touching the General tab atop the screen.

4. **Look at the item titled Android Version.**

   The number that's shown indicates the Android operating system version.

Don't fret if these steps confuse you: Review Part I of this book, and then come back here. (I'll wait.)

More assumptions:

You don't need to own a computer to use your Android tablet. If you have a computer, great. The Android tablet works well with both PC and Mac. When directions are specific to a PC or Mac, the book says so.

Programs that run on your Android tablet are *apps*, which is short for *applications*. A single program is an app.

Finally, this book assumes that you have a Google account, but if you don't, Chapter 2 explains how to configure one. Do so. Having a Google account opens up a slew of useful features, information, and programs that make using your tablet more productive.

How This Book Is Organized

This book is divided into five parts, each of which covers a certain aspect of the Android tablet or how it's used.

Part I: The Android Tablet Thing

Part I covers setup and orientation, to familiarize you with how the device works. It's a good place to start if you're new to the concept of tablet computing, mobile devices, or the Android operating system.

Part II: Stay in Touch

In Part II, you can read about various ways that an Android tablet can electronically communicate with your online friends. There's texting, e-mail, the web, social networking, and even the desired trick of using the non-phone Android tablet to make phone calls and do video chat.

Part III: Omni Tablet

The Android tablet is pretty much a limitless gizmo. To prove it, the chapters in Part III cover all the various and wonderful things the tablet does: It's an e-book reader, a map, a navigator, a photo album, a portable music player, a calendar, a calculator, and, potentially, much more.

Part IV: Nuts and Bolts

Part IV covers a lot of different topics. Up first is how to connect the Android tablet wirelessly to the Internet as well as to other gizmos, such as a Bluetooth printer. There's a chapter on sharing and exchanging files with a computer.

You'll find information on using the tablet elsewhere, even overseas. Then come the customization, maintenance, and troubleshooting chapters.

Part V: The Part of Tens

I wrap things up with the traditional *For Dummies* Part of Tens. Each chapter in this part lists ten items or topics. The chapters include tips, tricks, shortcuts, things to remember, and things not to forget — plus, a smattering of useful apps that no Android tablet should be without.

Icons Used in This Book

 This icon flags useful, helpful tips or shortcuts.

 This icon marks a friendly reminder to do something.

 This icon marks a friendly reminder not to do something.

 This icon alerts you to overly nerdy information and technical discussions of the topic at hand. Reading the information is optional, though it may win you the Daily Double on *Jeopardy!*

Where to Go from Here

Start reading! Observe the table of contents and find something that interests you. Or look up your puzzle in the index. When these suggestions don't cut it, just start reading Chapter 1.

My e-mail address is dgookin@wambooli.com. Yes, that's my real address. I reply to every e-mail I receive, and more quickly when you keep your question short and specific to this book. Although I enjoy saying Hi, I cannot answer technical support questions, resolve billing issues, or help you troubleshoot your tablet. Thanks for understanding.

My website is www.wambooli.com. This book has its own page on that site, which you can check for updates, new information, and all sorts of fun stuff. Visit often:

    www.wambooli.com/help/android/tablets

The publisher also offers its own helpful site, which contains official updates and bonus information. Visit the publisher's official support page at

    www.dummies.com/extras/androidtablets

You can also find this book's online Cheat Sheet at

    www.dummies.com/cheatsheet/androidtablets

Enjoy this book and your Android tablet!

Part I
The Android Tablet Thing

getting started with

Android Tablets

In this part . . .

- ✔ Get things set up on your new Android tablet.
- ✔ Work through activation and initial tablet configuration.
- ✔ Learn how to turn a tablet on and off and how to lock and unlock the screen.
- ✔ Discover the many sensual ways you can manipulate the touchscreen.
- ✔ Use the onscreen keyboard and dictation to create text.

That Out-of-the-Box Experience

In This Chapter

▶ Unboxing the tablet

▶ Charging the battery

▶ Locating important tablet-things

▶ Getting optional accessories

▶ Storing a tablet

*Y*our Android tablet adventure begins by opening the device's box. Sure, you've probably already done that. I don't blame you; I had already opened the box that my Android tablet came in before I read this chapter. No problem. So, to help you recall the ordeal, or to get you oriented if you found the process daunting, or just to prepare you for that out-of-the-box experience yet to come, this chapter provides you with a gentle introduction to your new Android tablet.

Initial Procedures

If you've purchased a cellular tablet, the folks who sold it to you may have already done some configuration before you left the store. That's great because an LTE tablet requires some extra setup before you can use the device. That duty is explained in Chapter 2. For now, all tablet owners — cellular and Wi-Fi — need to perform two basic tablet activities, described in this section.

Liberating the tablet from the box

Thanks to an excess of funds, your federal government has conducted numerous studies on how people use electronic devices. Men and women wearing white lab coats and safety goggles, and wielding clipboards, drew solid conclusions by thoroughly examining hundreds of Android tablets. The results were unanimous: An Android tablet works better when you first remove it from its box. Thank you, federal grant!

I assume that you're pretty good at the box-opening thing, so I probably don't need to detail that procedure. I can affirm, however, that it's perfectly okay to remove and throw away those plastic sheets stuck to the front, back, and sides of the tablet. And don't be embarrassed when, three weeks from now, you find yet another plastic sheet still clinging to the tablet. Remove the plastic sheet. Throw it away.

Along with the tablet, you'll find the following items in the box:

- ✔ **USB cable:** You can use it to connect the tablet to a computer or a wall charger.

- ✔ **Power adapter:** Use this thing (and the USB cable) to charge the tablet. The adapter may come in two pieces, both of which must be assembled.

- ✔ **Power charger and cable:** These are included with some tablets that don't use the USB cable to charge the battery.

- ✔ **Useless pamphlets:** If your tablet is like mine, you'll find that the safety and warranty information is far more extensive than the setup guide. That shows the priority our culture places on lawyers versus technology writers.

- ✔ **The 4G SIM card holder:** For the cellular tablet, you need a 4G SIM card. If you purchased your tablet at a phone store, someone there may have tossed the SIM card holder into the box as well. You can throw it out.

Go ahead and free the USB cable and wall charger from their clear plastic cocoons.

I recommend keeping the box for as long as you own your Android tablet. If you ever need to return the thing, or ship it anywhere, the original box is the ideal container. You can shove all those useless pamphlets and papers back into the box as well.

Charging the battery

The very first thing that I recommend you do with your tablet is give it a full charge. If the tablet comes with its own charging cord, connect the cord to the tablet and plug the cord into the wall. Otherwise, most Android tablets use the USB cable to charge the battery. Obey these steps:

1. **Assemble the power adapter and USB cable.**

   If necessary, assemble the power adapter's two pieces, and then plug the USB cable into the adapter. They snap together only one way.

2. **Plug the adapter into the wall.**

3. **Attach the USB cable to the Android tablet.**

   Look for the tiny connector on the tablet's bottom edge; typically, at the center. The connector might instead be located on the tablet's side.

Upon success, a large "battery charging" type of icon might appear on the Android tablet's touchscreen. This icon lets you know that the tablet is functioning properly — but don't be alarmed if the battery icon fails to appear.

If a Welcome screen or Setup screen appears when you charge the tablet, you can proceed with configuration. That process is covered in Chapter 2.

- Some tablets feature an HDMI connector, which looks similar to the USB or power connector. Don't jam the USB cable into that hole.

- Even if your Android tablet comes fully charged from the factory, I still recommend giving it an initial charge, to at least familiarize yourself with the process.

- The USB cable is also used for connecting the tablet to a computer to share information, exchange files, or use the tablet as a modem. The latter process. called *tethering,* is covered in Chapter 16.

- You can also charge the tablet by connecting it to a computer's USB port. As long as the computer is on, the tablet charges.

- The battery charges more efficiently if you plug it into a wall, as opposed to charging it from a computer's USB port.

- Most Android tablets I've seen don't feature a removable battery, so the battery cannot be replaced if it's defective. If the battery doesn't charge or keep a charge, you should return the tablet for a refund or replacement.

Tablet Exploration

One of the most expensive things to get fixed on a car is the franistan. Ho boy, that busted part can cost thousands of dollars to replace. The high price is due to the fact that there is no such thing as a franistan. It's made up. If you don't know that tidbit, you *will* pay a lot to get your car fixed.

Like an automobile, your tablet lacks a franistan. The way you know this tidbit is by reading this section to discover what is and what isn't part of the standard Android tablet.

Finding things on the tablet

Take heed of Figure 1-1, which is my attempt at illustrating a generic Android tablet's hardware features. Use this figure as a guide as you follow along on your own tablet to locate some key features.

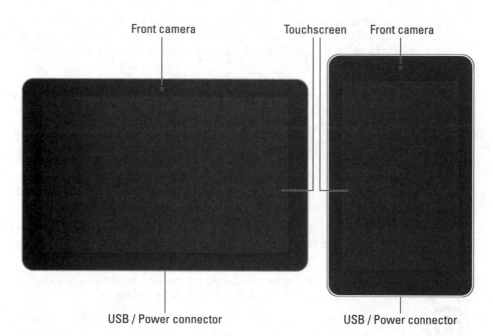

Figure 1-1: Things to find on your Android tablet.

Important items you'll find on the front of the tablet include:

Touchscreen display: The biggest part of the tablet is its touchscreen display, which occupies almost all the territory on the front of the device. The touchscreen display is a look-touch gizmo: You look at it but also touch it with your fingers to control the tablet.

Front camera: The Android tablet's front-facing camera is found above the touchscreen. On larger tablets, the camera is on top when the tablet is oriented horizontally (as shown on the left side of Figure 1-1). On small-format tablets, the camera is on top when the tablet is oriented vertically (as shown on the right side of Figure 1-1).

Light sensor: It's difficult to see, but a teensy light sensor is found near the front camera. The sensor is used to help adjust the brightness level of the touchscreen and probably serves other functions as well, none of which has to do with mind-reading.

Buttons or keys: Some Android tablets feature physical buttons or touch-activated buttons just below the touchscreen. These buttons are labeled with various icons, listed in Chapter 3. You use the buttons for navigation purposes, to control various apps that run on the tablet. (Other tablets display the same or similar buttons as part of the touchscreen display.)

Important items found on the tablet's edges include:

Power/Lock key: The Power/Lock key is labeled with the universal power icon, shown in the margin, although the icon may be difficult to see. Press this key to turn on the tablet, to lock it (put it to sleep), to wake it up, and to turn it off. Directions for performing these activities are found in Chapter 2.

Volume key: The tablet's volume control is two buttons in one. Press one side of the key to set the volume higher or the other side to set the volume lower. This key is often found next to the Power/Lock key. It's the larger of the two.

USB/Power connector: This slot is where you connect the USB cable, which is used both to charge the battery and to connect your Android tablet to a computer. The slot is also where the tablet connects to the dock, should one of those be available. See the later section "Optional Accessories."

External storage slot: The tablet's external storage is added by inserting a memory card into the external storage slot. Details on using this feature are covered in the next section.

SIM card cover: This spot is used to access the cellular tablet's SIM card, which is inserted into a slot beneath the cover.

Headphone jack: This hole is where you can connect standard headphones.

HDMI connector: Use this hole to plug in an HDMI cable. The other end of the cable fits into an HDMI TV or monitor, which you can use to view the tablet's content on a larger screen. Not every Android tablet features an HDMI connector.

Speaker(s): Stereo speakers are found left and right on the tablet, sometimes on the front, mostly on the sides, occasionally on the back.

Microphone: A miniscule circular opening serves as the device's microphone. Some tablets may feature two microphone holes. Don't worry if you can't find them; they're there.

The typical Android also has a back side. It's not shown earlier, in Figure 1-1, because the censors won't let me do an illustration and also because the back is boring: On it you may find the tablet's main camera and LED flash. That's it.

✔ Samsung tablets feature a Home button or Home key directly below the touchscreen. This physical button serves the same purpose as the Home icon on other Android tablets.

✔ Samsung tablets also feature Recent, Menu, and Back buttons. The Menu button is found only on older tablets; the Recent button is found on current Samsung tablets.

✔ Some tablets lack a rear-facing camera. To those tablet owners, I can recommend getting a painting program for your tablet and using it to paint the images you would otherwise photograph.

✔ Not every rear-facing camera features a flash.

✔ Some tablets use NFC, or Near Field Communications, so that you can send and receive information by touching your tablet with another NFC device. The NFC technology is internal, which means that you don't really see it on your tablet, although it's typically found on the back of the device.

✔ Be careful not to confuse the SIM card slot with the external storage slot. They're not the same thing. You'll rarely, if ever, access the SIM card.

✔ SIM stands for Subscriber Identity Module. The SIM card is used by your cellular provider to identify your tablet and keep track of the amount of data transmitted over the mobile data network. Yep, that's so you can be billed properly. The SIM also gives your cellular tablet a phone number, though that number is merely an account and not something you can dial into or use for sending a text message.

✔ Don't stick anything into the microphone hole. Yes, it's tempting, but don't. Only stick things into your tablet that you're supposed to, such as the USB cable, headphones, memory card, or SIM card.

Inserting the MicroSD card

External and removable storage is available on some Android tablets. The storage is in the form of a *MicroSD card,* which can be used for photos, videos, music, evil plans, and so on.

The MicroSD card is teensy. (That's a scientific description.) The card fits into a slot on the edge of your tablet but can also be inserted into your computer and read like any removable media card.

The MicroSD card can be insert into the tablet whether the device is on or off. Heed these directions:

1. **Locate the MicroSD card hatch on the tablet's edge.**

   Figure 1-2 illustrates the hatch's appearance, although it may look subtly different on your tablet. The card may be labeled *MicroSD.* Do not confuse it with the SIM card cover.

Lift here.

Figure 1-2: Opening the memory card hatch.

2. Insert a fingernail into the slot on the teensy hatch that covers the MicroSD slot, and then flip up the hatch.

There's a fingernail-size indentation on the slot cover, similar to the one shown in Figure 1-2. When pressure is applied, the hatch that covers the slot pops up and kind of flops over to the side. The slot cover may not come off completely.

3. Orient the MicroSD card so that the printed side faces up and the teeny triangle on the card points toward the open slot.

4. Use your fingernail or a paperclip to gently shove the card all the way into the slot.

The card makes a faint clicking sound when it's fully inserted.

If the card keeps popping out, you're not shoving it in far enough.

5. Close the hatch covering the MicroSD card slot.

If the tablet is on (and has been configured), you may see an onscreen prompt. If so, ignore the prompt and just touch the OK button on the tablet's touchscreen.

✔ Not every Android tablet features external storage. If you can't find a MicroSD card slot on the tablet's edge, that feature isn't available to your tablet.

✔ The tablet works with or without a MicroSD card installed.

✔ Almost always, the MicroSD card is a purchase you must make in addition to your Android tablet. Rarely does a tablet come with the MicroSD card preinstalled.

✔ MicroSD cards come in a smattering of capacities, measured in gigabytes (billions of bytes), abbreviated GB or just G. Common capacities include 8GB, 16GB, 32GB, and 64GB. The higher the capacity, the more stuff you can store but also the more expensive the card. But:

✔ Your tablet has a limit on the size of the MicroSD cards it can accept. For most Android tablets, that limit is 32GB. Newer (and more expensive) tablets can handle higher capacities. Check the tablet's box to determine the maximum size for external or removable storage.

✔ To use a MicroSD card with a computer, you need an SD card adapter. Insert the MicroSD card into the adapter, and then plug the SD card adapter into the computer. The adapter is an extra purchase, although some MicroSD cards come with such an adapter.

✔ SD stands for Secure Digital. It is but one of about a zillion media card standards.

✔ In addition to the MicroSD card, your Android tablet features internal storage. That storage is used for the programs you install on the tablet, as well as for the tablet's operating system and other control programs.

✔ Refer to Chapter 17 for more information on storage.

Removing the MicroSD card

Most of the time, you leave the MicroSD card inside your Android tablet. When the urge hits to remove it, heed these steps:

1. **Turn off your Android tablet.**

   You can damage the media card if you just yank it out of the tablet, which is why I recommend first turning off the tablet. Specific directions for turning off an Android tablet are found in Chapter 2.

2. **Open the itty-bitty hatch covering the MicroSD card slot.**

3. **Use your fingernail to press the MicroSD card inward a tad.**

   The MicroSD card is spring-loaded, so pressing it in eventually pops it outward.

4. **Pinch the MicroSD card between your fingers and remove it completely.**

The MicroSD card is too tiny to leave lying around. Put it into a MicroSD card adapter for use in your PC or another electronic device. Or store it inside a miniature box that you can label with a miniature pen in miniature letters: "MicroSD Card Inside." Don't lose it!

It's possible to remove the MicroSD card without turning off the tablet. To do that, you need to *unmount* the card while the tablet is running. This technical procedure is explained in Chapter 17.

Optional Accessories

Your credit card company will be thrilled when you discover that an assortment of handy Android tablet accessories are available for purchase. You can find them at the place where you purchased your tablet, online or in the real world. Here are just a few of the items that you can consider getting to complete your tablet experience:

Earphones: You can use any standard cell phone or portable media player earphones with an Android tablet. Simply plug the earphones into the headphone jack at the top of the tablet and you're ready to go.

HDMI cable: For tablets with an HDMI (video output) port, you can get an HDMI cable. The cable connects the tablet to an HD monitor, where you can view videos or pictures on a large-format screen.

Pouches and sleeves: Answering the question "Where do I put this thing?" is the handy Android tablet pouch or sleeve accessory. Try to get one designed for your tablet. If not, check the size before you buy. Not every 10-inch tablet fits into the same 10-inch pouch.

Screen protectors: These plastic, clingy things are affixed to the front of the tablet, right over the touchscreen. They help protect the touchscreen glass from finger smudges and sneeze globs while still allowing you to use the touchscreen.

Vehicle charger: You can charge the Android tablet in your car if you buy a vehicle charger. It's an adapter that plugs into your car's 12-volt power supply, in the receptacle that was once known as a cigarette lighter. The vehicle charger is a must if you plan on using the Android tablet's navigation features in your auto or when you need a charge on the road.

Docks, various and sundry: Most people manhandle their tablets. Tsk, tsk. You can be more refined and get your Android tablet a dock. There are several kinds, from the simple prop-dock that holds up the tablet at a pleasant viewing angle to docks that contain keyboards to multimedia docks that feature HDMI and USB ports.

Keyboard: Some docking stands double as tablet keyboards, but you can also obtain any Bluetooth keyboard for use with your Android tablet. See Chapter 16, which covers the Bluetooth connection.

USB Adapter: This USB adapter isn't the same thing as the USB cable that comes with your tablet. It's a dongle that plugs into the tablet's Power/USB jack to allow the tablet to host a USB device, such as a keyboard, mouse, modem, or external storage device (hard drive or optical drive).

Other exciting and nifty accessories might be available for your tablet. Check for new garnishes and frills frequently at the location where you bought your tablet.

✔ None of this extra stuff is essential to using your tablet.

✔ See Chapter 17 for more information on the HDMI connection and how to view tablet content on the "big" screen.

- You can use Bluetooth earphones or a cell phone Bluetooth headset with any Android tablet.

- If the earphones feature a microphone, you can use that microphone for dictation, recording, and even chatting with friends.

- If the earphones feature a button, you can use the button to pause and play music. Press the button once to pause, and again to play.

- Android tablets generally don't recognize more than one earphone button. For example, if you use earphones that feature a Volume button or Mute button, pressing that extra button does nothing.

- A useful accessory to get is a microfiber cloth to help clean the tablet's screen, plus a special cleaning solution wipe. See Chapter 20 for more information about cleaning an Android tablet's screen.

Where to Keep Your Tablet

Like your car keys, glasses, wallet, and phaser pistol, your Android tablet should be kept in a safe, easy-to-find, always handy place, whether you're at home, at work, or on the road or while orbiting the Klingon homeworld.

Making a home for the tablet

I recommend returning your Android tablet to the same spot whenever you finish using it. If you have a computer, my first suggestion is to make a spot right by the computer. Keep the charging cord handy, or just plug the cord into the computer's USB port so that you can synchronize information with your computer on a regular basis, not to mention keep the tablet charged.

Another handy place to keep the tablet is on your nightstand. That makes sense because, in addition to using the tablet for nighttime reading or video watching, it can serve as an alarm clock.

If you have a docking stand, plug your tablet into it whenever you're not toting it about.

Above all, avoid putting the tablet in a place where someone can sit on it, step on it, or otherwise damage it. For example, don't leave the tablet on a table or counter under a stack of newspapers, where it might get accidentally tossed out or put in the recycle bin.

Never leave the tablet on a chair!

As long as you remember to return the tablet to the same spot when you're done with it, you'll always know where it is.

Taking the Android tablet with you

If you're like me, you probably carry the Android tablet around with you to or from the office, at the airport, in the air, or in your car. I hope you're not using the tablet while you're driving. Regardless, it's best to have a portable place to store your tablet while you're on the road.

The ideal place for the tab is a specially designed pouch or sleeve. The pouch keeps the tablet from being dinged, scratched, or even unexpectedly turned on while it's in your backpack, purse, or carry-on luggage or wherever you put the tablet when you're not using it.

Also see Chapter 18 for information on using an Android tablet on the road.

Android Tablet On and Off

*T*he bestselling *Pencils For Dummies* has no chapter describing how to turn on a pencil. *Pens For Dummies* does have the chapter "Enabling the Pen to Write," but that's not really an on-off thing, and the author of that book does describe in great detail how awkward an On–Off switch or power button would be on a pen. Aren't you and I lucky to live in an age when such things are carefully described?

Your Android tablet is far more complex than a pen or a pencil, and, often, it's more useful. As such an advanced piece of technology, your tablet features not an On–Off button but, rather, a Power/Lock key. That key does more than just turn the Android tablet on or off, which is why this book has an entire chapter devoted to the subject.

Greetings, Android Tablet

The first time you turn on an Android tablet — the very first time — it prompts you to complete the setup process. This step is necessary, although it may have already been completed for you by the cheerful people who sold you the tablet. Better read this section, just to be sure.

 ✔ Initial tablet setup works best when you already have a Google, or Gmail, account. If you lack a Google account, see the section "Obtaining a Google account," later in this chapter, for details.

> ✔ The tablet will not start unless the battery is charged. Or unless you plug it in. See Chapter 1.

Turning on your Android tablet for the first time

The very, very first time you turn on your Android tablet, you're required to work through the setup process. It's a must, but it needs to be done only once. If your tablet has already been set up, skip to the next section, "Turning on the tablet."

The specifics of the setup-and-configuration process differ from tablet to tablet. For example, some tablets may prompt you to sign in to services like Dropbox. Tablets on certain cellular networks may require you to run specific setup apps, which you'll read about during the configuration process. Generally speaking, however, the process is similar on all tablets, which is what I've documented in this section.

I recommend reading through these steps first, and then turning on the tablet and working through them afterward — the process goes kind of fast, and the screen may dim if you spend too much time waiting between steps:

1. **Turn on the tablet by pressing the Power/Lock key.**

   You may have to press the button longer than you think; when you see the tablet's logo appear on the screen, the tablet has started.

   It's okay to turn on the tablet while it's plugged in and charging.

2. **Answer the question that's presented.**

   You're asked to select options for some, if not all, of these items:

   - Select your language
   - Activate the tablet on the cellular network
   - Choose a Wi-Fi network (can be done later)
   - Set the time zone
   - Sign in to your Google account
   - Add other online accounts
   - Set location information

   When in doubt, just accept the standard options as presented to you during the setup process.

   To fill in text fields, use the onscreen keyboard. See Chapter 4 for keyboard information.

   Other sections in this chapter, as well as throughout this book, offer information and advice on these settings. You can't screw up anything at this point; any selection you make can be changed later.

Having a Google account is important to the setup process. See the later section "Obtaining a Google account."

3. **After each choice, touch the Next button, or large triangle icon.**

   The Next button might appear on the screen, labeled with the text *Next,* or it might appear as a triangle button, shown in the margin.

4. **Touch the Finish button.**

   The Finish button appears on the last screen of the setup procedure.

The good news is that you're done. The better news is that you need to complete this setup only once on your Android tablet. From this point on, starting the tablet works as described in the next few sections.

After the initial setup, you're taken to the Home screen. Chapter 3 offers more Home screen information, which you should probably read right away, before the temptation to play with your new tablet becomes unbearable.

- ✔ You may find yourself asked various questions or prompted to try various tricks when you first start to use the tablet. Some of those prompts are helpful, but it's okay to skip some or to select the Do Not Show Again check box.

- ✔ Additional information on connecting your tablet to a Wi-Fi network is found in Chapter 16.

- ✔ Location settings relate to how the tablet knows its position on Planet Earth. I recommend keeping all these items activated to get the most from your Android tablet.

- ✔ It's not necessary to use any specific software provided by the tablet's manufacturer or your cellular provider. For example, if you don't want a Samsung account, you don't need to sign up for one; skip that step.

- ✔ By setting up your Google account, you coordinate with your new Android tablet whatever information you have on the Internet. This information includes your e-mail messages and contacts on Gmail, appointments on Google Calendar, and information and data from other Google Internet applications.

- ✔ See the later sidebar "Who is this Android person?" for more information about the Android operating system.

Turning on the tablet

To turn on your Android tablet, press and hold the Power/Lock button. After a few seconds, you see the tablet's start-up logo, perhaps some hypnotic animation, and maybe even a tune. Release the Power/Lock key; the device is starting.

Eventually, you see the standard slide or swipe lock screen, similar to the one shown in Figure 2-1. The screen may appear in a vertical orientation, depending on how you've oriented the tablet.

Swipe your finger across here.

Start-up apps

Figure 2-1: The basic unlocking screen.

To unlock the tablet, swipe your finger across the touchscreen, as illustrated in Figure 2-1. The tablet unlocks, and you can start using it.

- ✔ The tablet may provide animation to assist you with the unlocking process. Pay attention to it if you find yourself confused.

- ✔ You probably won't turn on your tablet much in the future. Mostly, you'll unlock the gizmo. See the later section "Unlocking the tablet."

Working the secure lock screens

The standard swipe-lock screen isn't a difficult lock to pick. In fact, it's known as the No Security screen lock on some tablets. If you've added more security, you might see any one of several different lock screens on your tablet, each illustrated in Figure 2-2.

The password lock is the most secure. It requires that you type a multicharacter password to unlock the tablet. Touch the Done button on the onscreen keyboard to accept the password and unlock the tablet.

The PIN lock is also considered secure. It requires that you type a secret number to unlock the tablet. Touch the OK button to unlock the tablet, or use the Del button to back up and erase.

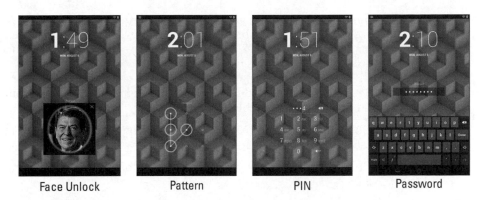

Face Unlock   Pattern   PIN   Password

Figure 2-2: Secure unlocking screens.

To work the pattern lock, trace your finger over the nine dots that appear on the screen (refer to Figure 2-2) along a preset pattern. After you match the pattern, the tablet is unlocked. This type of screen lock is more secure than the swipe lock, but not as secure as the password lock or PIN lock.

Some tablets may feature other lock screen options, such as the face lock screen, shown in Figure 2-2. Galaxy Note tablets feature a signature lock, which uses that tablet's S Pen. Though clever and fun, these locks are not considered secure, and they often require a password or PIN as a backup.

Whether or not you see these various lock screens depends on how you've configured your tablet's security. Specific directions for setting the locks, or for removing them and returning to the standard screen lock, are found in Chapter 19.

  ✔ The pattern lock can start at any dot, not necessarily the upper left dot, as shown in Figure 2-2.

  ✔ For additional information on working the onscreen keyboard, see Chapter 4.

Unlocking the tablet

You'll probably leave your Android tablet on all the time. That's great! Tablets are designed that way, and the battery supports keeping it on for lengthy periods. When your tablet is bored, or when you've ignored it for a while, it locks itself similarly to a computer entering Sleep mode. After the tablet is locked, the touchscreen turns off to save power.

To unlock the tablet, press the Power/Lock key. Unlike turning on the tablet, a quick press is all that's needed.

After unlocking the tablet, you see the lock screen (refer to Figure 2-1). Or, if you've configured the tablet for more security, you see one of the locking screens shown in Figure 2-2. Simply unlock the screen, and you can start using the device.

- ✔ See the section "Locking the tablet," later in this chapter, for information on how to lock the tablet.

- ✔ On Samsung tablets, you can press the Home button to unlock the tablet. The Home button is centered below the touchscreen.

- ✔ On the Samsung Galaxy Note, you can unlock the tablet by removing the S Pen.

- ✔ An Android tablet continues to run while it's sleeping. Mail is received, social networking updates are made, and so on. The tablet also continues to play music while it's locked.

- ✔ Touching the touchscreen doesn't unlock the tablet unless you've configured the tablet not to use a screen lock. See Chapter 19.

- ✔ Loud noises will not wake up your tablet.

- ✔ Android tablets don't snore while sleeping, but they can dream. See Chapter 21.

Who is this Android person?

Just like a computer, your Android tablet has an operating system. It's the main program in charge of all the software (apps) inside the tablet. Unlike a computer, however, Android is a mobile device operating system, designed primarily for use in tablets and cell phones.

Android is based on the Linux operating system, which is also a computer operating system, though it's much more stable and bug-free than Windows, so it's not as popular. Google owns, maintains, and develops Android, which is why your online Google information is synced with your tablet.

The Android mascot, shown here, often appears on Android apps or hardware. He has no official name, though most folks call him Andy.

Unlocking and running an app

Some tablets allow the lock screen to be adorned with app icons, such as those shown earlier, in Figure 2-1. You can both unlock the tablet and run an app: Touch the app icon and drag your finger across the touchscreen. The tablet unlocks, and the chosen app starts automatically.

> ✔ Only the swipe lock lets you unlock the tablet and immediately start an app.

> ✔ See Chapter 21 for information on choosing the apps to show on the lock screen.

Account Creation and Configuration

Your Android tablet can serve as home to your various online incarnations. That includes your e-mail accounts, online services, subscriptions, and other digital personas. I recommended adding those accounts to your tablet to continue the setup-and-configuration process.

Obtaining a Google account

It's possible to use your tablet without having a Google account, but you'd be missing out on a buncha features. So if you don't already have a Google account, drop everything (but not this book) and follow these steps to obtain one:

1. **Open your computer's web browser program.**

   Yes, it works best if you use your computer, not the tablet, to complete these steps.

2. **Visit the main Google page at** `www.google.com`.

   Type `www.google.com` into the web browser's address bar.

3. **Click the Sign In link or button.**

   Another page opens, and on it you can log in to your Google account. But you don't have a Google account, so:

4. **Click the link to create a new account.**

   The link is typically found beneath the text boxes where you would log in to your Google account. As I write this chapter, the link is titled Create an Account.

5. **Continue heeding the directions until you've created your own Google account.**

Eventually, your account is set up and configured.

To try things out, log off from Google and then log back in. That way, you ensure that you've done everything properly — and remembered your password. Your web browser may even prompt you to let it remember the password for you.

Your next step is to make your new Google account known to the tablet. Keep reading in the next section.

Adding accounts to the tablet

You don't have to add all your online accounts during the tablet setup-and-configuration process. If you skipped those steps, or when you have more accounts to add, you can easily do so. With your tablet turned on and unlocked, follow these steps:

1. **Go to the Home screen.**

   The Home screen is the main screen on your tablet. You can always get there by touching the Home icon, found at the bottom of the touchscreen.

2. **Touch the Apps icon.**

   The Apps icon is found at the bottom of the Home screen. It looks similar to the icon shown in the margin, although it has many variations. See Chapter 3 for the variety.

   When you touch the Apps icon, you view the Apps drawer, which lists all the apps available on your tablet.

3. **Choose the Settings icon to start the Settings app.**

   You may have to swipe the Apps Drawer screen left or right a few times, paging through the various apps, to find the Settings app icon. If you're having trouble, see Chapter 3 for specifics on how to swipe the screen.

   After touching the Settings icon, the Settings app runs. It shows commands for configuring and setting tablet options.

4. **Choose the Accounts category, or look for the Accounts heading.**

   On some Samsung tablets, you have to touch the General tab atop the Settings app screen to find the Accounts category. Otherwise, scroll down the screen by swiping upward with your finger to locate the Accounts category or heading.

   Some tablets may show the category as Accounts and Sync instead of Accounts.

5. **Touch the Add Account icon.**

   The icon may appear as a plus sign, shown in the margin, or it may be a button that says Add Account.

6. **Choose an account from the list that appears.**

   Don't worry if you don't see the exact type of account you want to add. You may have to add a specific app before an account appears. Chapter 15 covers adding apps.

7. **Follow the directions on the screen to sign in to your account.**

   The steps that follow depend on the type of account you're adding. Generally speaking, you sign in using an existing username and password.

When you're done, touch the Home icon to return to the Home screen, or you can continue adding accounts by repeating these steps.

✔ See Chapter 6 for specific information on adding e-mail accounts to your Android tablet.

✔ Chapter 8 covers social networking on your tablet. Refer there for specific information on adding Facebook, Twitter, and other social networking accounts.

The End of Your Android Tablet Day

I know of three ways to say goodbye to your Android tablet; only one of them involves renting a steamroller. The other two methods are documented in this section.

Locking the tablet

Locking the tablet is cinchy: Simply press and release the Power/Lock key. The display goes dark; your tablet is locked.

✔ Your Android tablet still works while locked; it receives e-mail and can play music, but it's not using as much power as it would with the display on.

✔ The tablet will probably spend most of its time locked.

✔ Locking the tablet isn't the same as turning off the tablet. It's more like a computer's Sleep mode. Indeed, a locked tablet is often described as a sleeping or snoozing tablet.

✔ Any timers or alarms you set still activate when your tablet is locked. See Chapter 14 for information on setting timers and alarms.

✔ To unlock your tablet, press and release the Power/Lock key. See the section "Unlocking the tablet," earlier in this chapter.

Setting the lock time-out

You can manually lock your tablet at any time by pressing the Power/Lock key. That's probably why it's called the Power/*Lock* key, although I have my doubts. Anyway, when you don't manually lock the tablet, it automatically locks after a given period of inactivity.

You can control the tablet's self-lock timeout value, which can be set anywhere from 15 seconds to 1 hour. Obey these steps:

1. **At the Home screen, touch the Apps icon.**

2. **Open the Settings app.**

3. **Choose Display.**

   On some Samsung tablets, you need to first choose the Device tab before you can locate the Display item.

4. **Choose the Screen Timeout item.**

   This option is titled Sleep on some tablets.

5. **Choose a time-out value from the list that's provided.**

   I prefer a value of 1 minute.

6. **Touch the Home icon to return to the Home screen.**

The lock timer begins after a period of inactivity. Specifically, when you don't touch the screen, the timer starts ticking. About 5 seconds before the time-out kicks in, the touchscreen dims. Then the touchscreen turns off and the tablet locks. If you touch the screen before then, the timer is reset.

Turning off your Android tablet

To turn off your tablet, heed these steps:

1. **Press and hold the Power/Lock key.**

   You see the Device Options menu, shown in Figure 2-3. Some tablets feature more items on this menu, although Figure 2-3 illustrates the basic commands.

Figure 2-3: The Device Options menu.

If you chicken out and don't want to turn off your tablet, touch the Back icon to dismiss the Device Options menu.

2. **Touch the Power Off item.**

   A confirmation message appears, although some tablets may instantly turn themselves off.

3. **Touch OK.**

   The Android tablet turns itself off.

The tablet doesn't run when it's off, so it doesn't remind you of appointments and doesn't collect e-mail, nor do you hear any alarms you've set. The tablet isn't angry with you for turning it off, though you may sense some resentment when you turn it on again.

- Varieties of the Device Options menu on various Android tablets include the Restart command as well as commands to silence the speakers or control vibration. I've also seen a Kid Mode command on some tablets.

- The Device Options menu is titled Tablet Options on some Android tablets. Other tablets may not title the menu at all.

- The tablet can be charged while it's off.

- Ensure that your tablet is kept in a safe place while it's turned off. Chapter 1 offers some suggestions.

3

How Android Tablets Work

*I*t used to be that you could judge how advanced something was by how many buttons it had. Starting with the dress shirt and progressing to the first computer, more buttons meant fancier technology. Your Android tablet tosses that rule right out the window. Beyond the Power/Lock key and Volume key, the device is shamefully bereft of buttons.

My point is that in order to use your tablet, you'll have to understand how a touchscreen works. That *touchscreen* is the tablet's main input device — the gizmo you'll use to do all sorts of wondrous and useful things. Using a touchscreen may be a new experience for you, so this chapter provides a general orientation to the touchscreen and how an Android tablet works.

Basic Operations

Your Android tablet's ability to frustrate you is only as powerful as your fear of the touchscreen and how it works. After you clear that hurdle, as well as understand some other basic operations, you'll be on your way toward mobile device contentment.

Touching the touchscreen

Minus any buttons and knobs, the way you control an Android tablet is to manipulate things on the touchscreen with one or two fingers. It doesn't matter which fingers you use, and you should feel free to experiment with other body parts as well, although I find fingers to be handy.

Here are the many ways the touchscreen can be touched, along with the terms attached to those techniques:

Touch: The simplest way to manipulate the touchscreen is to touch it. The touch operation is similar to a mouse click on a computer. Generally, you're touching an object such as an icon or a control. A touch may also be referred to as a *tap* or *press*.

Double-tap: Touch the screen twice in the same location. Double-tapping can be used to zoom in on an image or a map, but it can also zoom out. Because of the double-tap's dual nature, I recommend using the pinch or spread operation instead when you want to zoom.

Long-press: A long-press occurs whenever you touch part of the screen and keep your finger down. Depending on what you're doing, a pop-up menu may appear, or the item you're long-pressing may get "picked up" so that you can drag (move) it around. *Long-press* might also be referred to as *touch and hold* in some documentation. Moving an icon or another object is called a *long-press–drag*.

Swipe: To swipe, you touch your finger on one spot and then drag it to another spot. Swipes can go up, down, left, or right, which moves the touchscreen content in the direction you swipe. A swipe can be fast or slow. It's also called a *flick* or *slide*.

Pinch: A pinch involves two fingers, which start out separated and then are brought together. The effect is used to *zoom out,* to reduce the size of an image or to see more of a map.

Spread: The opposite of *pinch* is *spread.* You start out with your fingers together and then spread them. The spread is used to *zoom in,* to enlarge an image or see more detail on a map.

Rotate: A few apps let you rotate an image on the screen by touching with two fingers and twisting them around a center point. If you have trouble with this operation, pretend that you're turning the dial on a safe.

You can't manipulate the touchscreen while wearing gloves unless the gloves are specially designed for using electronic touchscreens, such as the gloves that Batman wears.

Using the navigation icons

Below the touchscreen dwells a series of icons. They can appear as part of the touchscreen itself; or, on some tablets, they may be part of the bezel or may even be physical buttons. These are the navigation icons, and they serve specific functions.

Traditionally, you'll find three navigation icons:

Back: The Back icon serves several purposes, all of which fit neatly under the concept of "back." Touch the icon once to return to a previous page, dismiss an onscreen menu, close a window, or hide the onscreen keyboard, for example.

Home: No matter what you're doing on the tablet, touching this icon displays the Home screen. When you're already viewing the Home screen, touching the Home icon returns you to the main, or center, Home screen.

Recent: Touching the Recent icon displays a list of recently opened or currently running apps. The list scrolls up and down, so when it's too tall for the screen, just swipe it with your finger to view all the apps. Choose an app from the list to switch to that app. To dismiss the list of recently used apps, touch the Back icon. See the later section "Switching apps" for more info.

Your tablet may not use the same symbols for the Back, Home, and Recent icons, as shown in this book. Some tablets offer subtle variations. You may even find additional icons beneath the touchscreen, but the three stock Android navigation icons are Back, Home, and Recent.

- ✔ On Android tablets without the Recent icon, press and hold the Home icon to see the Recent Apps list.

- ✔ Beyond Back, Home, and Recent, perhaps the most common icon found below the touchscreen is Menu. Touch this icon to display a pop-up menu from which you can choose commands. If nothing happens when you press the Menu icon, no pop-up menu is available.

- ✔ The Menu icon is essentially the same thing as the Overflow icon. See the section "Using common icons," later in this chapter.

- ✔ The three navigation icons may hide themselves when certain apps run. In most cases, the icons are still there — just invisible.

- ✔ The Back icon may change its appearance to the down caret, shown in the margin. Touch this icon to hide the onscreen keyboard, dismiss the recent app list, or perform other actions similar to the Back navigation icon.

Setting the volume

There are times when the sound level is too loud. There are times when it's too soft. And, there are those rare times when it's just right. Finding that just-right level is the job of the Volume key that clings to the side of your Android tablet.

Pressing the top part of the Volume key makes the volume louder; pressing the bottom part makes the volume softer. That is, unless the Volume key is on the top edge of the tablet, in which case the left part increases volume and the right part decreases volume.

As you press the Volume key, a graphic appears on the touchscreen to illustrate the relative volume level, similar to the one shown in Figure 3-1.

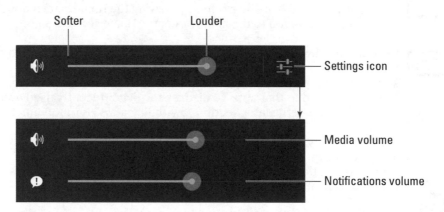

Figure 3-1: Setting the volume.

Touch the Settings icon, shown in Figure 3-1, to see more detailed volume controls. You can individually set the volume for media and notifications, as shown in the expanded onscreen volume control: Drag the dot left or right to set the volume.

Some tablets may show additional controls beyond the Media and Notifications controls, illustrated in Figure 3-1.

  ✔ The Settings icon may appear as the Gear icon, shown in the margin, instead of as the icon referenced later in this chapter, in Figure 3-2.

  ✔ When the volume is set all the way down, the tablet is silenced.

Vertical orientation   Horizontal orientation

Figure 3-2: Android tablet orientation.

> **TIP**
>
> ✏ Silencing the tablet by sliding down the volume level may place it into Vibration mode.
>
> ✏ A Silence command is also available on the Device Options menu: Press and hold the tablet's Power/Lock key to see the Device Options menu.
>
> ✏ The Volume key works even when the tablet is locked (when the touchscreen display is off). That means you don't need to unlock the tablet if you're playing music and only need to adjust the volume.
>
> ✏ Refer to Chapter 19 for information on placing the tablet into Vibration mode.

Changing the orientation

Your Android tablet features an *accelerometer* gizmo. It determines in which direction the tablet is pointed or whether you've reoriented the device from an upright position to a horizontal one (or vice versa) or even upside down. That way, the information displayed on the tablet's screen always appears upright, no matter how you hold it.

To demonstrate how the tablet orients itself, rotate the tablet to the left or right. Most apps change their orientation to match however you've oriented the tablet, such as the Home screen, shown in Figure 3-2.

The Rotation feature may not work for all apps, and it may not even work for the Home screen. In that case, open the web browser app to experiment with rotation.

✓ Most games present themselves in one orientation only.

✓ You can lock the orientation if the rotating screen bothers you. See the section "Taking Quick Actions," later in this chapter.

✓ eBook apps feature special commands to lock the tablet's orientation as you read. See Chapter 14 for information on eBooks.

✓ A great application for demonstrating the Android tablet accelerometer is the game *Labyrinth*. You can purchase it at the Google Play Store or download the free version, *Labyrinth Lite*. See Chapter 15 for more information about the Google Play Store.

There's No Place Like Home Screen

The main base from which you begin domination of your Android tablet is the *Home screen*. It's the first thing you see after unlocking the tablet, and it's the place you go to whenever you leave an app.

To view the Home screen at any time, touch the Home icon found at the bottom of the touchscreen. Some tablets feature a physical Home button or key, which performs the same duties as the Home icon.

Touring the Home screen

The typical Android tablet Home screen is illustrated in Figure 3-3. In the horizontal orientation, the items appear in generally the same location, although the Apps icon may move to the lower right corner of the screen.

Several fun and interesting things appear on the Home screen. Find these items on your own tablet's Home screen:

Notification icons: These icons come and go, depending on what happens in your digital life. For example, new icons appear whenever you receive a new e-mail message or have a pending appointment. The section "Checking notifications," later in this chapter, describes how to deal with notifications.

Status icons: These icons represent the tablet's current condition, such as the type of network to which it's connected, signal strength, and battery status, as well as whether the tablet is connected to a Wi-Fi network or is using Bluetooth, for example.

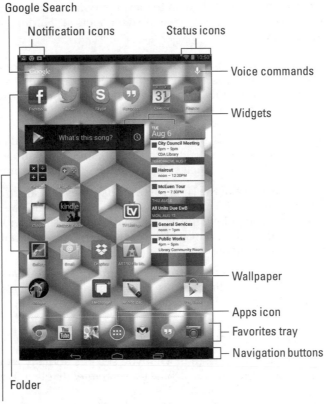

Google Search

Notification icons   Status icons

Voice commands

Widgets

Wallpaper

Apps icon

Favorites tray

Navigation buttons

Folder

App icons

Figure 3-3: The Home screen.

App icons: The meat of the meal on the Home screen plate is the App icon. Touching an icon runs a program, or *app*.

Widgets: A widget is a teensy program that can display information, let you control the tablet, access features, or do something purely amusing. For example, the Google Search widget is used to invoke a powerful search of the items stored on the Android tablet or the entire Internet. You can read more about widgets in Chapter 19.

Folders: Multiple apps can be stored in a folder. Touch the folder to see a pop-up window listing all the apps.

Wallpaper: The background image you see on the Home screen is the wallpaper.

Favorites Tray: The lineup of icons near the bottom of the screen contains slots for popular apps.

Apps icon: Touch this icon to view the collection of apps and widgets available on your tablet. See the later section "Finding an app in the Apps drawer."

Ensure that you recognize the names of the various parts of the Home screen because these terms are used throughout this book and in whatever other scant Android tablet documentation exists. Directions for using the Home screen gizmos are found throughout this chapter.

✔ The Home screen is entirely customizable. You can add and remove icons from the Home screen, add widgets and shortcuts, and even change wallpaper (background) images. See Chapter 19 for more information.

✔ Touching a part of the Home screen that doesn't feature an icon or a control does nothing. That is, unless you're using the *live wallpaper* feature. In that case, touching the screen changes the wallpaper in some way, depending on the wallpaper that's selected. You can read more about live wallpaper in Chapter 19.

✔ You may see numbers affixed to certain Home screen icons. Those numbers indicate pending actions, such as unread e-mail messages, indicated by the icon shown in the margin.

Accessing multiple Home screens

The Home screen is more than what you see. It's actually an entire street of Home screens, with only one Home screen *panel* displayed at a time.

To switch from one panel to another, swipe the Home screen left or right. There are pages to the left of the main Home screen page, and pages to the right. The number of panels depends on the tablet. Many tablets let you add or remove panels; see Chapter 19 for details.

Figure 3-4 illustrates the Home screen index, used on some tablets to help you determine which Home screen is displayed. You can swipe the index or touch one of the dots to zoom to a specific Home screen panel.

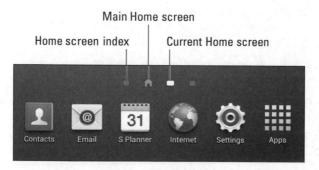

Figure 3-4: The Home screen panel index.

✓ When you touch the Home icon, you return to the last Home screen page you viewed. To return to the main Home screen panel, touch the Home icon a second time.

✓ Some tablets may reserve the far left Home screen panel for the Google Now app. See Chapter 14 for information on Google Now.

✓ The main Home screen is often the center Home screen panel, though some Android tablets let you choose any page as the main one.

Reviewing notifications

Notifications appear as icons at the top of the Home screen, as illustrated earlier, in Figure 3-3. To review them, you pull down the notifications drawer by dragging your finger from the top of the screen downward. The notifications drawer is illustrated in Figure 3-5.

Scroll through the list of notifications by swiping the shade up and down. To peruse a specific notification, touch it. Choosing a notification displays more information, and it may also dismiss the notification.

You can dismiss a notification by sliding it to the right. If the Close icon appears to the right of the notification, touching that icon dismisses the notification. To dismiss all notifications, touch either the Dismiss All or Clear button.

To hide the notifications drawer, touch the Back icon, the X (Close) icon on the notifications drawer, or anywhere else on the Home screen.

✓ Some tablets require you to swipe the screen from the top-left edge to see the notifications shade. When you swipe from the top-right edge, you see the Quick Settings shade. See the next section.

✓ When more notifications are present than can be shown on the status bar, you see the More Notifications icon displayed, similar to the one shown in the margin.

✓ Dismissing some notifications doesn't prevent them from appearing again in the future. For example, notifications to update your programs continue to appear, as do calendar reminders.

✓ Ongoing notifications cannot be dismissed. They include items such as USB (refer to Figure 3-5), Bluetooth, and Wi-Fi connections.

✓ Some programs, such as Facebook and the various Twitter apps, don't display notifications unless you're logged in. See Chapter 8.

✓ Your Android tablet plays a sound, or *ringtone,* whenever a new notification floats in. You can choose which sound plays; see Chapter 19 for more information.

✓ See Chapter 14 for information on dismissing calendar reminders.

Drag down from here to
see the notifications.

Swipe a notification to
the right to dismiss it.

Dismiss all notifications.

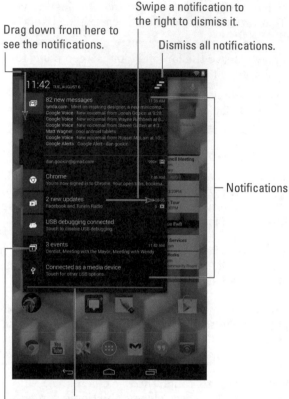

— Notifications

Notifications drawer handle

Choose a notification
to see more details.

Figure 3-5: The notifications drawer.

Taking Quick Actions

Quick Actions are a clutch of popular tablet features, such as Bluetooth, Wi-Fi, Airplane mode, and Auto Rotate. Shortcuts to popular places, such as the Settings app, might also be in with the Quick Actions. The point is to keep these items handy in one, specific location. What drives you nuts, of course, is finding where the Quick Actions lurk.

Some Android tablets feature Quick Actions as their own drawer, accessed by swiping down from the upper right area of the screen, as shown in Figure 3-6.

Other Android tablets may crowd up the notifications drawer with Quick Actions, as illustrated in Figure 3-7.

Figure 3-6: The Quick Actions shade.

Figure 3-7: Quick Actions sharing the notification drawer.

Dismiss the Quick Actions drawer by touching either the Back or Home icon.

> ✔ The Settings icon in the Quick Actions drawer provides instant access to the Settings app, a popular place to visit as you learn about your Android tablet.
>
> ✔ Quick Actions may also be referred to as *quick settings*.

The World of Apps

You probably didn't purchase a tablet so that you could enjoy the thrill-a-minute punch that's packed by the Android operating system. No, an Android tablet's success lies with the apps you obtain. Knowing how to deal with apps is a vital to being a successful, happy Android tablet user.

Starting an app

It's blissfully simple to run an app on the Home screen: Touch its icon. The app starts.

> ✔ App is short for *app*lication. It's another word for *program* or *software*.
>
> ✔ Not all apps appear on the Home screen, but all of them appear whenever you display the Apps drawer. See the later section "Finding an app in the Apps drawer."

Quitting an app

Unlike on a computer, you don't need to quit apps on your Android tablet. To leave an app, touch the Home icon to return to the Home screen. You can keep touching the Back icon to back out of an app. Or you can touch the Recent icon to switch to another running app.

> ✔ Some apps feature a Quit command or Exit command, but for the most part you don't quit an app on your tablet — not like you quit an app on a computer.
>

> ✔ If necessary, the Android operating system shuts down apps you haven't used in a while. You can directly stop apps run amok, which is described in Chapter 15.

Finding an app in the Apps drawer

The place where you find all the apps installed on your tablet is the *Apps drawer*. Even though you can find app icons (shortcuts) on the Home screen, the Apps drawer is where you need to go to find *everything*.

Wonderful widgets

Like apps, widgets appear on the Home screen. To use a widget, touch it. What happens after that depends on the widget and what it does.

For example, the YouTube widget lets you peruse videos. The Calendar widget shows a preview of your upcoming schedule. A Twitter widget may display recent tweets. Other widgets do interesting things, display useful information, or give you access to the tablet's settings or features.

New widgets are obtained from the Google Play Store, just like apps. See Chapter 15 for information. Also see Chapter 19 for details on adding widgets to the Home screen.

To view the Apps drawer, touch the Apps icon on the Home screen. This icon has a different look to it, depending on your tablet. Figure 3-8 illustrates various looks to the Apps icon, though more varieties may exist.

Figure 3-8: Apps icon varieties.

After you touch the Apps icon, you see the Apps drawer. Swipe through the icons left and right across the touchscreen.

To run an app, touch its icon. The app starts, taking over the screen and doing whatever magical thing that app does.

- As you add new apps to your tablet, they appear in the Apps drawer. See Chapter 15 for information on adding new apps.

- Some tablets allow you to create folders in the Apps drawer. These folders contain multiple apps, which helps keep things organized. To access apps in the folder, touch the icon.

- The Apps drawer displays apps alphabetically. On some tablets, you can switch to a non-alphabetical viewing grid. With that feature active, it's possible to rearrange the app icons in any order you like.

- The Apps drawer also lists widgets. They may appear at the end of the list of apps, or you may have to touch a Widgets tab to view the widgets.

- For apps you use all the time, consider creating launcher icons or shortcuts on the Home screen. Chapter 19 describes how.

Switching apps

The apps you run on your tablet don't quit when you dismiss them from the screen. For the most part, they stay running. To switch between running apps, or to any app you've recently opened, touch the Recent icon. Choose the app to switch to from the list that's displayed, similar to what's shown in Figure 3-9.

Scroll up for more.

App thumbnails

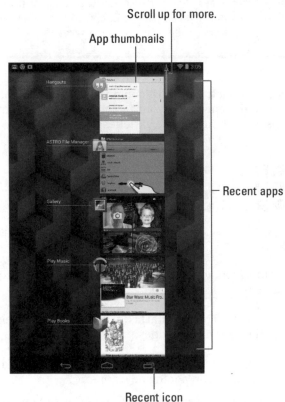

Recent apps

Recent icon

Figure 3-9: Recently used apps.

To reopen an app, choose it from the list. You can hide the Recently Used Apps list by touching the Back icon. On some tablets, the Back icon changes to the Hide icon, looking like the down-pointing chevron shown in the margin.

- For tablets that lack the Recent icon, press and hold the Home icon to see recent apps.

- Consider creating shortcuts on the Home screen for the apps you use all the time. Chapter 19 describes how to create shortcuts for apps, as well as shortcuts to popular contacts, shortcuts for e-mail, and all sorts of fun stuff.

✔ Some tablets feature extra buttons on the Recent Apps screen. For example, you can touch a button to view a Task Manager app, which allows for further control over all running apps.

Using common icons

In addition to the navigation icons, various other icons appear while you use your Android tablet. These icons serve common functions in your apps as well as in the Android operating system. Table 3-1 lists the most common icons and their functions.

Table 3-1		Common Icons
Icon	*Name*	*Function*
	Action Bar	Displays a pop-up menu. This teensy icon appears in the lower right corner of a button or image, indicating that actions (commands) are attached.
	Add	Adds or creates a new item. The plus symbol (+) may be used in combination with other symbols, depending on the app.
	Close	Closes a window or clears text from an input field.
	Delete	Removes one or more items from a list or deletes a message.
	Done	Dismisses an action bar, such as the text-editing action bar.
	Edit	Lets you edit an item, add text, or fill in fields.
	Microphone	Lets you use your voice to dictate text.
	Overflow	Displays a menu or list of commands.

(continued)

Table 3-1 *(continued)*

Icon	Name	Function
	Refresh	Fetches new information or reloads.
	Search	Search the tablet or the Internet for a tidbit of information.
	Settings	Adjusts options for an app.
	Share	Shares information stored on the tablet via e-mail, social networking, or other Internet services.
	Star	Flags a favorite item, such as a contact or a web page.

Various sections throughout this book give examples of using the icons. Their images appear in the book's margins where relevant.

- ✔ Some tablets use the Menu icon to display onscreen menus. This icon serves the same function as the Overflow icon, shown in Table 3-1. The icon is found as a button on the device.

- ✔ The Gear icon, shown in the margin, is also used to represent settings. In fact, you may see both the Settings icon, shown in Table 3-1, and the Gear icon, used to represent the Settings command on some tablets.

- ✔ Other common symbols are used on icons in various apps. For example, the standard Play and Pause icons are used as well as variations on the symbols shown in Table 3-1.

- ✔ Some older Android tablets feature the Screen Capture icon, shown in the margin. Touch that icon to convert the image on the screen into a picture file. To access the screen capture feature, use the Gallery app. See Chapter 12 for more information on the Gallery app.

4

Creating and Editing Text

In This Chapter

▶ Using the onscreen keyboard
▶ Choosing another keyboard
▶ Creating text
▶ Accessing special characters
▶ Dictating text with voice input
▶ Editing text
▶ Selecting, cutting, copying, and pasting text

Human beings create text in a variety of ways. From stone tablets to paper, text was mostly crafted by hand. With the advent of the typewriter, humans typed their text. Then came the computer and word processing. It's easy to assume that for the past 100 years or so, text was created by using some form of keyboard.

Your Android tablet lacks a keyboard — a real one, at least. To sate the tablet's text-input desires, you use something called an *onscreen keyboard*. It works like a real keyboard, but with the added frustration that it lacks moveable keys. Don't fret! You can add a real keyboard to your tablet, and you can even forgo typing and just dictate your text. It's all covered here.

Everybody Was Touchscreen Typing

The old mechanical typewriters required a lot of effort to press their keys: clackity-clack-clack. Electronic typewriters made typing easier. And, of course, the computer is the easiest thing to type on. A tablet? That device takes some getting used to, because its keys are merely flat rectangles on a touchscreen. Whether your fingers love it or hate it, you must tolerate it.

Using the onscreen keyboard

When you touch a text field or you're given the opportunity to type something, an onscreen keyboard pops up conveniently. The stock Android onscreen keyboard layout is shown in Figure 4-1. You'll be relieved to know that it's similar to the standard computer keyboard, though some of the keys change their appearance and function depending on what you're typing. Computer keyboards are incapable of that feat, unless you provide them with an ample supply of hallucinogens.

Figure 4-1: The Google Voice Typing onscreen keyboard.

The stock Android onscreen keyboard's Alphabetic mode is illustrated in Figure 4-1. You see keys from A through Z, albeit not in that order. You also see the Shift key for changing the letter case, and the Delete key, which backspaces and erases. Your tablet may show more keys — such as Tab and Caps Lock — or it may show fewer keys.

The Enter key changes its look depending on what you're typing. Five variations are shown in Figure 4-1. Here's what each one does:

Enter (or Return): Just like the Enter key or Return key on your computer keyboard, this key ends a paragraph of text. It's used mostly when filling in long stretches of text or when multiline input is available.

Go: This action key directs the app to proceed with a search, accept input, or perform another action.

Search: You see this key appear when you're searching for something on the tablet. Touching the key starts the search.

A real keyboard?

If typing is your thing and the onscreen keyboard doesn't do it for you, consider getting your Android tablet a real keyboard. You can do so in two ways. First, you can see whether your tablet features an optional *keyboard dock*. This docking stand props up the tablet at a good viewing angle and also provides a laptop-size keyboard.

When no docking station is available, you can obtain a Bluetooth keyboard for your tablet. The Bluetooth keyboard connects wirelessly, giving you not only a larger, full-action keyboard but also all the divine goodness that wireless brings. You can read more about Bluetooth in Chapter 16.

Next: This key appears whenever you're typing information in multiple fields. Touching this key switches from one field to the next, such as when typing a username and password.

Done: This key appears whenever you've finished typing text in the final field of a screen that has several fields. Sometimes it dismisses the onscreen keyboard; sometimes it doesn't.

The large key at the bottom center of the onscreen keyboard is the Space key. It's flanked left and right by other keys that may change, depending on the context of what you're typing. For example, the www key or .com key may appear in order to assist in typing a web page or e-mail address. Though these and other keys may change, the basic alphabetic keys remain the same.

✔ To display the onscreen keyboard, touch any text field or spot on the screen where typing is permitted.

✔ If you pine for a real keyboard, one that exists in the fourth dimension, you're not stuck. See the nearby sidebar, "A real keyboard?"

✔ To dismiss the onscreen keyboard, touch the Back icon. It may appear as the Hide icon, shown in the margin.

✔ Some onscreen keyboards label the Space key with a large, ugly U symbol.

✔ You may find a Keyboard Settings key, labeled with the Settings (Gear) icon, which you use to make adjustments to the onscreen keyboard. In Figure 4-1, that key is shared with the Microphone key; long-press the Microphone key to see the Keyboard Settings key.

✔ The keyboard changes its width when you reorient the tablet. The keyboard's horizontal presentation is wider and easier for typing.

✔ The Microphone key is used for dictation. If you don't see the Microphone key on the keyboard, dictation must be activated. See the section "Activating voice input," later in this chapter, for the secret instructions.

Selecting another onscreen keyboard

The onscreen keyboard that your tablet presents is preset by the tablet's manufacturer. It may be the stock Android or Google Voice keyboard, or it may be a custom keyboard. To determine which onscreen keyboard you're using, or to switch to another keyboard, heed these steps:

1. **At the Home screen, touch the Apps icon.**

   The Apps drawer appears, listing all apps on your tablet.

2. **Open the Settings app.**

3. **Choose Language & Input.**

   On Samsung tablets, you may have to choose the Controls tab before you can choose the Language and Input item. (Samsung uses the word *and* instead of the ampersand, which pleases my editor to no end.)

The Language and Input screen shows the variety of keyboards available under the heading Keyboard and Input Methods. You should see Google Keyboard as well as Google Voice Typing. Any other available keyboards also appear in this list.

To use another keyboard, choose it from the list. To use that keyboard exclusively, remove the check mark by other keyboards. Likewise, to switch back to the Google keyboard, choose that item from the list and remove the check mark from other items.

 ✔ Samsung tablets refer to their standard keyboard as the *Samsung keyboard.* You may find only that option and not the Google keyboard.

 ✔ You can quickly access keyboard settings by long-pressing the Microphone key on the keyboard. Choose the Settings icon that appears in order to display the Input Options menu.

 ✔ Alternative keyboards are available at the Google Play Store. See Chapter 15 for information on the Play Store.

Hunt and Peck and Swipe

Typing should be a basic activity. It *should* be. Typing on a touchscreen keyboard can be, well, touchy. Use my advice in this section to get some basics and perhaps discover a few tricks.

Typing one character at a time

The onscreen keyboard is pretty easy to figure out: Touch a letter to produce the character. It works just like a computer keyboard in that respect. As you type, the key you touch is highlighted. The tablet may give a wee bit of feedback in the form of a faint click or vibration.

- ✔ To type in all caps, press the Shift key twice. The Shift key may appear highlighted, the shift symbol may change color, or a colored dot may appear on the key, all of which indicate that Shift Lock is on.

- ✔ Tap the Shift key again to turn off Shift Lock.

- ✔ Above all, it helps to *type slowly* until you get used to the onscreen keyboard.

- ✔ When you make a mistake, touch the Delete key to back up and erase.

- ✔ A blinking cursor on the touchscreen shows where new text appears, which is similar to how typing text works on a computer.

- ✔ When you type a password, the character you type appears briefly, but for security reasons, it's then replaced by a black dot.

- ✔ Need more room for your stubby fingers? Turn the tablet horizontally, and the keyboard grows in size.

- ✔ See the later section "Text Editing" for more details on editing your text so that you can fix those myriad typos and boo-boos.

Accessing special characters

You're not limited to typing only the symbols you see on the alphabetic keyboard. Touch the 123 key to get access to additional keyboard layouts, samples of which are shown in Figure 4-2.

In Figure 4-2, the symbol keys are accessed by touching the key labeled ~\{, although some tablets label that key as Sym (for *sym*bols).

A 123 key on the keyboard may merely access the numeric keys.

Tablets with multiple sets of symbol keys let you page through them by touching the 1/2 and 2/2 keys. Some tablets may have three sets of symbol keyboards, in which case the keys are labeled 1/3, 2/3, and 3/3.

To return to the standard alphabetic keyboard (refer to Figure 4-1), touch the ABC key.

You can access special character keys from the main alphabetic keyboard, *if* you know a secret: *Long-press* (touch and hold) a key. When you do, you see a pop-up palette of additional characters, similar to the ones shown for the A key in Figure 4-3.

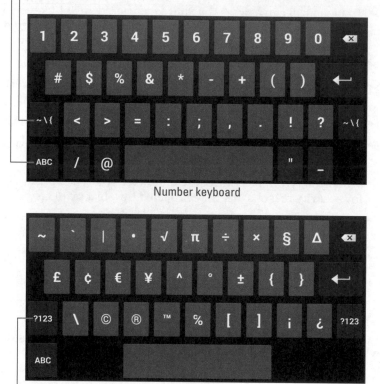

Figure 4-2: The number and symbol keyboards.

Choose a character from the pop-up palette. If you choose the wrong character, tap the Delete key on the onscreen keyboard to erase the mistyped symbol.

Not every character has a special pop-up palette.

Typing quickly by using predictive text

Many Android tablets sport a predictive-text feature, which suggests words before you type them. For example, you may type **abo** and a list of words starting with *abo* appears: *above*, *about*, *abode*, and so on. Touch a word to choose it.

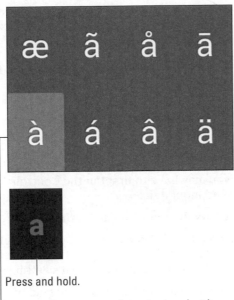

Press and hold.

Drag your finger over a character to select it.

Figure 4-3: Special-symbol pop-up palette-thing.

As you use predictive text, it may even suggest the next word to type. For example, in Figure 4-4, I typed the word *I*. The keyboard has suggested the words *have*, *am*, and *can*. Long-pressing the word *am* displayed the pop-up list of 15 other suggestions. Choose a word to insert it into your text.

To choose more suggestions, long-press
the three-dotted word and drag your finger upward.

can't	didn't	need
hope	love	could
know	want	just
think	do	would
was	don't	will

| have | **am** | can |

Suggested word   Touch a suggestion.

Figure 4-4: Predictive text in action.

When the desired word doesn't appear, continue typing: The Predictive Text feature begins making suggestions, based on what you've typed so far. Touch the correct word when it appears.

To ensure that predictive text has been activated on your tablet, follow these steps:

1. **At the Home screen, touch the Apps icon.**

2. **Open the Settings app.**

3. **Choose Language & Input.**

   On Samsung tablets, you may have to first tap the Controls tab and then choose the Language and Input item.

4. **Touch the Settings icon by the item Google Keyboard.**

   Choose the Settings icon (shown in the margin) by the Google Keyboard item. Another item, Google Voice Typing, might also appear in the list, but you want to choose the Google Keyboard item's Settings icon.

   On Samsung tablets, choose Samsung Keyboard instead of Google Keyboard. Also, the icon may appear as a gear, as shown in the margin.

   The Google Keyboard Settings screen appears.

5. **Ensure that a check mark appears by the item Next-Word Suggestions.**

   This item may be titled Show Suggestions. Or, on Samsung tablets, it's named Predictive Text, and you must slide the Master Control icon to the right to activate that setting.

When you type a word that the tablet doesn't recognize, you might be prompted to add the word to the tablet's dictionary. (Yes, the tablet has a dictionary.) Choose that option. Also see Chapter 21 for more information about the tablet's dictionary.

Activating keyboard gestures

If you're really after typing speed, consider using gesture typing. It allows you to type words by swiping your finger over the onscreen keyboard, like mad scribbling but with a positive result.

To ensure that this feature is enabled, follow Steps 1 through 4 from the preceding section to view the Google Keyboard Settings screen. Place a check mark by the item Enable Gesture Typing. While you're at it, ensure that all the items in the Gesture Typing section are enabled; a check mark should be found by each one.

For some Samsung tablets, the setting is called Keyboard Swipe. Activate it from the Samsung Keyboard Settings screen by choosing the SwiftKey Flow item.

You use gesture typing by dragging your fingers over letters on the keyboard. Figure 4-5 illustrates how the word *taco* would be typed in this manner.

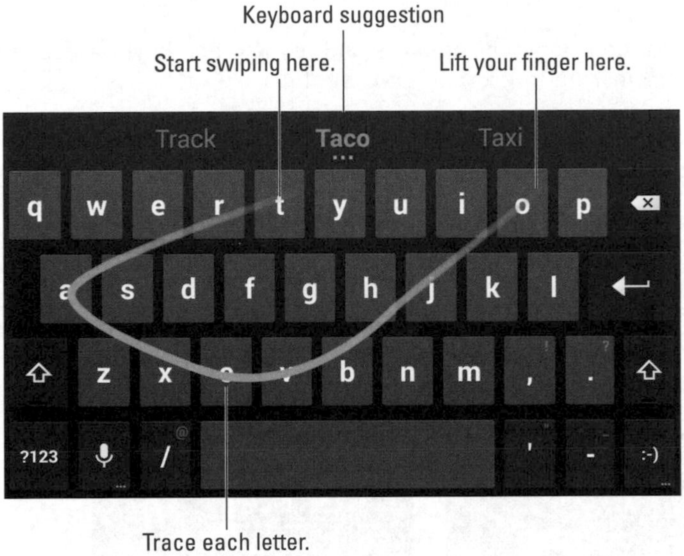

Keyboard suggestion

Start swiping here.   Lift your finger here.

Trace each letter.

Figure 4-5: Using gesture typing to type *taco*.

The gesture typing feature may not be active when you need to type a password or for specific apps. When it doesn't work, use the onscreen keyboard one letter at a time.

Android Tablet Dictation

The Android tablet has the amazing capability to interpret your dictation as text. It works almost as well as computer dictation in science fiction movies, though I can't seem to find the command to locate intelligent life.

Activating voice input

The tablet's voice input feature is officially known as Google Voice Typing. To ensure that this feature is active, obey these steps:

1. **At the Home screen, touch the Apps icon.**

2. **Open the Settings app.**

3. **Choose Language & Input.**

   Some Samsung tablets title this item Language and Input, and it's found on the Controls tab.

4. **Ensure that a check mark appears next to Google Voice Typing.**

   If not, touch the box to place a check mark there.

5. **Touch the Home icon to return to the Home screen.**

The Microphone key now appears on the onscreen keyboard. See the next section for instructions on how to use this key.

Speaking instead of typing

Talking to your tablet really works, and works quite well, if you touch the Microphone key on the keyboard and properly dictate your text.

After touching the Microphone key, you see a special window at the bottom of the screen, similar to the one shown in Figure 4-6. When the text *Speak Now* appears, dictate your text, speaking directly at the tablet. Try not to spit.

Google Voice typing active

Google Voice typing paused

Figure 4-6: Google Voice typing.

As you speak, a Microphone graphic on the screen flashes. The flashing doesn't mean that the Android tablet is embarrassed by what you're saying. No, the flashing merely indicates that the tablet is listening, detecting the volume of your voice.

As you blab, the tablet digests what you say, and the text you speak — or a close approximation — appears on the screen. It's magical and sometimes comical.

✔ The first time you try voice input, you might see a description displayed. Touch the OK button to continue.

✔ You can edit your voice input just as you edit any text. See the section "Text Editing," later in this chapter.

✔ If you don't like a word that's chosen by the dictation feature, touch the word on the screen. You see a pop-up list of alternatives from which to choose.

✔ Speak the punctuation in your text. For example, you would say, "I'm sorry comma and it won't happen again" to have the tablet produce the text *I'm sorry, and it won't happen again* or something close to that.

✔ Common punctuation you can dictate includes the comma, period, exclamation point, question mark, and colon.

✔ You cannot dictate capital letters. If you're a stickler for such things, you have to go back and edit the text.

✔ Dictation may not work where no Internet connection exists.

Uttering s**** words

The Android tablet features a voice censor. It replaces those naughty words you might utter, placing the word's first letter on the screen, followed by the appropriate number of asterisks.

For example, if *spatula* were a blue word and you uttered *spatula* when dictating text, the dictation feature would place *s******* on the screen rather than the word *spatula*.

Yeah, I know: silly. Or should I say "s****."

The tablet knows a lot of blue terms, including George Carlin's infamous "Seven Words You Can Never Say on Television," but apparently the terms *crap* and *damn* are fine. Don't ask me how much time I spent researching this topic.

See Chapter 21 if you'd like to disable the dictation censor.

Text Editing

You'll probably do more text editing on your Android tablet than you anticipated. That editing includes the basic stuff, such as spiffing up typos and adding a period here or there as well as complex editing involving cut, copy, and paste. The concepts are the same as you find on a computer, but the process can be daunting without a physical keyboard and a mouse. This section irons out the text-editing wrinkles.

Moving the cursor

The first part of editing text is to move the cursor to the right spot. The *cursor* is that blinking, vertical line where text appears. On most computing devices, you move the cursor by using a pointing device. The Android tablet has no pointing device, but you do: your finger.

To move the cursor, simply touch the spot on the text where you want to move the cursor. To help your accuracy, a cursor tab appears below the text, similar to the one shown in the margin. You can move that tab with your finger to precisely locate the cursor in your text.

After you move the cursor, you can continue to type, use the Delete key to back up and erase, or paste text copied from elsewhere.

- ✔ You may see the Paste Command button appear above the cursor tab. This button is used to paste in text, as described in the later section "Cutting, copying, and pasting text."

- ✔ You can also move the cursor around by dragging your finger over the onscreen keyboard. This trick doesn't work when the Gesture Typing feature is activated. See the section "Typing quickly by using gestures," earlier in this chapter.

Selecting text

Selecting text on an Android tablet works just like selecting text in a word processor: You mark the start and end of a block. That chunk of text appears highlighted on the screen. How you get there, however, can be a mystery — until now!

Text selection starts by long-pressing a chunk of text. Sometimes you have to press for a while, and you might try double-tapping the text, but eventually you see the Text Selection toolbar appear at the top of the screen. You also see a chunk of selected text, as shown in Figure 4-7.

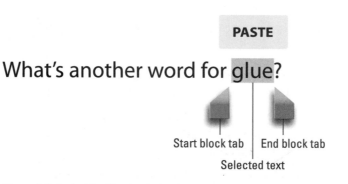

Figure 4-7: Android tablet text selection.

Drag the start and end markers around the touchscreen to define the block of selected text.

When text is selected, the Contextual action bar appears atop the screen. The stock Android version of the action bar appears in Figure 4-8, although your tablet may sport a custom action bar. Either way, you use the action bar to deal with the selected text.

| ✓ DONE | ⬛ SELECT ALL | ✂ CUT | 📋 COPY | 📋 PASTE |

Close Action bar   Select All   Cut   Copy   Paste
and deselect text.

Figure 4-8: Text selection Contextual action bar.

After you select the text, you can delete it by touching the Delete key on the onscreen keyboard. You can replace the text by typing something new. Or you can cut or copy the text. See the later section "Cutting, copying, and pasting text."

To cancel text selection, touch the Done button on the action bar, or just touch anywhere in the text outside the selected block.

- ✏ Seeing the onscreen keyboard is a good indication that you can edit and select text.

- ✏ The action bar's Select All command can be used to mark all text as a single block.

Selecting text on a web page

Grabbing a bit of text from a web page works similarly to selecting text elsewhere on your Android tablet. The difference is that you must long-press the text to start the selection process. (Double-tapping a web page activates the zoom-in feature.) After long-pressing, you can drag the selection tabs to mark the block or use the Select All command on the Action Bar toolbar to select all text on the page.

Unlike selecting text elsewhere, selecting text on a web page opens access to some special features. For example, you can choose the action bar's Share command to send the chunk o' text to another app, send it in an e-mail message, or post it to a social networking site. Use the Web Search command to perform a Google search on the selected text.

Touch the Done button on the action bar to cancel the web page text selection. With some web browser apps, you merely have to wait, and the action bar disappears.

Also note that the action bar lacks the Cut command when text is selected on a web page. Use Copy instead of Cut.

Cutting, copying, and pasting text

Selected text is primed for cutting or copying, which works just like it does in your favorite word processor. After you select the text, choose the proper command from the Contextual action bar. To copy the text, choose the Copy command. To cut the text, choose Cut.

Just like on a computer, cut or copied text on an Android tablet is stored on a clipboard. To paste any previously cut or copied text, move the cursor to the spot where you want the text pasted.

✔ A quick way to paste text is to look for the Paste command button above the cursor tab. To see that button, touch anywhere in the text. Touch the Paste command button to paste in the text.

✔ Some tablets feature a Clipboard app, which lets you peruse, review, and select previously cut or copied text or images. You might even find the Clipboard button on the action bar or onscreen keyboard.

✔ You can paste text only into locations where text is allowed. Odds are good that if you see the onscreen keyboard, you can paste text.

Part II
Stay in Touch

Get more from the tablet's address book by organizing your contacts into groups. Find out how at www.dummies.com/extras/androidtablets.

In this part . . .

- ✔ Organize your contacts in the tablet's address book, keeping them handy for e-mail, social networking, voice chat, or video chat.

- ✔ Send and receive e-mail using your tablet.

- ✔ Explore the web using the tablet's web browser or the innovative Google Chrome app.

- ✔ Share your life using your Android tablet and various social networking apps.

- ✔ Secretly turn your tablet into a phone using the Talk and Skype apps.

5

All Your Friends

It may seem puzzling that your Android tablet features an address book, chock-full of contact information. Such a thing makes sense for a phone. After all, how good are you at keeping phone numbers in your head? So why bother with phone numbers on a tablet — a device that isn't a phone? The answer is communications.

To best use your tablet for communications, you need to keep track of people. That means having their e-mail information, website addresses, social networking info, and phone numbers because — and this isn't really a secret — it's possible to make phone calls with your tablet. That communication all starts with keeping all your friends' information in a single app.

EMAIL

potus@whitehouse.gov
WORK

CONNECTIONS

⊕ Add connection

ADDRESS

1600 Pennsylvania Ave
Washington , D.C. 20006
HOME

ʹNTS

The Tablet's Address Book

You most likely already have contacts in your Android tablet's address book because your Google account was synchronized with the tablet when you first set things up. All your Gmail contacts, as well as other types of contacts on the Internet, were duplicated on the tablet, so you already have a host of friends available. The place where you can access these folks is the tablet's address book.

🖊 The tablet's address book app is named either People or Contacts. The stock Android name is People; Samsung tablets tend to use the name Contacts.

🖊 Whether the app is called Contacts or People — or even something else — it does basically the same thing. For the sake of consistency, this chapter refers to the app as the People app.

🖊 If you haven't yet set up a Google account, refer to Chapter 2.

🖊 Adding more contacts is covered later in this chapter, in the section "Even More Friends."

🖊 Contact information from the People app is used by most apps on the Android tablet, including Email, Gmail, Hangouts, and any other app that lets you share information, such as photographs or videos.

Using the address book

To peruse your Android tablet's address book, start the People or Contacts app. You may be blessed to find that app's icon on the Home screen. If not, touch the Apps icon on the Home screen, and then touch the appropriate app icon in the Apps drawer.

The address book app shows a list of all contacts in your Android tablet, organized alphabetically by first name. Figure 5-1 illustrates a version of the People app.

Scroll the list by swiping your finger on the touchscreen. You can use the index on the side of the screen (refer to Figure 5-1) to quickly scroll the list up and down. Large letters may appear as you scroll, to help you find your place.

To do anything with a contact, you first have to choose it: Touch a contact name and you see detailed information on the right side of the screen, as shown in Figure 5-1. The list of activities you can do with the contact depends on the information that's shown and on the apps installed on your tablet. Here are some options:

Place a phone call. No, An Android tablet isn't a phone, but when you install Skype, touching a contact's phone number activates that app and you can use the tablet to make a call. See Chapter 9 for details.

Send e-mail. Touch the contact's e-mail address to compose an e-mail message using either the Gmail or Email app. When the contact has more than one e-mail address, you can choose to which one you want to send the message. Chapter 6 covers using e-mail on your tablet.

Quickly scroll.   Search contacts.

View   Add new contact.

Edit contact.

Contact's photo

Favorite

Contact's name

Contacts

Figure 5-1: The People app.

View a social networking status. Contacts who are also your social networking buddies can display their current status. The status may appear at the bottom of the info list in the contact's Details screen. You might see a View Profile item or a Social Network Feeds button, which lets you see all social networking status updates for that contact. See Chapter 8 for more information on social networking.

View an address on a map. When the contact has a home or business address, you can choose that item to view the address using the Maps app. When you choose the Maps app, you can then get directions, look at the place using the Street View tool, or do any of a number of interesting things, as covered in Chapter 10.

Some tidbits of information that show up for a contact don't have an associated action. For example, the tablet doesn't sing *Happy Birthday* whenever you touch a contact's birthday information.

The Address Book app features three modes for viewing contacts: All Contacts, Favorites, and Groups. When looking for individuals, ensure that the All Contacts item is chosen. In Figure 5-1, use the View action bar to choose All Contacts. In Figure 5-2, touch the Contacts tab to view all contacts.

Search contacts.

View contact groups.

View favorites. View all contacts.

Delete contact.

Edit contact.

Add new contact.

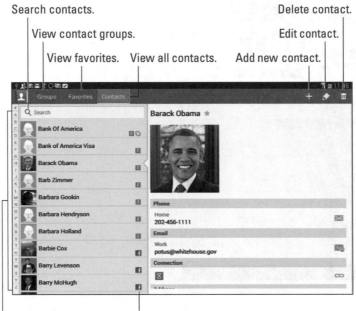

Contact index   Contact type

Figure 5-2: The Contacts app.

✔ Some versions of the address book display contact details full-screen. If so, touch the Back icon to view the main address book list after you're done viewing the contact's information.

✔ Not every contact has a picture, and the picture can come from a number of sources (Gmail or Facebook, for example). See the section "Adding a contact picture" for more information.

✔ When a contact is referred to as a *joined contact*, it means that the information you see comes from multiple sources, such as Gmail or Facebook. See the later section "Joining identical contacts" for information on joining contacts, as well as the later section "Separating contacts" for information on splitting improperly joined contacts.

Sorting the address book

The tablet's address book displays contacts in a certain order. Most often, that order is alphabetically by first name. You can change this order if the existing arrangement drives you nuts. Here's how:

1. **Open the tablet's address book.**

   Start the People or Contacts app.

2. **Touch the Action Overflow icon.**

   On some tablets, touch the Menu icon instead.

3. **Choose Settings.**

   The screen that appears contains options for viewing your contacts.

4. **Choose the Sort List By or List By command.**

   This command sorts contacts by first name or by last name. Some tablets may use *given name* for *first name* and *family name* for *last name.* It's European.

5. **Choose View Contact Names By or Display Contacts By.**

   This command specifies how the contacts appear in the list: first name first or last name first.

There's no right or wrong way to display your contacts — only the method you prefer.

Searching contacts

You might have a massive number of contacts. Although the address book app doesn't provide a running total, I'm certain that I have more than 250,000 contacts on my tablet. That's either because I know a lot of people or they just owe me money.

Rather than endlessly scroll the Contacts list and run the risk of rubbing your fingers down to nubs, you can employ the tablet's powerful Search command. Touch the Search icon or use the Search or Find Contacts text field, if it's visible. Type the name you want to locate. The list of contacts quickly narrows to show only the contacts matching the text you type.

✔ To clear a search, touch the X at the right side of the search text box.

✔ No, there's no correlation between the number of contacts you have and how popular you are in real life.

Even More Friends

Having friends is great. Having more friends is better. Keeping all those friends is best. You and all your new friends will be thrilled to know the myriad ways to add friends or create contacts for your tablet's address book app. This section lists a few of the more popular and useful methods.

Building a contact from scratch

Sometimes it's necessary to create a contact when you actually meet another human being in the real world. Or maybe you finally got around to transferring information to the tablet from a traditional address book. In either instance, you have information to input, and it starts like this:

1. **Open the tablet's address book app.**

   The app may be named People or Contacts or Unwashed Masses or something similar.

2. **Touch the Add Contact icon.**

   Refer to Figures 5-1 and 5-2 for this icon's potential location and design. If you don't see the Add Contact icon, ensure that you're viewing all contacts and not a specific contact group: Choose All Contacts from the View action bar, or touch the All Contacts tab at the top of the screen.

3. **If prompted, choose an account as the place to store the contact.**

   I recommend choosing Google, unless you use another account listed as your main Internet mail account, such as Yahoo!.

4. **Fill in the contact's information as best you can.**

   Fill in the text fields with the information you know. The more information you provide, the better.

   Use the action bar (shown in the margin) to expand a field. You may see a pop-up window with specific controls, commands, or options. Use the pop-up to help fill in the field or provide specific information, such as whether a phone number is a mobile, work, or home number.

   Some items may have a large Plus icon next to them, or you may see the text *Add New*. Use that icon to add another phone number or e-mail address or another item. A Minus or Cancel icon is used to remove multiple items.

   At the bottom of the New Contact screen, you'll find the Add Another Field button. Use that button when you can add more details for the contact, such as their birthday or website address.

5. **Touch the Done or Save button to complete editing and add the new contact.**

The new contact is created. As a bonus, it's also automatically synced with your Google account, or with whichever account you chose in Step 3.

Creating a contact from an e-mail message

Perhaps one of the easiest ways to build up the tablet's address book is to create a contact from an e-mail message. Follow these general steps when you receive a message from someone not already in your Android tablet's address list:

1. **Touch either the contact's name in the From field or the picture by the contact's name at the top of the message.**

   The contact's name or picture is really a menu, as shown by the Action Bar icon. It's your clue that a menu exists.

2. **Choose whether to create a contact or add the e-mail address to an existing contact:**

   - *For an existing contact:* Scroll through the address book to choose the contact. The e-mail address is added to that contact.

   - *For a new contact:* Fill in the rest of the contact's information on the New Contact screen or Add Contact screen. Building the contact works just like creating a contact from scratch, though the e-mail address and, potentially, the person's name is already available.

3. **Touch the OK, Done, or Save button to create the contact.**

If you accidentally create a contact when you already have that contact, you can join the two. See the later section "Joining identical contacts" for information on combining two address book entries.

Importing contacts from a computer

Your computer's e-mail program is doubtless a useful repository of contacts you've built up over the years. You can export these contacts from your computer's e-mail program and then import them into your tablet. It's not simple, but it's possible.

The key is to save or export your computer e-mail program's records in the *vCard* (.vcf) file format. These records can then be imported by the Android tablet into the address book app. The method for exporting contacts varies, depending on the e-mail program:

- **In the Windows Live Mail program,** choose Go⇨Contacts and then choose File⇨Export⇨Business Card (.VCF) to export the contacts.

- **In Windows Mail,** choose File⇨Export⇨Windows Contacts, and then choose vCards (Folder of .VCF Files) from the Export Windows Contacts dialog box. Click the Export button.

- **On the Mac,** open the Address Book program and choose File⇨Export⇨ Export vCard.

After the vCard files are created on your computer, connect the Android tablet to the computer and transfer them. Transferring files from your computer to the Android tablet is covered in Chapter 17.

With the vCard files stored on your tablet, follow these steps in the Address Book app to complete the process:

1. **Touch the Action Overflow or Menu icon.**

2. **Choose the Import/Export command.**

3. **Choose Import from Storage.**

    The command might instead read Import from USB Storage or Import from SD Card.

4. **Choose an account to save the contacts.**

    I recommend choosing your Google account, unless you have another account, such as Yahoo!, that you use primarily.

5. **Choose the Import All vCard Files option.**

6. **Touch the OK button.**

    The contacts are saved on your tablet and also synchronized to your Gmail account, which instantly creates a backup copy.

The importing process may create some duplicates. That's okay: You can join two entries for the same person in your tablet's address book. See the section "Joining identical contacts," later in this chapter.

If you're using Microsoft Outlook and have an exchange server, add your Outlook contacts by adding your exchange server account as one of the tablet's accounts. Once added, all your Outlook contacts, as well as scheduling and other information, are automatically synchronized with your Android tablet. See Chapter 2 for information on adding accounts.

Beaming contacts

A quick, handy, and extremely high-tech way to send a contact from one device to another is to use the Android Beam feature. To make it happen, both devices must be capable of Near Field Communications, or NFC, and they must sport the Android Beam feature.

To share the contact, open the tablet's Address Book app and display the contact's information. Place the back of your tablet (where the NFC field is located) against the other Android device. When the text *Touch to Beam* appears on the screen, tap the screen. The contact information is sent to the other device.

See Chapter 16 for additional information on NFC and Android Beam.

Bringing in social networking contacts

You can pour your whole gang of friends and followers into your Android tablet from your social networking sites. The operation is automatic: Simply add the social networking site's app to the tablet's app inventory as described in Chapter 8. At that time, either you're prompted to sync the contacts or they're added instantly to the tablet's address book.

A side effect of the social networking importing process is that it may create duplicate address book entries. Depending on the Address Book app, you may also find improperly joined entries, such as two people with similar names having a single, combined account. To remedy these situations, refer to the later section "Joining identical contacts" as well as the later section "Separating contacts."

Finding a new contact on the map

It's not possible to directly translate a location from the Maps app into the tablet's address book. Instead, you can flag found locations as favorites. After you flag a favorite location, you can use the Maps app to locate contact information or to obtain directions to that location.

See Chapter 10 for details on using the Maps app.

Manage Your Friends

Don't let your friends just sit there, occupying valuable storage space inside your tablet! Put them to work. Actually, the tablet does the work; you just give the orders. This section lists some routine and common address book chores and activities.

Editing contact information

To make minor touch-ups on any contact, start by locating and displaying the contact's information. Touch the Edit icon (at the top of the screen) to start making changes. When the Edit icon isn't visible, touch the Action Overflow or Menu icon and choose the Edit command.

Change or add information by touching a field and then typing using the onscreen keyboard. You can edit information as well: Touch the field to edit and change whatever you want.

Some contact information cannot be edited. For example, fields pulled in from social networking sites can be edited only by that account holder on the social networking site.

When you're finished editing, touch the Save or Done button.

Adding a contact picture

Nothing can be more delicious than snapping an inappropriate picture of someone you know and using the picture as his or her contact picture on your Android tablet. Then, every time the person e-mails you, that embarrassing, potentially career-ending photo comes up.

Oh, and I suppose you could use nice pictures as well, but what's the fun in that?

The simplest way to add a picture to a contact is to have the image already stored in the tablet. You can snap a picture and save it, grab a picture from the Internet, or use any image that's already stored in the Gallery app. The image doesn't even have to be a picture of the contact — any image will do.

After you store the contact's photo or any other suitable image on your tablet, follow these steps to update the contact's information:

1. **Locate and display the contact's information.**

2. **Edit the contact's information.**

   Touch the Edit icon or, if it's unavailable, touch the Action Overflow or Menu icon and choose the Edit command or Edit Contact command.

3. **Touch the icon where the contact's picture would go, or touch the existing picture assigned to the contact.**

   The icon shows a generic human image when no picture is assigned.

4. **Choose Picture or Album to fetch the image from the tablet's storage.**

   If you have other image management apps on your tablet, you can instead choose the app's command from the list. Otherwise:

5. **Choose Gallery.**

   The photo gallery is displayed. It lists all photos and videos stored on your tablet.

6. **Browse the photo gallery to look for a suitable image.**

   See Chapter 12 for more information on using the Gallery app.

7. **Touch the image you want to use for the contact.**

8. **Crop the image.**

   Use Figure 5-3 as a guide to how to crop the image.

9. **Save the cropped image.**

   Touch the OK, Save, or Done button.

   The image is cropped but not yet assigned.

Crop image.

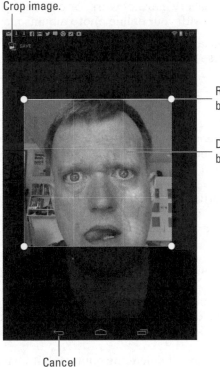

Resize cropping box.

Drag cropping box.

Cancel

Figure 5-3: Cropping a contact's image.

10. Touch the OK, Save, or Done button to finish editing the contact.

The image is now assigned, and it appears whenever the contact is referenced.

The contact's image appears whenever they contact you, such as by sending e-mail, in a Google hangout, as well as other instances when the contact is referenced in your tablet.

✔ If you would rather use the tablet to take a picture of the contact, choose the Take Photo, Take Picture, or Take New Photo command in Step 4. Use the tablet's Camera app to take a picture; see Chapter 11 for details on using the Camera app. After you've taken the picture, touch the OK icon or the Check Mark icon, and then proceed with cropping the image.

✔ Pictures can also be added by your Gmail friends and contacts when they add their own images to their accounts.

✔ You may also see pictures assigned to your contacts based on pictures supplied on Facebook or other social networking sites.

     ✔ Some images in the Gallery may not work for contact icons. For example, images synchronized with your online photo albums may be unavailable.

     ✔ To remove or change a contact's picture, follow Steps 1 through 3 in the preceding list. Choose the Remove Photo command to get rid of the existing image.

Making a favorite

A *favorite* contact is someone you stay in touch with most often. The person doesn't have to be someone you like — just someone you (perhaps unfortunately) contact often, such as your bookie.

To make a contact a favorite, display the contact's information and touch the Favorite (star) icon by the contact's image, as shown in Figure 5-1. When the star is filled, the contact is one of your favorites and is stored in the Favorites group.

To remove a favorite, touch the contact's star again, and it loses its highlight.

The favorite contacts are all found by accessing the Starred group or Favorites group. To view that group, choose the Favorites command from the View action bar (refer to Figure 5-1), or choose the Favorite tab (refer to Figure 5-2).

     ✔ Removing a favorite doesn't delete the contact, but instead removes it from the Favorites group.

     ✔ The Favorites group may be named the Starred group on some tablets.

     ✔ By the way, contacts have no idea whether they're among your favorites, so don't believe that you're hurting their feelings by not making them favorites.

Joining identical contacts

Your tablet pulls contacts from multiple sources, such as Gmail, Facebook, Yahoo!, and even other apps such as Skype. Because of that, you may discover duplicate contact entries in the tablet's address book. Rather than fuss over which entry to use, you can join the contacts. Here's how:

1. **Wildly scroll the address book until you locate a duplicate.**

   Well, maybe not *wildly* scroll, but locate a duplicated entry. Because the address book is sorted, the duplicates usually appear close together (though that may not always be the case).

2. **Select one of the duplicate contacts.**

3. **Touch the Action Overflow or Menu icon and choose either the Join or Link Contact command.**

   You may have to edit the contact first and then touch the Action Overflow or Menu icon to find the command.

After choosing the command, you see a list of contacts that the tablet guesses might be identical. You also see the entire list of contacts, in case the guess is incorrect. Your job is to find the duplicate contact.

4. **Choose a matching contact in the list to join the two contacts.**

The contacts are merged, appearing as a single entry in the address book.

Joined contacts aren't flagged as such in the address book, but you can easily identify them: When looking at the contact's information, a joined contact looks like a single, long entry, often showing two sources or accounts from which the contact's information is pulled.

Separating contacts

The topic of separating contacts has little to do with parenting, although separating bickering children is the first step in avoiding a fight. Contacts in the address book might not be bickering, but occasionally the tablet may automatically join two contacts that aren't really the same person. When that happens, you can split them by following these steps:

1. **Display the improperly joined contact.**

As an example, I'm a Facebook friend with other humans named Dan Gookin. My tablet accidentally joined my address book entry with another Dan Gookin.

2. **Touch the Action Overflow or Menu icon and choose the Separate command.**

The command might not be available, in which case you need to edit the contact, as described earlier in this chapter. At that point, touch the Action Overflow or Menu icon to choose the Separate command.

The Separate command might also be called Separate Contacts.

3. **Touch the OK button to confirm that you're splitting the contacts.**

You don't need to actively look for improperly joined contacts as much as you'll just stumble across them. When you do, feel free to separate them, especially if you detect any bickering.

Removing a contact

Every so often, consider reviewing your tablet's address book. Purge the folks whom you no longer recognize or you've forgotten. It's simple: View the forlorn contact and touch the Trash icon, shown in the margin. Touch the OK button to confirm. Poof! They're gone.

On some tablets, you may have to touch the Action Overflow or Menu icon and then choose a Delete command. Touch the OK button to remove the contact.

✔ Because the tablet's address book is synchronized with your Google account, the contact is also removed there.

✔ You may not be able to delete contacts associated with specific accounts, such as your social networking friends. To remove those contacts, you need to go to the source, such as Facebook or Twitter.

✔ Removing a contact doesn't kill the person in real life.

You've Got E-Mail

The first e-mail message was sent back in the early 1970s. Programmer Ray Tomlinson doesn't remember the exact text but guesses that it was probably something like "QWERTYUIOP." Although that's not as memorable as the first telegraph that was sent ("What hath God wrought?") or the first telephone message ("Mr. Watson, come here. I want you."), it's one for the history books.

Today, e-mail has become far more functional and necessary, well beyond Mr. Tomlinson's early tests. Although you could impress your e-mail buddies by sending them "QWERTYUIOP," you're more likely to send and reply to more meaningful communications. Your Android tablet is more than up to the task.

Android Tablet E-Mail

Electronic mail is handled on the Android tablet by two apps: Gmail and Email.

The Gmail app hooks directly into your Google Gmail account. In fact, they're exact echoes of each other: The Gmail you receive on your computer is received also on your tablet.

You can also use the Email app to connect with non-Gmail electronic mail, such as the standard mail service provided by your ISP or a web-based e-mail system such as Yahoo! Mail or Windows Live Mail.

Regardless of the app, electronic mail on the Android tablet works just like it does on a computer: You can create, send, receive, and forward e-mail to a group of contacts, and work with attachments, for example. As long as the tablet can find an Internet connection, e-mail works just peachy.

✔ Both the Gmail and Email apps are located in the Apps drawer. You may also find shortcuts to the apps on the Home screen.

✔ The Gmail app is updated frequently. To review any changes since this book went to press, visit my website at

    www.wambooli.com/help/android/gmail

✔ Although you can use your tablet's web browser to visit the Gmail website, you should use the Gmail app to pick up your Gmail.

✔ If you forget your Gmail password, visit this web address:

    www.google.com/accounts/ForgotPasswd

Setting up an Email account

The Email app is used to access web-based e-mail, or *webmail,* from Yahoo! Mail, Windows Live, and what-have-you. It also lets you read e-mail provided by an Internet service provider (ISP), an office, or another large, intimidating organization. To get things set up regardless of the service, follow these steps:

1. **Start the Email app.**

   Look for it in the Apps drawer.

   If you've run the Email app before, you see the Email inbox and you're done. See the next section for information on adding e-mail accounts.

   If you haven't yet run the Email app, the first screen you see is Account Setup.

2. **Type the e-mail address you use for the account.**

3. **Type the password for that account.**

4. **Touch the Next button.**

   If you're lucky, everything is connected and you can move on to Step 5. Otherwise, you have to specify the details as provided by your ISP, including the incoming and outgoing server information, often known by the bewildering acronyms POP3 and SMTP. Plod through the steps on the screen, although the tablet really just wants to know the incoming and outgoing server names.

   Your ISP most likely has a support web page for setting up e-mail accounts. That page may list specific account setup information for an Android device. Use it.

5. **Set the account options on the aptly named Account Options screen.**

   You might want to reset the Inbox Checking Frequency option to something other than 15 minutes.

   If the account will be your main e-mail account, place a check mark next to the Send Email from This Account By Default option.

6. **Touch the Next button.**

7. **Give the account a name and check your own name.**

   The account is given the name of the mail server, which may not ring a bell when you receive your e-mail. I name my ISP's e-mail account Main because it's my main account.

   The Your Name field lists your name as it's applied to outgoing messages. So if your name is really, say, Cornelius the Magnificent and not wally78, you can make that change now.

8. **Touch the Next or Done button.**

   You're done.

The next thing you see is your e-mail account inbox. Your tablet synchronizes any pending e-mail you have in your account, updating the inbox immediately. See the later section "Message for You!" for what to do next.

Adding more e-mail accounts

The Email app can be configured to pick up mail from multiple sources. If you have a Yahoo! Mail or Windows Live account and maybe an evil corporate account in addition to your ISP's account, you can add them. Follow through with these steps:

1. **In the Email app, touch the Action Overflow or Menu icon.**

2. **Choose the Settings command.**

   If you don't see the Settings command, you probably aren't at the top level of the Email app: Touch the app icon in the upper left corner of the screen until you see the Email app's main screen.

3. **Touch the Add Account button.**

   The Account Setup or Account Options screen appears. From this point forward, adding the account works as described in the preceding section, starting at Step 2.

You can also add new Email accounts by using the Settings app. Obey these directions:

1. **Start the Settings app.**

   It's found in the Apps drawer; touch the Apps icon on the Home screen to view the Apps drawer.

2. **In the Accounts area, choose Add Account.**

   On some Samsung tablets, touch the General tab and then choose the Accounts item. The Add Account command is found on the right side of the screen, near the bottom of the account list.

3. **Select the type of e-mail account you want to add.**

   If you see the account type listed, such as AOL or Yahoo!, choose it. Otherwise, choose the Email option. If the IMAP or POP3 options are available, choose IMAP for web-based e-mail (such as Yahoo! or Windows Live) and POP3 for an ISP e-mail account. The Corporate option is available for organizations with an Exchange Server.

4. **Continue working through the e-mail setup as described in the preceding section.**

   Start with Step 2, where you type your user account name and password.

You can repeat the steps in this section to add more e-mail accounts. E-mail from the accounts you configure is accessed by using the Email app.

> ✔ Be on the lookout for e-mail–specific apps, although not every tablet has them. For example, I've seen a Yahoo! Mail app. If you find such an app that's specific to your e-mail service, be sure to use it.

> ✔ I highly recommend getting the necessary information from your organization's friendly IT people if you decide to add a corporate e-mail account.

> ✔ For some corporate accounts, you may be prompted to activate the device administrator. That feature gives your corporate IT overlords remote access to your Android tablet to control e-mail. If you're shackled to corporate e-mail, you've probably already agreed to such a thing when you signed up to be an employee. Otherwise, keep in mind that you can always get your corporate e-mail at work and may not really need to use your Android tablet for that purpose.

Message for You!

All Android tablets work flawlessly with Gmail. In fact, if Gmail is already set up to be your main e-mail address, you'll enjoy having access to your messages all the time by using your tablet.

Non-Gmail e-mail, handled by the Email app, must be set up before it can be used, as covered earlier in this chapter. After completing the quick and occasionally painless setup, you can receive e-mail on your tablet just as you can on a computer.

Getting a new message

You're alerted to the arrival of a new e-mail message in your tablet by a notification icon. The icon differs, depending on the e-mail's source.

 For a new Gmail message, the New Gmail notification, similar to the one shown in the margin, appears at the top of the touchscreen.

 For a new e-mail message, you see the New Email notification.

Conjure the notification drawer to review your e-mail notifications. You see either a single notification representing the most recent message or the total number of pending messages listing the various senders and subjects.

Choosing an e-mail notification takes you to the appropriate e-mail inbox.

Checking the inbox

To peruse your Gmail, start the Gmail app. The Gmail inbox is shown in Figure 6-1.

Sidebar   All Mail inbox   Message

Figure 6-1: The Gmail inbox.

To check your Email inbox, open the Email app. You either see a single account's inbox or you can choose to view the universal inbox, shown as Combined view in Figure 6-2.

Mailbox overview   File attachment

Account menu   Compose new message.

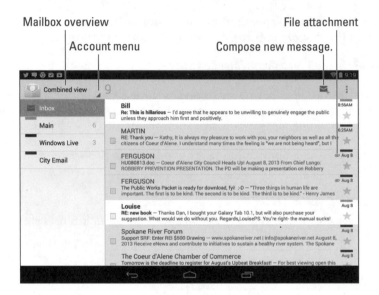

Figure 6-2: Messages in the Email app.

Don't bother looking for your Gmail inbox in the Email app. Gmail is its own app; your Gmail messages don't show up in the Email app, even when you choose Combined View from the Account menu.

✔ Search your Gmail messages by touching the Search icon, shown in Figure 6-1.

✔ Gmail is organized using labels, not folders. To see your Gmail labels from the inbox, touch the Folder Overview button. It's found in the upper left corner of the screen.

✔ Multiple e-mail accounts that are gathered in the Email app are color coded. When you view the combined inbox, you see the color codes to the left of each message — as long as messages from multiple accounts are available.

✔ To view an individual account's inbox, choose the account from the navigation drawer.

Reading e-mail

As mail comes in, you can read it by choosing a new e-mail notification, as described earlier in this chapter. Reading and working with the message operate much the same whether you're using the Gmail or Email app.

Touch a message in either the Gmail or Email app to read it. Swipe the message up or down by using your finger.

To work with the message, use the icons that appear above the message. These icons, which may not look exactly like those shown in the margin, cover common e-mail actions:

Reply: Touch this icon to reply to a message. A new message window appears with the To and Subject fields reflecting the original sender(s) and subject.

Reply All: Touch this icon to respond to everyone who received the original message, including folks on the Cc line. Use this option only when everyone else must get a copy of your reply.

Forward: Touch this icon to send a copy of the message to someone else.

Delete: Touch this icon to delete a message. This icon is found atop the message.

You may not see the Reply All and Forward icons when the tablet is in its vertical orientation. Turn the tablet horizontally to see all three icons, along with the Favorite icon.

Additional e-mail commands can be found by tapping the Action Overflow icon. The commands available depend on what you're doing in the Gmail or Email app at the time you touch the icon.

- ✔ Browse between messages by swiping the screen left or right.

- ✔ Favorite messages can be viewed or searched separately, making them easier to locate later.

- ✔ If you've properly configured the Email program, you don't need to delete messages you've read. See the section "Configuring the Server Delete option," later in this chapter.

Write a New E-Mail Message

The Gmail and Email apps not only receive electronic mail but can also be used to spawn new mail. This section describes the various ways to create a message using your tablet.

Starting a message from scratch

Creating a new e-mail epistle works similarly in both the Gmail and Email apps. The key is to touch the Compose icon, found atop the screen. Figure 6-3 shows how the e-mail composition screen might look. Its features should be familiar to you if you've ever written e-mail on a computer.

Figure 6-3: Writing a new e-mail message.

Fill in the To, Subject, and message content fields. As you type in the To field, matching contacts from the tablet's address book appear. Choose one from the list that appears. As with any e-mail message, you can send to multiple recipients.

■ If you can't see the CC and BCC fields, touch the Action Overflow icon and choose the Add Cc/Bcc command.

■ When you have more than one e-mail account configured for the Email app, you can select which account to use for sending the message. Choose the sending account as shown in Figure 6-3. The account being used appears on the screen, such as Main, shown in the figure.

To send the message, touch the Send icon, illustrated in Figure 6-3. The Send icon might also appear as shown in the margin.

✔ To cancel a message, choose the Discard command (refer to Figure 6-3). This command might be found by first touching the Action Overflow or Menu icon. Touch either the OK or Discard button to confirm.

✔ Copies of the messages you send in the Email app are stored in the Sent mailbox. For Gmail, sent messages are saved in your Gmail account.

✔ The Compose icon may look different on your tablet. Occasionally, the Pencil icon (shown in the margin) is used.

✔ Save a message by choosing the Save Draft command from the Action Overflow menu. Drafts are saved in the Drafts folder. You can open them there for further editing or sending.

✔ Some tablets feature a formatting toolbar in the Email app. Use the toolbar to change the way the text looks in your message.

Sending e-mail to a contact

A quick and easy way to compose a new message is to find a contact and then create a message using that contact's information. Heed these steps:

1. **Open the tablet's address book app.**

   The stock Android app is named People, although the name Contacts is also popular.

2. **Locate the contact to whom you want to send an electronic message.**

3. **Touch the contact's e-mail address.**

4. **Choose Gmail or Email to compose the message.**

   Other options may be available for composing the message. For example, a custom e-mail app you've downloaded may show up there as well.

At this point, creating the message works as described in the preceding section.

At Step 4, you may be prompted to use the selected app always or just once. I recommend choosing Just Once until you become more familiar with the e-mail apps. Refer to Chapter 21 for more information on the Always/Just Once choice.

Message Attachments

The key to understanding e-mail attachments on your Android tablet is to look for the paperclip icon. When you find that icon, you can either deal with an attachment for incoming e-mail or add an attachment to outgoing e-mail.

Receiving an attachment

The difference between attachments in the Gmail and Email apps is the way they look. The stock Android method of displaying a message attachment is shown in Figure 6-4. That's how Gmail displays attachments, and it might also be the way the Email app displays them, though your tablet may highlight the attachment differently.

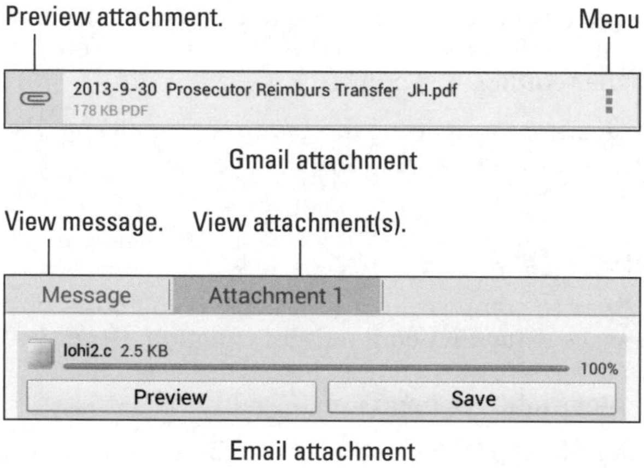

Preview attachment.   Menu

	2013-9-30 Prosecutor Reimburs Transfer JH.pdf	
	178 KB PDF	⋮

Gmail attachment

View message.   View attachment(s).

Message	**Attachment 1**	
lohi2.c 2.5 KB		100%
Preview		Save

Email attachment

Figure 6-4: Attachment methods and madness.

To deal with the attachment, touch it. In most cases, the attachment opens using a given app on your tablet. The app that's used depends on the type of attachment. For example, a PDF attachment might be opened by the Quickoffice app.

Touching the Action Overflow icon (refer to Figure 6-4) displays commands related to the attachment. Here's a smattering of what you may see:

Preview: Open the attachment for viewing.

Save: Save the attachment to the tablet's storage.

Download Again: Fetch the attachment from the mail server.

As with e-mail attachments received on a computer, the only problem you may have is that the tablet lacks the app required to deal with the attachment. When an app can't be found, you have to either suffer through not viewing the attachment or simply reply to the message and direct the person to resend the attachment in a common file format.

✔ Sometimes, pictures included in an e-mail message aren't displayed. You can touch the Show Pictures button in the message to display the pictures.

✔ Common file formats include PNG and JPEG for pictures, and HTML and RTF for documents. PDF and DOCX for Adobe Acrobat and Microsoft Word documents (respectively) are also common.

✔ You may see a prompt displayed when several apps can deal with the attachment. Choose one and touch the Just This Once button to view the attachment. Also see Chapter 21 for information on the Always/Just This Once prompt.

✔ Attachments are saved in the Downloads folder or Download folder on either the tablet's internal storage or its removable storage (the MicroSD card). You can view that folder by using the Downloads app. If that app isn't available, look for the My Files app, or you can obtain a file management app from the Google Play Store, as covered in Chapter 15. Chapter 17 covers Android tablet storage.

Sending an attachment

The most common e-mail attachment to send from a tablet is a picture or video. Some tablets may limit you to that choice, but other tablets may allow you to attach documents, music, and even random files, if you're so bold.

The key to adding an attachment to an outgoing message is to touch the Paperclip (Add Attachment) icon in the Compose window. This technique works in both the Gmail and Email apps. After touching the Add Attachment icon, you see the Choose Attachment menu. The number of items on that menu depends on what's installed on your Android tablet. There are a few basic items:

Gallery: Pluck a picture or video from the Gallery app.

Quickoffice: Choose a document you've saved on your tablet.

Select music track: Choose music stored in the music library. (Not every tablet allows you to share music.)

Other items: If you've installed another photo manager or a file manager, it also appears on the list.

The number of items you see depends on which apps are installed on your Android tablet. Also, the variety is different between the Gmail and Email apps.

You'll use the program you've chosen to locate the specific file or media tidbit you plan to send. That item is attached to the outgoing message.

To select more than one attachment, touch the paperclip icon again.

 It's also possible to send an attachment by using the various Share commands and icons located in various apps. After choosing the Share icon, select Gmail or Email as the app to use for sharing whatever it is you want to share. For example, view an image in the Gallery app, touch the Share icon, and then choose Gmail or Email to compose a new message with the image as an attachment.

  ✔ It's possible to attach multiple items to a single e-mail message. Just keep touching the attachment icon for the message to add additional goodies.

  ✔ The variety of items you can attach depends on which apps are installed on the tablet.

  ✔ The Gmail and Email apps sometimes accept different types of attachments. So if you cannot attach something by using the Gmail app, try using the Email app instead.

E-Mail Configuration

You can have oodles of fun and waste oceans of time confirming and customizing the e-mail experience on your Android tablet. The most interesting things you can do are to modify or create an e-mail signature, specify how mail you retrieve on the tablet is deleted from the server, and assign a default e-mail account for the Email app.

Creating a signature

I highly recommend that you create a custom e-mail signature for sending messages from your Android tablet. Here's my signature:

```
DAN

This was sent from my Android tablet.
Typos, no matter how hilarious, are unintentional.
```

To create a signature for Gmail, or to change the existing signature, obey these directions:

1. **At the Gmail app's main screen, touch the Action Overflow or Menu icon.**

2. **Choose your Gmail account from the list.**

   Touch your e-mail address as it's shown on the touchscreen.

3. **Choose Signature.**

   Any existing signature appears on the screen, ready for you to edit or replace it.

4. **Type or dictate your signature.**

5. **Touch OK.**

To set a signature for the Email app, heed these steps:

1. **In the Email app, touch the Action Overflow or Menu icon.**

2. **Choose the Settings or Email Settings command.**

   You may have to first choose the More command to find the Settings command. Or you may be lucky and find the Signature command directly.

3. **If prompted, choose an e-mail account from the list.**

   You create a separate signature for each e-mail account, so when you have multiple accounts, you need to repeat these steps for each one.

4. **Choose the Signature command or Add Signature command.**

   If you don't see either command, choose an account from the left side of the screen.

5. **Type or dictate your new, outgoing e-mail signature, or edit any existing signature.**

6. **Touch the OK, Save, or Done button.**

When you have multiple e-mail accounts, repeat these steps to configure a signature for each one.

Configuring the server delete option

Non-Gmail e-mail that you fetch on your Android tablet is typically left on the e-mail server. That's because, unlike a computer's e-mail program, the Email app doesn't delete messages after it picks them up. The advantage is that you can retrieve the same messages later using a computer. The disadvantage is that you end up retrieving mail you've already read and, possibly, replied to.

You can control whether the Email app removes messages after they're picked up. Follow these steps:

1. **Open the Email app and visit the inbox.**

2. **Touch the Action Overflow icon and choose the Settings command.**

   On some tablets, touch the Menu icon to see the Settings command.

3. **Choose an e-mail account.**

4. **Choose the Incoming Settings command.**

   If there's no such command, you're dealing with a web-based e-mail account, in which case there's no need to worry about the Server Delete option.

5. **Touch the Delete Email from Server item.**

   The item is an Action Bar menu, shown by the triangle in the lower right corner.

6. **Choose the When I Delete from Inbox option.**

7. **Touch the Done button.**

After you make or confirm this setting, messages you delete in the Email app are also deleted from the mail server. That means the message won't be picked up again, not by the tablet, another mobile device, or any computer that fetches e-mail from that same account.

Tablet Web Browsing

In This Chapter

▶ Browsing the web on your tablet

▶ Adding a bookmark

▶ Working with tabs

▶ Searching for text on a web page

▶ Sharing web pages

▶ Downloading images and files

▶ Configuring the web browser app

I'm certain that the World Wide Web was designed to be viewed on a computer. The monitor is big and roomy. Web pages are displayed amply, like Uncle Carl on the sofa watching a ballgame. The smaller the screen, however, the more difficult it is to view web pages designed for those roomy monitors. The web on a cell phone? Tragic. But on an Android tablet?

Your tablet doesn't have the diminutive screen of a cell phone, nor does it have a widescreen computer monitor. Instead, the tablet's screen is a good size in between, like a younger, thinner version of Uncle Carl. That size is enjoyable for viewing the web, especially when you've read the tips and suggestions in this chapter.

NIC-lawsuit-rev-5-
opencda.com
Complete 208 KB

LCDC-Projects_Sou
opencda.com
Complete 796 KB

648px-Conversion_
upload.wikimedia.org
Complete 147 KB

    ✔ If possible, activate the tablet's Wi-Fi connection before you venture out on the web. Although you can use the cellular data connection, a Wi-Fi connection incurs no data usage charges.

    ✔ Many places you visit on the web can instead be accessed directly and more effectively by using specific apps. Facebook, Gmail, Twitter, YouTube, and other popular web destinations have apps that you may find already installed on your tablet or are otherwise available for free from the Google Play Store.

The Web on Your Tablet

It's difficult these days to find someone who has no experience with the World Wide Web. More common is someone who has used the web on a computer but has yet to sample the Internet waters on a mobile device. If that's you, consider this section your quick mobile web orientation.

Using the web browser app

All Android tablets feature a web browsing app. The stock Android app is Google's own Chrome web browser. Your tablet may have another web browser app, which may be named Web, Browser, or Internet. The good news is that all web apps work in a similar way and offer comparable features.

- If your tablet doesn't have the Chrome app, you can obtain a free copy at the Google Play Store. See Chapter 15.

- As with all apps, you can find a copy of the web browser app in the Apps drawer. A shortcut icon might also be found on the Home screen.

- Chrome is also the name of Google's computer web browser. An advantage of using Chrome is that your bookmarks, web history, and other features are shared between all copies of Chrome that you use.

- The first time you fire up the web browser app on certain Samsung tablets, you may see a registration page. Register your device to receive sundry Samsung bonus stuff — or not. Registration is optional.

Viewing the web

When you first open the web browser app, you're taken to the home page. That may be the tablet manufacturer's home page, the cellular provider's home page, or a home page you've set. For the Chrome app, you see the last page you viewed on the app, or you may see Google's main page, illustrated in Figure 7-1.

Here are some handy Android tablet web browsing and viewing tips:

- Pan the web page by dragging your finger across the touchscreen. You can pan up, down, left, or right when the page is larger than the tablet's screen.

- Pinch the screen to zoom out or spread two fingers to zoom in.

- Double-tap the screen to zoom in.

- Long-press the screen to see a magnification window, which makes it easier to read items and to touch links.

- You can orient the tablet vertically to read a web page in Portrait mode. Doing so may reformat some web pages, which can make long lines of text easier to read.

Back
Forward
Refresh   Tabs
Close tab   Address box
New tab
Incognito tab
Bookmark page

Web page content

Figure 7-1: The Chrome app beholds the Google home page.

Visiting a web page

To visit a web page, type its address in the Address box (refer to Figure 7-1). You can also type a search word or phrase if you don't know the exact address of a web page. Touch the Go button on the onscreen keyboard to search the web or visit a specific web page.

If you don't see the Address box, touch the web page's tab atop the screen. The Address box, along with the various icons left and right, appears on the screen.

You "click" links on a page by touching them with your finger. If you have trouble stabbing the right link, zoom in on the page and try again. You can also long-press the screen to see a magnification window to make accessing links easier.

✔ The Go icon might appear in the Address box while you're typing a web page address. If it doesn't, check the onscreen keyboard for the Go key.

✔ To reload a web page, touch the Refresh icon. If you don't see that icon on the screen, touch the Action Overflow or Menu icon to find the Refresh or Reload command. Refreshing updates a website that changes often, and the command can also be used to reload a web page that may not have completely loaded the first time.

✔ To stop a web page from loading, touch the Stop (X) icon that appears by the Address box.

    ✔ Many websites feature special mobile editions, which automatically appear when you visit those sites using a device like the Android tablet. If you'd prefer not to automatically visit the mobile version of a website, touch the Action Overflow or Menu icon and choose the command Request Desktop Site. After that item is selected, the web browser app no longer shows the mobile version of a website.

Browsing back and forth

To return to a web page, you can touch the Back icon at the top of the screen (refer to Figure 7-1). If that icon isn't visible, you can also use the Back navigation icon, shown in the margin.

Touch the Forward icon (refer to Figure 7-1) to go forward or to return to a page you were visiting before you touched Back.

To review web pages you've visited in the long term, visit the web browser's history page. In Chrome, choose History from the Action Overflow menu. Other web browser apps may show your web page history on the Bookmarks page: Choose Bookmarks from the Action Overflow menu and touch the History tab.

To clear the history list in the Chrome app, touch the Clear Browsing Data button while viewing the web page history. Ensure that there's a check mark by the Clear Browsing History item, and then touch the Clear button.

Working with bookmarks

Need to remember a favorite website? For heaven's sake, don't fold down the corner of your tablet! Instead, just create a bookmark for that site. It's cinchy: Touch the Favorite icon near the Address box. Tap that icon and you see the Add Bookmark window, similar to the one shown in Figure 7-2.

I typically edit the name to something shorter, especially if the web page's title is long. Shorter names look better in the Bookmarks window. Touch the Save button or OK button to create the bookmark.

After the bookmark is set, it appears in the list of bookmarks. To see the bookmark list in the Chrome app, touch the Action Overflow or Menu icon and choose the Bookmarks command. Chrome has three categories of bookmarks: Desktop Bookmarks, Other Bookmarks, and Mobile Bookmarks. (You choose the category from the Add Bookmark window; refer to Figure 7-2.)

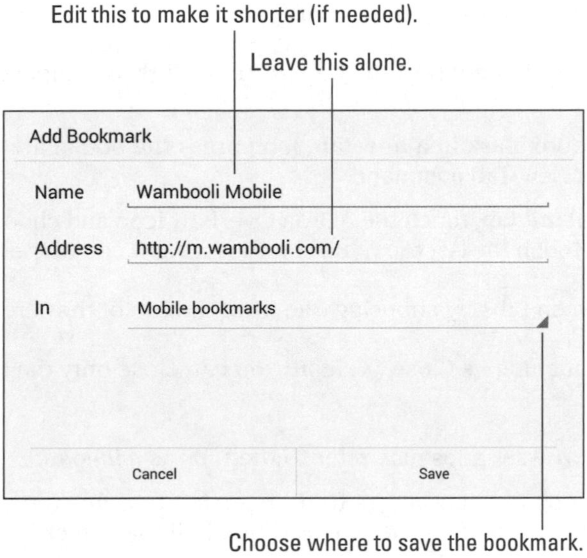

Edit this to make it shorter (if needed).

Leave this alone.

Add Bookmark

Name   Wambooli Mobile

Address   http://m.wambooli.com/

In   Mobile bookmarks

Cancel   Save

Choose where to save the bookmark.

Figure 7-2: Creating a bookmark.

The Desktop Bookmarks folder contains any bookmarks you've used in the desktop version of Chrome, which is a handy way to import your computer's bookmarks. That information is coordinated with your Android tablet, courtesy of your Google account.

To browse bookmarks, open a bookmark folder. If necessary, touch a sub-folder icon to open it. Then touch a bookmark to visit that page.

- ✔ Remove a bookmark by long-pressing its entry in the Bookmarks list. Choose the Delete Bookmark command.
- ✔ Bookmarked websites can also be placed on the Home screen: Long-press the bookmark thumbnail, and choose the Add to Home Screen command.

- ✔ A handy way to create new bookmarks is to review the most visited sites in the Chrome app: When perusing your bookmarks, touch the Most Visited tab at the bottom of the screen. Touch a web page thumbnail to view that page, and then touch the Favorite icon to bookmark that page.

Managing web pages in multiple tabs

The Chrome app, as well as other tablet web browsers, uses a tabbed interface to help you access more than one web page at a time. Refer to Figure 7-1 to see various tabs marching across the Chrome app's screen, just above the Address box.

You can do various interesting things with tabs:

- ✔ **To open a link in another tab,** long-press the link and choose the command Open in New Tab from the menu that appears.

- ✔ **To open a bookmark in a new tab,** long-press the bookmark and choose the Open in New Tab command.

- ✔ **To open a blank tab,** touch the Action Overflow icon and choose New Tab. Or you can touch the last tab "stub" on the far right end of the tab list.

You switch between tabs by choosing one from the top of the screen.

Close a tab by touching its Close (X) icon; you can close only the tab you're viewing.

- ✔ Some web browser apps may refer to the tabs as *windows.*

- ✔ The tabs keep marching across the screen, left to right. You can scroll the tabs to view the ones that have scrolled off the screen.

- ✔ If you close all the tabs, you see a blank screen in the Chrome app. The New Tab command appears atop the screen.

- ✔ New tabs open to the last web page you viewed. Or if you were viewing the bookmarks, the tab opens with the bookmarks.

- ✔ Shhh! For secure browsing, you can open an *incognito* tab: Touch the Action Overflow or Menu icon, and choose the New Incognito Tab command. When you go incognito, the web browser doesn't track your history, leave cookies, or provide other evidence of which web pages you've visited. A short description appears on the incognito tab page, describing how it works.

- ✔ To switch between your incognito tabs and regular tabs, touch the rectangle that appears in the upper right corner of the Chrome app's screen (refer to Figure 7-1).

Searching the web

The handiest way to find things on the web is to use the Google Search widget, often found floating on the Home screen. You can also use Google Now, which is covered in Chapter 14. And, of course, you can visit Google's main search page by using the tablet's web browser app.

Or, what-the-hey: Be different and use Bing: www.bing.com.

Finding text on a web page

To locate text on a web page, touch the Action Overflow or Menu icon and choose the Find in Page command. Type the search text into the Find in Page box. As you type, found text is highlighted on the screen. Use the up and down chevrons to the right of the search box to page through the document. Touch the Back icon to dismiss the Find in Page contextual action bar after you've finished searching.

Sharing a web page

There it is! That web page you just *have* to talk about to everyone you know. The gauche way to share the page is to copy and paste it. Because you're reading this book, though, you know the better way to share a web page. Heed these steps:

1. **Go to the web page you desire to share.**

   Actually, you're sharing a *link* to the page, but don't let my obsession with specificity deter you.

2. **Touch the Action Overflow or Menu icon and choose the Share command.**

   The command might also be called Share Page or Share Via. Either way, you see an array of apps displayed. The variety and number of apps depends on what's installed on the tablet.

3. **Choose a method to share the page.**

   For example, choose Email to send the link by e-mail, or Facebook to share the link with your friends.

4. **Do whatever happens next.**

   Whatever happens next depends on how you're sharing the link: Compose the e-mail, write a comment in Facebook, or whatever. Refer to various chapters in this book for specific directions.

You cannot share a page you're viewing on an Incognito tab.

If your Android tablet sports the NFC feature, you can share a web page by using the Android Beam feature. Simply visit the web page you want to share, and touch the back of your Android to the other device's rear (or wherever NFC is enabled on that device). To send the page you're viewing, touch the screen when you see the prompt Touch to Beam.

The Art of Downloading

There's nothing to downloading, other than understanding that most people use the term without knowing exactly what it means. Officially, a *download* is a transfer of information over a network from another source to your gizmo. For your Android tablet, that network is the Internet, and the other source is a web page.

- ✔ The Downloading Complete notification appears after your tablet has downloaded something. You can choose that notification to view the downloaded item.

- ✔ Most people use the term *download* when they really mean *transfer* or *copy*. Those people must be shunned.

- ✔ New apps are installed on your tablet by using the Play Store app, covered in Chapter 15. Installing a new app is a type of downloading, but it's not the same as the downloading described in this section.

- ✔ The opposite of downloading is *uploading*. That's the process of sending information from your gizmo to another location on a network.

Grabbing an image from a web page

The simplest thing to download is an image from a web page: Long-press the image. You see a pop-up menu appear, from which you choose the Save Image command.

To view images you download from the web, you use the Gallery app. Downloaded images are saved in the Download album.

- ✔ Refer to Chapter 12 for information on the Gallery app.

- ✔ The image is stored in the tablet's internal storage. The location of the Download folder, where the files are stored, depends on the tablet. You can read about Android tablet file storage in Chapter 17.

Downloading a file

The web is full of links that don't open in a web browser window. For example, some links automatically download, such as links to PDF files or Microsoft Word documents or other types of files that a web browser is too afeared to display.

To save other types of links that aren't automatically downloaded, long-press the link and choose the Save Link command from the menu that appears. If this command doesn't appear, your tablet is unable to save the file, either because the file is of an unrecognized type or because there may be a security issue.

You view the saved file by using the Downloads app. See the next section.

Reviewing your downloads

To review a history of your downloaded stuff, from the web as well as from e-mail attachments you've saved, open the Downloads app in the Apps drawer. You see the list of downloads sorted by date, similar to what's shown in Figure 7-3.

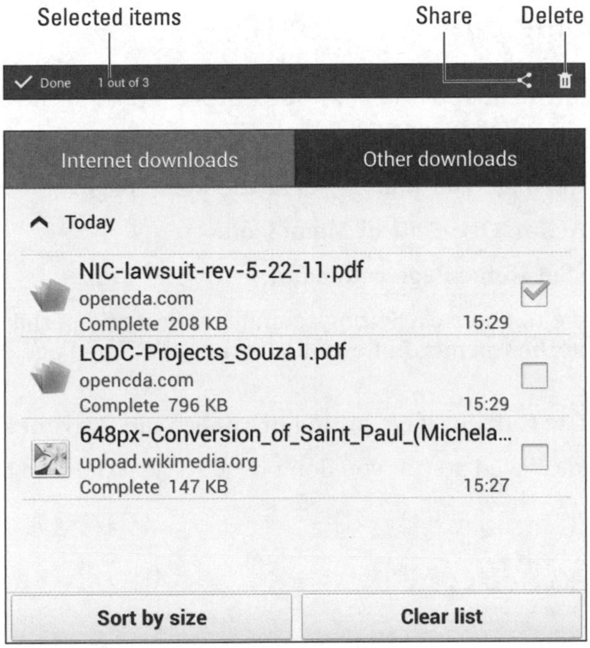

Selected items   Share   Delete

Figure 7-3: The Download Manager.

To view a download, choose it from the list. The Android tablet opens the appropriate app to view the download.

REMEMBER

- You can quickly review any download by choosing the Download notification.

- To remove an item from the Downloads list, place a check mark in its box, as shown in Figure 7-3. Touch the Trash icon at the top of the screen to remove that download.

- Sharing a downloaded item is done by placing a check mark by the downloaded file and choosing the Share icon at the top of the screen (refer to Figure 7-3).

Web Browser Controls and Settings

More options and settings and controls exist for web browser apps than for just about any other Android app I've used. Rather than bore you with every dang-doodle detail, I thought I'd present just a few of the options worthy of your attention.

Setting a home page

The *home page* is the first page you see when you start a web browser app. Well, every web browser app except for the Chrome app. For the others, heed these directions to set a home page:

1. **Browse to the page you want to set as the home page.**

2. **Touch the Action Overflow or Menu icon.**

3. **Choose the Set Home Page command.**

   You may have to choose a Settings command first and perhaps even dig through other menus, but eventually the Set Home Page command appears.

4. **Touch the Use Current Page button or choose the Current Page item.**

   Because you obeyed Step 1, you don't need to type the web page's address.

5. **Touch OK.**

   The home page is set.

If you want your home page to be blank (not set to any particular web page), choose the Blank Page item from the Set Home Page menu. When this item isn't available, type **about:blank** as the home page address. That's the word *about,* a colon, and then the word *blank,* with no period at the end and no spaces in the middle.

I prefer a blank home page because it's the fastest web page to load. It's also the web page with the most accurate information.

Setting privacy and security options

As far as your tablet's web browser app settings go, most of the security options are already enabled, including the blocking of pop-up windows (which normally spew ads).

If information retained by the web browser concerns you, you can clear it: In the web browser app, touch the Action Overflow or Menu icon and choose the Settings command. Choose either the Privacy or Privacy and Security category. Review the items presented to see which information the app is keeping and which it's not.

Choose the Clear Browsing Data command to remove any memorized information you may have typed on a web page. Choose items from the list that's presented, which can be cleared from the tablet's internal storage. Touch the Clear button to remove that information, such as browsing history, cookies, saved passwords, and data from online forms you've filled in.

Remove the check mark from Remember Form Data. These two settings prevent any characters you've input into a text field from being summoned automatically by someone who may steal your tablet.

You might be concerned about various warnings regarding location data. What the warnings refer to is the tablet's ability to track your location on Planet Earth. That ability comes from the device's GPS, or global satellite positioning system. It's a handy feature, but one that some people find overly intrusive. See Chapter 10 for information on changing the GPS settings if you prefer to wander stealthily.

With regard to general online security, my advice is always to be smart and *think* before doing anything questionable on the web. Use common sense. One of the most effective ways that the Bad Guys win is by using *human engineering* to try to trick you into doing something you normally wouldn't do, such as click a link to see a cute animation or a racy picture of a celebrity or politician. As long as you use your noggin, you should be safe.

Also, if security concerns you, most definitely apply a PIN lock or password lock to your tablet. See Chapter 19.

Digital Social Life

*L*ong ago, social networking eclipsed e-mail as the number-one reason for using the Internet. It has nearly replaced e-mail, has definitely replaced having a personalized website, and has become an obsession for millions across the globe. Your Android tablet is ready to meet your social networking desires. This chapter covers the options.

Your Life on Facebook

Of all the social networking sites, Facebook is the king. It's *the* online place to go to catch up with friends, send messages, express your thoughts, share pictures and video, play games, and waste more time than you ever thought you had.

▶ Although you can access Facebook on the web by using your tablet's web browser app, I highly recommend that you use the Facebook app described in this section.

▶ If your tablet didn't ship with the Facebook app, you can easily obtain it from the Google Play Store. See the later section "Getting the Facebook app."

Setting up your Facebook account

The best way to use Facebook is to have a Facebook account, and the best way to do that is to sign up at www.facebook.com by using a computer. Register for a new account by setting up your username and password.

Don't forget your Facebook username and password!

Eventually, the Facebook robots send you a confirmation e-mail. You reply to that message, and the online social networking community braces itself for your long-awaited arrival.

After you're all set up, you're ready to access Facebook on your Android tablet. To get the most from Facebook, you need a Facebook app. Keep reading in the next section.

Getting the Facebook app

If your Android tablet doesn't come with a Facebook app preinstalled, you can get the Facebook app for free from the Google Play Store. That app is your red carpet to the Facebook social networking kingdom.

The official name of the app is *Facebook for Android*. It's produced by the Facebook organization itself. You can search for this app at the Google Play Store. See Chapter 15.

✐ After you install the Facebook app, you may see the Facebook notification icon. Choose that icon and complete the steps required to complete installation.

✐ Some tablets may come with a social networking app. The app provides a central location for all your social networking accounts, including Facebook. You can use that app instead of, or in addition to, the Facebook app.

Running Facebook on your tablet

The first time you behold the Facebook app, you'll probably be asked to sign in. Do so: Type the e-mail address that you used to sign up for Facebook, and then type your Facebook password. Touch the Log In button or the onscreen keyboard's Done key.

When asked to synchronize your contacts, do so. I synchronize all my Facebook contacts with the tablet's address book. That way, my friends' Facebook status and other information appears in the address book app.

Eventually, you see the Facebook news feed, similar to the one shown in Figure 8-1.

Friend requests

Set your status.

Facebook notification

Upload photo.

App icon

Messages

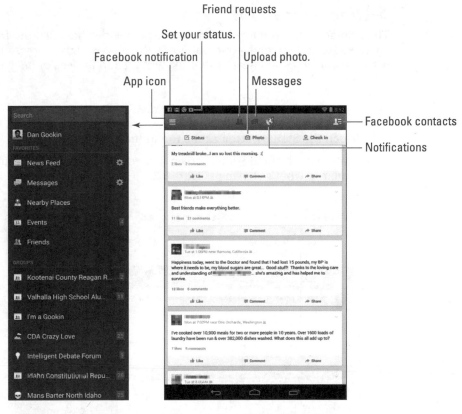

Facebook contacts

Notifications

Navigation drawer

Figure 8-1: Facebook on an Android tablet.

To set Facebook aside, touch the Home icon to return to the Home screen. The Facebook app continues to run until you either sign out of the app or turn off your Android tablet. To sign out of the Facebook app, touch the Menu icon (at the bottom right of the screen) and choose the Logout command.

- ✔ Show the navigation drawer by touching the Facebook app icon in the upper left corner of the screen. To hide the drawer, touch that icon again.

- ✔ Refer to Chapter 19 for information on placing a Facebook app shortcut or widget on the Home screen. The Facebook widget displays recent status updates and allows you to share your thoughts directly from the Home screen.

- ✔ The news feed can be updated by swiping down the screen.

- ✔ The Facebook app generates notifications for new news items, mentions, chat, and so on. Look for them on the status bar along with the tablet's other notifications.

Setting your status

The primary thing you live for on Facebook, besides having more friends than anyone else, is to update your status. It's the best way to share your thoughts with the universe, far cheaper than skywriting and far less offensive than a robocall.

To set your status, follow these steps in the Facebook app:

1. **Touch the Status button at the top of the screen.**

   You see the Update Status screen, where you can type your musings, similar to what's shown in Figure 8-2.

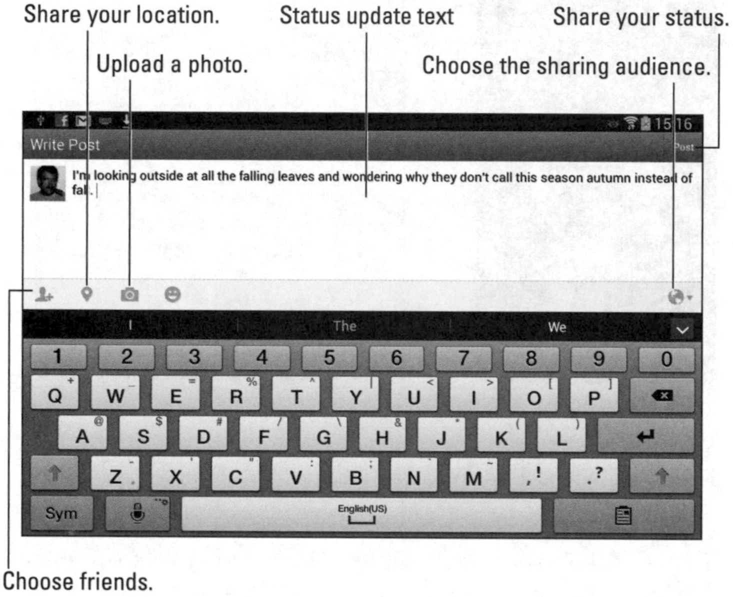

Choose friends.

Figure 8-2: Updating your Facebook status.

2. **Type something pithy, newsworthy, or typical of the stuff you read on Facebook.**

3. **Touch the Post button.**

You can set your status also by using the Facebook widget on the home page, if it's been installed: Touch the text box, type your important news tidbit, and touch the Share button.

Uploading a picture to Facebook

One of the many things your Android tablet can do is take pictures. Combine this feature with the Facebook app and you have an all-in-one gizmo designed for sharing the various intimate and private moments of your life with the ogling throngs of the Internet.

The picture posting process starts by touching the Photo icon in the Facebook app. Refer to Figures 8-1 and 8-2 for popular Photo icon locations on the main screen and the Write Post screen. After touching the Photo icon, you have two choices:

- First, you can select an image from pictures shown on the Photo Selection screen. These are images found on the tablet. Touch an image, or touch several images to select a bunch, and then proceed with the steps listed later in this section.

- Second, you can take a picture by using the tablet's camera.

If you elect to use the camera to take a picture, touch the Camera icon on the Photo Selection screen. (It's in the lower left corner.) You then find yourself thrust into Facebook's camera app, shown in Figure 8-3. This is not the same app as the Camera app, covered in Chapter 11.

Use the onscreen controls to take your picture. Or you can shoot a quick video by touching the Record Video icon, shown in Figure 8-3. When you're done, touch the Gallery icon, also shown in Figure 8-3.

To proceed with uploading the image, follow these steps:

1. **Touch an image on the Photo Selection screen to select it.**

2. **Tap the image to (optionally) add a tag.**

   You can touch someone's face in the picture and then type their name. Choose from a list of your Facebook friends to apply a name tag to the image.

3. **Use the Rotate button to reorient the image, if necessary.**

   The button's icon is shown in the margin. Please don't try to annoy me on Facebook by posting improperly oriented images.

4. **Touch the Compose button.**

   The Compose button is shown in the margin.

5. **Add a message to the image.**

   At this point, posting the image works just like adding a status update, similar to what's shown in Figure 8-2.

6. **Touch the Post button.**

   The image is posted as soon as it's transferred over the Internet and digested by Facebook.

Flash control (not all tablets)

Switch cameras (front/back).

Record video.   Return to Gallery.

Take picture.

Figure 8-3: Snapping a pic for Facebook.

The image can be found as part of your status update or news feed, but it's also saved to Facebook's Mobile Uploads album.

✒ To view your Facebook photo albums, touch the app icon in the upper left corner of the main Facebook screen. Choose your account from the top of the navigation drawer, and then on your account screen, choose the Photos item to view albums and pictures associated with your Facebook account.

✒ Facebook appears also on the Share menus you find in various tablet apps. Choose Facebook from the Share menu to send to Facebook whatever it is you're looking at. (Other chapters in this book give you more information about the various Share menus and where they appear.)

Configuring the Facebook app

The commands that control Facebook are stored on the Settings screen, which you access while viewing the main Facebook screen: Touch the app icon in the upper left corner of the screen to view the navigation drawer. Choose the App Settings command found near the bottom of the navigation drawer.

Choose Refresh Interval to specify how often the tablet checks for Facebook updates. If you find the one-hour value too long for your active Facebook social life, choose something quicker. To disable Facebook notifications, choose Never.

The following two options determine how your tablet reacts to Facebook updates:

Vibrate: Vibrates the tablet

Notification Ringtone: Plays a specific ringtone

For the notification ringtone, choose the Silent option when you want the tablet not to make noise upon encountering a Facebook update.

Not every tablet may feature the Vibrate setting.

Touch the Back icon to close the navigation drawer and return to the main Facebook screen.

The Tweet Life

Twitter is a social networking site, similar to Facebook but far briefer. On Twitter, you write short spurts of text that express your thoughts or observations, or you share links. Or you can just use Twitter to follow the thoughts and twitterings, or *tweets,* of other people.

- ✔ A message posted on Twitter is a *tweet.*

- ✔ A tweet can be no more than 140 characters long, including spaces and punctuation.

- ✔ You can post messages on Twitter and follow others who post messages. It's a good way to get updates and information quickly, from not only individuals but also news outlets, corporations, various organizations, and evil robots.

- ✔ They say that of all the people who have accounts on Twitter, only a small portion of them actively use the service.

Setting up Twitter

The best way to use Twitter on the Android tablet is to already have a Twitter account. Start by going to `http://twitter.com` on a computer and following the directions there for creating a new account.

After you've established a Twitter account, obtain the Twitter app for your Android tablet. The app can be obtained from the Google Play Store. Get the Twitter app from Twitter, Inc. (The Play Store features lots of Twitter apps, or *clients*.) Refer to Chapter 15 for additional information on downloading apps to your Android tablet.

When you start the Twitter app for the first time, touch the Sign In button. Type your Twitter username or e-mail address, and then type your Twitter password. After that, you can use Twitter without having to log in again — until you turn off the tablet or exit the Twitter app.

Figure 8-4 shows the Twitter app's main screen, which shows the current tweet feed.

Figure 8-4: The Twitter app.

See the next section for information on *tweeting,* or updating your status using the Twitter app.

Tweeting

The Twitter app provides an excellent interface to the many wonderful and interesting things that Twitter does. Of course, the two most basic tasks are reading and writing tweets.

To read tweets, choose the Home category, shown in Figure 8-4, to view the timeline. Recent tweets are displayed in a list, with the most recent information at the top. Scroll the list by swiping it with your finger.

To tweet, touch the New Tweet icon (refer to Figure 8-4). Use the New Tweet screen, shown in Figure 8-5, to compose your tweet.

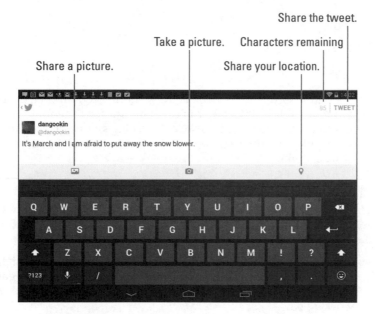

Figure 8-5: Creating a tweet.

Touch the Tweet button to share your thoughts with the twitterverse.

- You have only 140 characters, including spaces, for creating your Tweet.
- The character counter in the Twitter app lets you know how close you're getting to the 140-character limit.
- Twitter itself doesn't display pictures, other than your account picture. When you send a picture to Twitter, you use an image-hosting service and then share the link, or *URL*, to the image. All that complexity is handled by the Twitter app.

> ✔ The Twitter app appears on various Share menus in other apps on your Android tablet. You use those Share menus to send to Twitter whatever you're looking at.

Even More Social Networking

The Internet is brimming with social networking opportunities. Facebook may be the king, but lots of landed gentry are eager for that crown. It almost seems as though a new social networking site pops up every week. Beyond Facebook and Twitter, other social networking sites include, but are not limited to

> ✔ Google+
> ✔ LinkedIn
> ✔ Meebo
> ✔ Myspace

I recommend first setting up the social networking account on a computer, similar to the way I describe earlier in this chapter for Facebook and Twitter. After that, obtain an app for the social networking site using the Google Play Store. Set up and configure that app on your Android tablet to connect with your existing account.

> ✔ See Chapter 15 for more information on the Google Play Store.
> ✔ The HootSuite app can be used to share your thoughts on a multitude of social networking platforms. It can be obtained from the Play Store, as described in Chapter 15.
> ✔ As with Facebook and Twitter, your social networking apps might appear on various Share menus on the Android tablet. That way, you can easily share your pictures and other types of media with your online social networking pals.

9

Text Chat, Video Chat, and Phone Calls

In This Chapter

▶ Setting up Google Talk

▶ Adding friends to the Talk app

▶ Doing a video chat

▶ Chatting on Skype

▶ Texting with Skype

▶ Making a Skype video call

▶ Using Skype to make phone calls

*T*he holy grail of communications has always been video chat. Back in the 1960s, the video phone was touted as the harbinger of the future. The film *2001: A Space Odyssey* features a key character making a video phone call to his daughter on the "Bell network." (Cost: $1.70.) Obviously, seeing and speaking on a phone was considered a big deal.

More than a decade after that film was to have taken place, a video phone call is more commonly known as a video chat. It's a feature that your Android tablet is more than capable of offering, along with text messaging, voice chat, and even real phone calls. The future is here — and rather than costing $1.70 for a two-minute video call, it's *free*.

Type a name, email, number, u...

Aug 11

Aug 10

▸ call

Aug 10

▸ call

Aug 10

Jeremiah

PEOPLE YOU HANGOUT WITH

Jeremiah Gook

⚭ Famil...

Can We Hangout?

The great Googly way to text-message, voice-chat, and video-chat with your online pals is to use the Hangouts app. It's a communications app, designed by Google to let you connect with one or more of your friends to, well, hang out. It's also a great communications tool, which anyone who has an Android phone or tablet can use.

Using Hangouts

You may find the Hangouts app lurking as an icon on the tablet's Home screen. If not, dig it up in the Apps drawer. On the remote chance that you may not find it in either location, pick up a free copy from the Google Play Store, as described in Chapter 15.

Hangouts hooks into your Google account. If you have any previous conversations, they're listed on the main part of the screen, shown in Figure 9-1. On the right side of the screen you see a specific conversation, although it just peeks in when the tablet is held vertically.

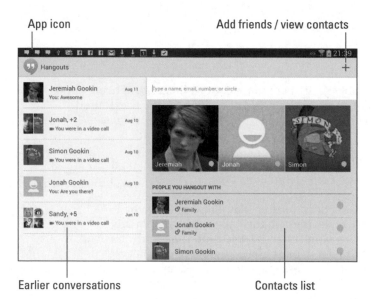

App icon

Add friends / view contacts

Earlier conversations

Contacts list

Figure 9-1: Google Hangouts.

The Hangouts app listens for incoming conversation requests, or you can start your own. You're alerted via notification of an impending hangout request. The notification icon is shown in the margin.

To sign out of the app, which means that you won't receive any notifications, touch the Action Overflow or Menu icon. Choose Settings, and then choose Sign Out. Touch OK to quit.

- ✒ If you can't find the Hangouts app in the Apps drawer, look in the Google folder.

- ✒ When using the tablet in the vertical orientation, you need to swipe the touchscreen right-to-left to see previous conversations or the contacts list.

- ✒ Conversations are archived in the Hangouts app. To peruse a previous text chat, choose it from the list, shown in Figure 9-1. Part of the previous chat shows up on the right side of the screen.

- ✒ Video calls aren't archived, but you can review when the call took place, and with whom, by choosing a video chat item.

- ✒ To remove a previous conversation, long-press it. Touch the Trash icon that appears on the contextual Action bar atop the screen. You can also swipe a conversation left or right to remove it.

- ✒ To use Hangouts, your friends must have Google accounts. They can be using computers or mobile devices — it doesn't matter which — but they must have cameras available to enable video chat.

Typing at your friends

Text chatting is one of the oldest forms of communication on the Internet. It's where people type text back and forth at each other, which can be tedious, but it remains popular. To text-chat in the Hangouts app, obey these steps:

1. **Choose a contact listed on the screen, or fetch one by touching the Add icon.**

   When you touch the Add icon, you're starting a new hangout. Choosing a contact already on the screen continues a hangout. Even an earlier video hangout can become a text hangout.

   When you choose a hangout with multiple people, all of them receive a copy of the message.

2. **Type your message.**

   Touch the Send a Message box, shown in Figure 9-2. Up pops the onscreen keyboard so that you can type a message.

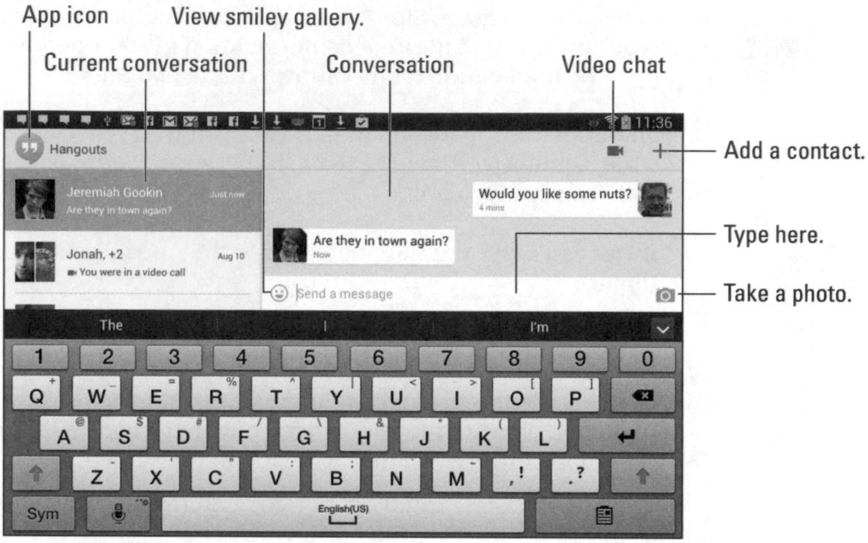

App icon   View smiley gallery.

Current conversation   Conversation   Video chat

Add a contact.

Type here.

Take a photo.

Figure 9-2: Text-chatting.

3. **Touch the Send icon to send your comment.**

   The Send icon replaces the Photo icon when you start to type.

You type, your friend types, and so on until you grow tired or the tablet's battery dies.

Adding more people to the hangout is always possible: Touch the Action Overflow or Menu icon and choose New Group Hangout. Choose a friend from those listed to invite them into the hangout.

When you're chatting, or I should say "hanging out," with a group, everyone in the group receives the message.

You can leave the conversation at any time to do other things with your tablet. To return to any ongoing hangout, choose the Hangouts notification, shown in the margin.

Talking and video chat

Take the hangout up a notch by touching the Video Chat icon (refer to Figure 9-2). When you do, your friend receives a pop-up invite, as shown in Figure 9-3. Touch the Answer button to begin talking.

Figure 9-3: Someone wants to video-chat!

Figure 9-4 shows what an ongoing video chat might look like. The person you're talking with appears in the big window; you're in the smaller window. Other video chat participants appear at the bottom of the screen as well, as shown in the figure.

The onscreen controls (shown in Figure 9-4) may vanish after a second; touch the screen to see the controls again.

To end the conversation, touch the Exit button. Well, say goodbye first, and then touch the button.

- ✔ When you're nude, or just ugly, decline the video-chat invite. After that, you can choose that contact and reply with a text message or voice chat instead. Explain your embarrassment.

- ✔ Use the Speaker icon to choose how to listen when you video-chat. You can choose to use the tablet's speaker, headphones, and so on.

- ✔ When video chatting with multiple contacts, choose a contact from the bottom of the screen to see them in a larger format in the center of the screen.

- ✔ If you want to make eye contact, look directly into the tablet's front-facing camera. It's right above the touchscreen, either centrally located or to the left or right.

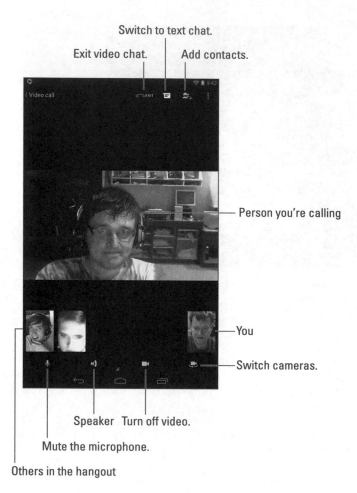

Switch to text chat.

Exit video chat.   Add contacts.

Person you're calling

You

Switch cameras.

Speaker Turn off video.

Mute the microphone.

Others in the hangout

Figure 9-4: Video chat in the Hangouts app.

Connect to the World with Skype

A versatile app for converting your "It's not a phone!" Android tablet into a phone is Skype. It's one of the most popular Internet communications programs, allowing you to text-, voice-, or video-chat with others on the Internet as well as use the Internet to make real, honest-to-goodness phone calls.

Obtaining Skype for your tablet

The typical Android tablet doesn't come with the Skype app preinstalled. To get Skype, visit the Google Play Store and obtain the Skype app. In case you find multiple apps, get the one that's from the Skype company itself.

To use Skype, you need a Skype account. You can sign up while using the app, or you can visit www.skype.com on a computer to complete the process by using a nice, full-size keyboard and widescreen monitor.

When you start the Skype app for the first time, work through the initial setup screens. You can even take the tour. Be sure to have Skype scour the tablet's address book for contacts you can Skype. This process may take a while, but if you're just starting out, it's a great help.

✔ Skype is free to use. Text chat is free. Voice and video chat with one other Skype user is also free. When you want to call a real phone, or video-chat with a group, you need to boost your account with Skype Credit.

✔ It's doesn't cost extra to do a gang video chat in the Hangouts app.

✔ Don't worry about getting a Skype number, unless you plan to receive Skype phone calls on your tablet. Those phone calls include calls from any phone, not just a mobile device using the Skype app. So, unless it's your ultimate desire to transform your Android tablet into a cell phone, don't bother with the Skype number.

Chatting with another Skype user

Text chat with Skype works similarly to texting on a cell phone. The only difference is that the other person must be a Skype user. So in that respect, Skype text chat works a lot like Hangouts chat, covered earlier in this chapter.

To chat, follow these steps:

1. **Start the Skype app and sign in.**

   You don't need to sign in when you've previously run the Skype app. Like most apps, Skype continues to run until you sign out or turn off the tablet.

2. **At the main Skype screen, touch the People tab and choose a contact.**

   Or you can choose one of the contact icons shown on the main screen.

3. **Type your text in the text box.**

   The box is found at the bottom of the screen. It says Type a Message Here.

4. **Touch the blue arrow icon to send the message.**

   As long as your Skype friend is online and eager, you'll be chatting in no time.

At the far right end of the text box, you find a Smiley icon. Use this icon to insert a cute graphic into your text.

✔ The Skype Chat notification, shown in the margin, appears whenever someone wants to chat with you. It's handy to see, especially when you may have switched away from the Skype app to use another app. Choose that notification to get into the conversation.

✔ To stop chatting, touch the Back icon. The conversation is stored in the Skype app, even after the other person has disconnected.

✔ For the chat to work, the other user must be logged in on Skype and available to chat.

Seeing on Skype (video call)

Placing a video call with Skype is easy: Start up a text chat as described in the preceding section. After the conversation starts, touch the Video Call icon. The call rings through to the contact, and if that person wants to video-chat, they pick up in no time and you're talking and looking at each other.

When someone calls you on Skype, you see the Skype incoming-call screen, similar to the one shown in Figure 9-5. Touch the Answer icon to take the call. You may also see a Video button to accept an incoming video call. Touch Decline to dismiss the call, especially when it's someone who annoys you.

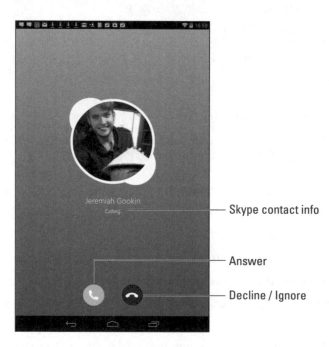

Figure 9-5: An incoming Skype voice call.

The incoming-call screen (see Figure 9-5) appears even when the tablet is sleeping; the incoming call wakes up the tablet, just as a real call would.

When you're in a Skype video chat, the screen looks like Figure 9-6. Touch the screen to see the onscreen controls, if they disappear.

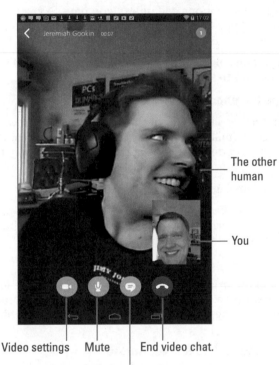

The other human

You

Video settings   Mute   End video chat.

Switch to text chat.

Figure 9-6: A Skype video call.

Touch the red End Call icon to end the call.

- ✔ Voice and video chat on Skype over the Internet are free. When you use a Wi-Fi connection, you can chat without incurring a loss of your cellular plan's data minutes.

- ✔ You can chat with any user in your Skype contacts list by using a mobile device, a computer, or any other gizmo on which Skype is installed.

- ✔ Video chat may be available only over Wi-Fi or 4G connections. You may see a warning displayed before using video chat on the mobile data network.

- ✔ It's impossible to tell whether someone has dismissed a Skype call or simply hasn't answered. And Skype has no voice mail so that you can leave a message.

Placing a Skype phone call

Ah. The big enchilada: Skype can be used to turn your Android tablet into a cell phone. It's an amazing feat. And it works quite well. Heed these steps:

1. **Ensure that you have Skype Credit.**

   You can't make a "real" phone call unless you have Skype Credit on your account. You add Skype Credit by touching the Profile button on the main Skype screen and choosing Skype Credit.

2. **From the Skype app's main screen, choose a contact to dial or use the Phone Handset icon to type a number.**

3. **Choose or type the phone number to dial.**

   When typing a number, always input the full phone number when making a Skype phone call, including the country code (which is +1 for the United States) and the area code. The Skype app may already supply the +1 for you.

4. **Touch the big green Call button to place the call.**

   This step works just like using a cell phone. Indeed, at this point, your tablet has been transformed by the Skype app into a cell phone (albeit a cell phone that uses Internet telephony to make the call).

5. **Talk.**

   You see a per-minute price listed below the contact's name in the upper left corner of the screen. It's a good reminder that the real phone call you're making is costing you money — not a lot, but something to be aware of.

6. **To end the call, touch the End Call button.**

7. **If the number you dialed isn't a current Skype contact, touch the Add Contact icon to create a Skype contact for that person.**

   Skype contacts are separate from your tablet's address book contacts. By touching the Add Contact icon, you create a phone number contact for the number you just dialed.

Lamentably, you can't receive a phone call using Skype on your Android tablet. The only way to make that happen is to pay for a Skype online number. In that case, you can use Skype to both send and receive regular phone calls. This book doesn't cover the Online Number option.

- ✏ I recommend getting a good headset if you plan on using Skype often to place phone calls.

- ✏ In addition to the per-minute cost, you may be charged a connection fee for making the call.

- ✏ You can check the Skype website at www.skype.com for a current list of call rates, for both domestic and international calls.

✔ Unless you've paid Skype to let you use a specific phone number, the phone number shown on the recipient's Caller ID screen is something unexpected — often, merely the text *Unknown*. Because of that, you might want to e-mail the person you're calling and let him or her know that you're placing a Skype call. That way, the call won't be skipped because the Caller ID isn't recognized.

Part III
Omni Tablet

In this part . . .

- ✔ Discover your location, find interesting things nearby, and never be lost again.

- ✔ Augment your digital photo album by capturing images and recording video.

- ✔ Learn how to record an image's location and then find that location again by using the Maps app.

- ✔ Transfer music from your computer and enjoy it on your Android tablet.

- ✔ Schedule your personal and professional life by using the tablet's Calendar app.

- ✔ Enjoy an e-book on the road or wherever you take your tablet.

There's a Map for That

I'm hoping that teleportation becomes a reality someday. It would be so convenient to travel instantly, to get where you're going without sitting in a cramped cabin. In fact, the only mystery will be whether teleportation has the same knack of losing your luggage as air travel.

One thing our fortunate descendants probably won't complain about is being lost. That's because their Android tablets and the Maps app will tell them exactly where they are. They'll be able to find all sorts of things, from tacos in pill form to used flying cars to Hello Kitty light sabers. Because it's the future, they might even be able to use the futuristic version of an Android tablet to find their lost luggage.

A Map That Needs No Folding

You can find your location, as well as the location of things near and far, by using the Maps app on your Android tablet. Good news: You run no risk of improperly folding the Maps app. Better news: The Maps app charts the entire country, including freeways, highways, roads, streets, avenues, drives, bike paths, addresses, businesses, and points of interest.

Using the Maps app

You start the Maps app by choosing Maps from the Apps drawer. If you're starting the app for the first time or it has been recently updated, you can read its What's New screen; touch the OK button to continue.

Your tablet communicates with Global Positioning System (GPS) satellites to hone in on your current location and display it on a map, similar to Figure 10-1. (See the later sidebar, "Activate your locations!") The position is accurate to within a given range, as shown by a faint blue circle around your location.

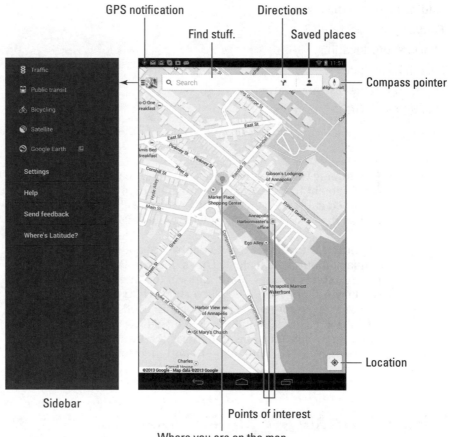

Figure 10-1: Your location on a map.

Here are some fun things you can do when viewing the basic street map:

Zoom in: To make the map larger (to move it closer), double-tap the screen. You can also spread your fingers on the touchscreen to zoom in.

Zoom out: To make the map smaller (to see more), pinch your fingers on the touchscreen.

Pan and scroll: To see what's to the left or right or at the top or bottom of the map, drag your finger on the touchscreen; the map scrolls in the direction you drag.

Rotate: Using two fingers, rotate the map clockwise or counterclockwise. Touch the Compass Pointer icon (labeled in Figure 10-1) to reorient the map with north at the top of the screen.

Location: Touch the Location icon to zero in on your current location.

Perspective: Touch the screen with two fingers and swipe up or down to view the map in perspective. You can also tap the Location icon to switch to Perspective view, although that trick works only for your current location. To return to flat-map view, touch the Compass Pointer icon (refer to Figure 10-1).

The closer you zoom in on the map, the more detail you see, such as street names, address block numbers, businesses, and other sites — but no tiny people.

- ✔ The blue triangle (shown in the center of Figure 10-1) shows in which general direction the tablet is pointing.

- ✔ When the tablet's direction is unavailable, you see a blue dot as your location on the map.

Activate your locations!

The Maps app works best when you activate all of your tablet's location technology. I recommend that you turn on all available location settings. From the Apps drawer, open the Settings app. In the Settings app, choose the Location item to view the Location screen. On some Samsung tablets, touch the Connections tab and then choose the Location Services item to view the settings.

The Master Control icon is found atop the Location screen. Use the icon to activate the tablet's location services; ensure that the button reads ON. If it doesn't, touch the Master Control icon or slide the OFF button to the right so that it says ON. When the Master Control icon isn't present, ensure that a check mark appears by the item Access to My Location.

You may find additional settings on the Location screen, I recommend you ensure that each one is activated by placing a check mark by the service name.

Any apps listed on the Location screen use location information. You can choose an app icon to examine further how it uses the tablet's location technology, although in some cases you won't find any specific controls to disable the app's location requests.

Location information is enhanced when the tablet's Wi-Fi is activated. See Chapter 16 for details on Wi-Fi.

✔ To view the navigation drawer, touch the app icon, shown in Figure 10-1. Swipe the navigation drawer to the left to return to the Maps app.

✔ When all you want is a virtual compass, similar to the one you lost as a kid, get a compass app from the Google Play Store. See Chapter 15 for more information about the Google Play Store. Search for *compass*.

Adding layers

You add details from the Maps app by applying layers: A *layer* can enhance the map's visual appearance, provide more information, or add other fun features to the basic street map. For example, the Satellite layer is shown in Figure 10-2.

The key to accessing layers is to touch the app icon in the lower left corner of the screen. The navigation drawer displays several layers you can add, such as the Satellite layer, shown in Figure 10-2. Another popular layer is Traffic, which lists updated travel conditions.

To remove a layer, choose it again from the navigation drawer; any active layer appears highlighted. When a layer isn't applied, Street view appears.

Your approximate
location and direction

Main roads

Figure 10-2: The Satellite layer.

It Knows Where You Are

It's common to use a map to find out where you're going. New is the concept of using a map to find out where you are. You no longer need to worry about being lost. Using your tablet's Maps app, you can instantly find out where you are and what's nearby. You can even send a message to someone in the tablet's address book to have that person join you — or rescue you.

Discovering your location

The Maps app shows your location as a compass arrow or blue dot on the screen. But *where* is that? I mean, if you need to contact a tow truck, you can't just say, "I'm the blue triangle on the gray slab by the green thing."

Well, you *can* say that, but it probably won't do any good.

To find your current street address, or any street address, long-press a location on the Maps screen. Up pops a card, similar to the one shown in Figure 10-3. The card gives your approximate address.

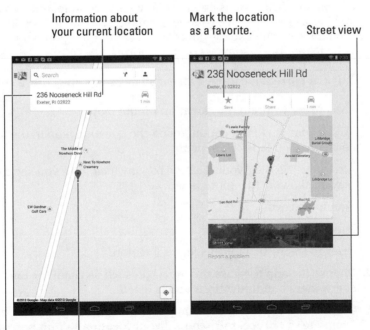

Information about your current location

Mark the location as a favorite.

Street view

Long-press a location to see the address.

Touch the card to see more info.

Figure 10-3: Finding an address.

If you touch the card, you see a screen with more details and additional information, shown on the right in Figure 10-3.

Route

- ✔ This trick works only when the tablet has Internet access. When Internet access isn't available, the Maps app can't communicate with the Google map servers.

- ✔ To make the card go away, touch anywhere else on the map.

- ✔ The time under the Travel icon (the car in Figure 10-3) indicates how far away the address is from your current location. If the address is too far away, you see the Route icon, shown in the margin.

- ✔ When you have way too much time on your hands, play with the Street View command. Choosing this option displays the location from a 360-degree perspective. In Street view, you can browse a locale, pan and tilt, or zoom in on details to familiarize yourself with an area, for example — whether you're familiarizing yourself with a location or planning a burglary.

Helping others find your location

It's possible to use the Maps app to send your current location to a friend. If your pal has a mobile device (phone or tablet) with smarts similar to your Android tablet, he can use the coordinates to get directions to your location. Maybe he'll even bring some tacos in pill form!

To send your current location in an e-mail message, obey these steps:

1. **Long-press your current location on the map.**

   To see your current location, touch the Location icon in the lower right corner of the Maps app screen.

   After long-pressing your location (or any location), you see a card displayed, showing the approximate address.

2. **Touch the card.**

3. **Touch the Share icon.**

   Refer to Figure 10-3 for this icon's location.

4. **Choose the app to share the message, such as Gmail or Email or whichever other communications app is listed.**

5. **Continue using the selected app to choose a recipient and otherwise complete the process of sending your location to that person.**

When the recipients receive the message, they can touch the link to open your location in the Maps app — providing that they have an Android tablet or some other Android device. When the location appears, they can follow my advice in the later section "Getting directions" for getting to your location. And don't loan them this book, either; have them purchase their own copy. Thanks.

Find Things

The Maps app can help you find places in the real world, just like the Google Search app helps you find places on the Internet. Both operations work basically the same.

Open the Maps app and type something to find in the Search text box, as illustrated in Figure 10-1. You can type a variety of terms in the Search box, as explained in this section.

Looking for a specific address

To locate an address, type it in the Search box. For example:

```
1313 N. Harbor Blvd., Anaheim, CA 92803
```

Touch the Search key on the onscreen keyboard, and that location is shown on the map. The next step is getting directions, which you can read about in the later section "Getting directions."

- ✔ You don't need to type the entire address. Oftentimes, all you need is the street number and street name and then either the city name or zip code.
- ✔ If you omit the city name or zip code, the Maps app looks for the closest matching address near your current location.
- ✔ Touch the X button in the Search box to clear the previous search.

Finding a business, restaurant, or point of interest

You may not know an address, but you know when you crave sushi or Hungarian or perhaps the exotic flavors of Wyoming. Maybe you need a hotel or a gas station, or you have to find a place that buys old dentures. To find a business entity or a point of interest, type its name in the Search box. For example:

```
Movie theater
```

This command flags movie theaters on the current Maps screen or nearby.

Have the Maps app jump to your current location, as described earlier in this chapter, to find locations near you. Otherwise, the Maps app looks for places near the area shown on the screen.

Or you can be specific and look for businesses near a certain location by specifying the city name, district, or zip code, such as

```
Liquor 02554
```

After typing this command and touching the Search key, you see a smattering of tippling establishments found in or near Nantucket, Massachusetts, similar to the ones shown in Figure 10-4.

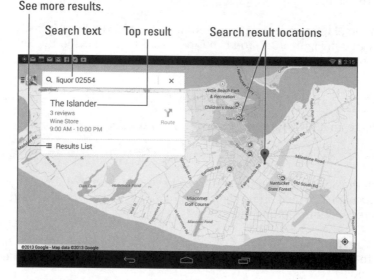

Figure 10-4: Finding booze in and near Nantucket, Massachusetts.

To see more information about a result, touch it. You can touch either the item in the search results list or the pin that's dropped on the map, as shown in Figure 10-4. You see a pop-up cartoon bubble, which you can touch to get even more specific information.

You can touch the Route icon on the location's Details screen to get directions; see the later section "Getting directions."

Route

- Every letter or dot on the screen represents a search result (refer to Figure 10-4).

- Spread your fingers on the touchscreen to zoom in on the map.

- If you *really* like the location, touch the Save (Star) icon. That action directs the Maps app to keep the location as one of your favorite places. The location shows up as a star on the Maps app screen. See the next section.

Making a favorite place

Just as you can bookmark favorite websites on the Internet, you can mark favorite places in the real world by using the Maps app. The feature is called Saved Places.

To visit your favorite places or browse your recent map searches, touch the Saved Places icon at the top of the Maps app screen. If you don't see the icon, touch the X icon in the Search box.

The Saved Places window sports various categories of places you've *starred* (marked as favorites), locations you've recently searched for, or places you've been.

✔ Mark a location as a favorite by touching the Star icon when you view the location's details.

✔ The Recently Accessed Places list allows you to peruse items you've located or searched for recently.

✔ Touch the app icon (in the upper left corner of the screen) to return to the Maps app when you're done looking at saved places.

Locating a contact

The secret to finding a contact's location is to touch the contact's address as it appears in the tablet's address book app. Sometimes, the Place icon (shown in the margin) is used to help display a location on the Maps app. Even when the Place icon isn't there, just touch the contact's address. The Maps app zooms onto the screen, displaying that location.

✔ If you see the Complete Action Using prompt after touching a contact's location, choose the Maps app and then touch the Always button. That way, you'll never be bothered by the prompt again.

✔ The tablet's address book is covered in Chapter 5. The app might be named Contacts or People or something completely unexpected.

Android the Navigator

Finding something is only half the job. The other half is getting there, or sending someone else there, if it's an unpleasant place. Your Android tablet is ever-ready, thanks to the various direction and navigation features nestled in the Maps app.

If you use your tablet in your auto, I strongly recommend that someone else hold it and read the directions. Or use voice navigation and, for goodness sake, don't look at the tablet while you're driving!

Getting directions

Route

One command associated with locations found in the Maps app deals with getting directions. The command is called Route, and it shows either the Route icon (see the margin) or a mode of transportation, such as a car, bike, or bus. Here's how it works:

1. **Touch the Route icon on a location's card.**

   After touching the Route icon, you see a screen similar to the one shown in Figure 10-5.

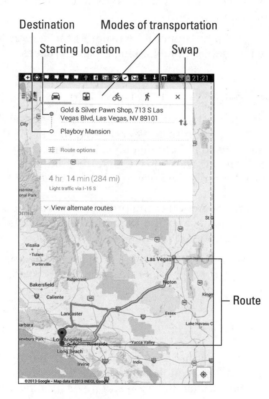

Figure 10-5: Planning a trip.

2. **Choose a method of transportation.**

   The available options vary, depending on your location. In Figure 10-5, the items are (from left to right) Car, Public Transportation, Bicycle, and On Foot.

3. **Set a starting point.**

   You can type a location or choose from one of the locations shown on the screen, such as your current location, home location, or any location you've previously searched. Touch the Starting Location item to choose another location.

4. **Ensure that the starting location and destination are what you want.**

    If they're backward, touch the Swap icon (refer to Figure 10-5).

5. **Choose a route card.**

    One or more routes are listed on the screen. In Figure 10-5, one card is shown, which indicates the adventure's duration of 4 hours and 14 minutes.

6. **Peruse the results.**

The map shows your route, highlighted as a blue line on the screen. Detailed directions also appear.

See the next section for turn-by-turn navigation instructions.

- ✓ The Maps app alerts you to any toll roads on the specified route. As you travel, you can choose alternative, non-toll routes, if available. You're prompted to switch routes during navigation; see the next section.

- ✓ The blue line appears only on the tablet screen, not on streets in the real world.

- ✓ You may not get perfect directions from the Maps app, but it's a useful tool for places you've never visited.

Navigating to your destination

To use navigation, obey these steps:

1. **Choose a location on the map.**

    It must be a spot other than your current location. You can search for a spot, type a location, or long-press any part of the map.

2. **Choose a card from the search results.**

    This process works identically to finding any location; see the earlier section "Find Things."

Route

3. **Touch the Route icon.**

    The Route icon can look like the icon shown in the margin, though most often it looks like a car.

4. **Ensure that My Location is chosen on the next screen, similar to what's shown in Figure 10-6.**

    If you don't see My Location, touch the top entry (refer to Figure 10-6) where it should be, and then choose the My Location item from the next screen.

Directions

Travel details

Trip overview   Preview (navigation)

Road alert   Page between waypoints.

Swipe down for more.

Figure 10-6: Plotting your course.

5. Choose a card representing the route you want to take.

Sometimes, only one card is available, though others may appear. The variety depends upon traffic conditions, toll roads, zombie attacks, and similar things you might want to avoid.

6. Touch the Start icon.

And you're on your way.

While you're navigating, the tablet displays an interactive map that shows your current location and turn-by-turn directions for reaching your destination. A digital voice tells you how far to go and when to turn, for example, and gives you other nagging advice, such as to sit up, be nice to other drivers, and call your mother once in a while.

To exit navigation, touch the Close icon at the bottom of the screen.

✔ The neat thing about tablet navigation is that whenever you screw up, a new course is immediately calculated.

✔ When you tire of hearing the navigation voice, touch the Action Overflow icon and choose the command Mute Voice Guidance.

✔ The tablet stays in Navigation mode until you exit. The Navigation notification can be seen atop the touchscreen while you're in Navigation mode.

✔ While navigating with the tablet, touch the Action Overflow icon and choose Step By Step List to review your journey. The Route Preview command lets you see the big picture.

✔ In Navigation mode, the Android tablet consumes a lot of battery power. I highly recommend that you plug the tablet into your car's power adapter (cigarette lighter) for the duration of the trip. Any Android cell phone power adapter works, or any adapter with a micro-USB connector.

Adding a navigation widget to the Home screen

When you visit certain places often — such as a Turkish bathhouse — you can save yourself the time you would spend repeatedly inputting navigation information. All you need to do is create a navigation widget on the Home screen. Here's how:

1. **Touch the Apps icon to display the Apps drawer.**

2. **Touch the Widgets tab atop the screen.**

3. **Long-press the Directions widget and drag it to a position on the Home screen.**

   You need to scroll over a few pages to find the Directions widget.

4. **Type a destination, a contact name, an address, or a business in the text box.**

   As you type, suggestions appear in a list. You can choose a suggestion to save yourself some typing.

5. **Choose a traveling method.**

   Your options are Car, Public Transportation, Bicycle, and On Foot.

6. **Type a shortcut name.**

7. **Touch the Save button.**

   The navigation shortcut is placed on the Home screen.

To use the shortcut, simply touch it on the Home screen. Instantly, the Maps app starts and enters navigation mode, steering you from wherever you are to the location referenced by the shortcut.

See Chapter 19 for additional information on adding widgets to the Home screen. Information on Turkish bathhouses can be found on the Internet at www.dummies.com.

The Whole Google Earth

The Earth app is similar to the Maps app, but with one huge difference: It covers the entire planet. And though you can get around and explore your locale or destination using the Maps app, Earth is more of a look-and-see, interactive world atlas.

Your tablet may or may not have come supplied with the Earth app. If so, you'll find it in the Apps drawer. Otherwise, visit the Google Play Store and download a free copy.

If you're familiar with the Google Earth program on a computer, the Earth app should be familiar to you. Its interface is shown in Figure 10-7. It has similar features to the Maps app, but it's customized for viewing *the globe*.

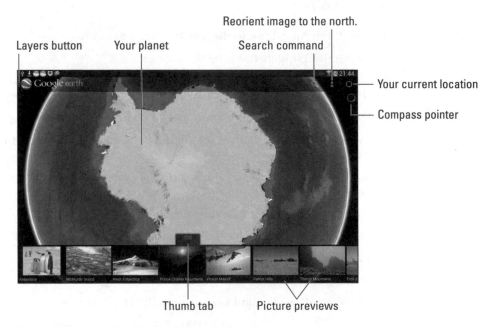

Figure 10-7: Earth, most likely your home planet.

The best advice for using the Earth app is to explore: Drag your finger around the screen to pan and tilt the globe; pinch and spread your fingers to zoom out and zoom in, respectively.

- ✔ Items in the Layers navigation drawer are used to show or hide map details.

- ✔ Use the thumb tab to slide the picture previews up or down.

- ✔ If you enjoy looking up as much as you enjoy looking down, consider getting the Sky Map app. Search the Google Play Store for the Sky Map app, from Sky Map Devs. (It was once known as Google Sky Map.)

11

Everyone Say "Cheese!"

I have no idea why people say "Cheese" when they get their pictures taken. Supposedly, it's to make them smile. Even in other countries, where the native word for *cheese* can't possibly influence the face's smile muscles, they still say their native word for *cheese* when a picture is taken. Apparently, it's a tradition that's present everywhere. Well, except for maybe the moon, where it's rumored that Buzz Aldrin said "Green cheese."

When you hear folks say "Cheese" around your Android tablet, it will most likely be because you're taking advantage of the tablet's photographic and video capabilities. Or I suppose that you could use the tablet as a festive cheese platter. But when you opt to take pictures or shoot video, turn to this chapter for helpful words of advice.

Android Tablet Camera 101

An Android tablet isn't the world's best camera. And I'm sure that Mr. Spock's tricorder wasn't the best camera in the *Star Trek* universe, either, but it could take pictures. That comparison is kind of the whole point: Your Android tablet is an incredible gizmo that does many things. One of those things is to take pictures, which is the responsibility of the Camera app.

Though the Camera app is one of the most common apps on Android tablets, it's also perhaps the one that's the most customized. This chapter refers to the stock Android Camera app, which is available at the Google Play Store as Google Camera.

- ✔ The Camera app is typically found on the Home screen — often, in the Favorites tray. Like every other app, a copy also dwells in the Apps drawer.

- ✔ When you use the Camera app, the touchscreen navigation icons (Back, Home, Recent) turn into tiny dots. The icons are still there, and they still work, but you may find them difficult to see.

- ✔ When you first start the Camera app, it asks about location settings. I recommend accepting the settings as presented. You can change them afterward, if you like. See the section "Setting the image's location," elsewhere in this chapter.

- ✔ The tablet's primary camera is on the back of the device. The secondary camera faces you as you look at the touchscreen.

- ✔ Not all Android tablets feature a rear-facing camera. If yours doesn't, the tablet most likely didn't come with an app that can shoot pictures or videos.

Capturing the moment

After it's started, the Camera app takes over the tablet, turning the touchscreen into a viewfinder. The stock Android version of the Camera app is shown in Figure 11-1. Your tablet may use a customized version of the Camera app that presents the onscreen controls in a different manner.

In Figure 11-1, the Camera app is in single shot, or Camera, mode. The Shutter icon reflects the mode; touch that icon to take a still picture. The camera focuses, you may hear a mechanical shutter sound play, and the flash may go off. You're ready to take the next picture.

To record video, switch the Camera app into Video mode: In the stock Android Camera app, swipe your finger from the left edge of the screen toward the center. You see a list of shooting modes, as shown in Figure 11-2. Choose Video.

Some variations of the Camera app may feature a sliding switch to switch between single-shot and video modes, such as the Samsung Camera app, shown in Figure 11-3.

 When Video mode is active, the Shutter icon changes to the Video icon, shown in the margin. In some Camera apps, a Record icon (a red dot) is used instead. Touch that icon to start recording.

Action Overflow

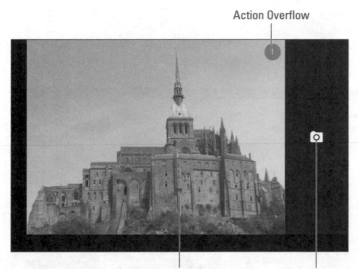

Image preview   Shutter icon

Figure 11-1: The stock Android Camera app.

Swipe in from here to
view the shooting modes.   Settings icon

Photo Sphere

Panorama

Lens Blur

Camera

Video

Figure 11-2: Stock Android Camera app shooting modes.

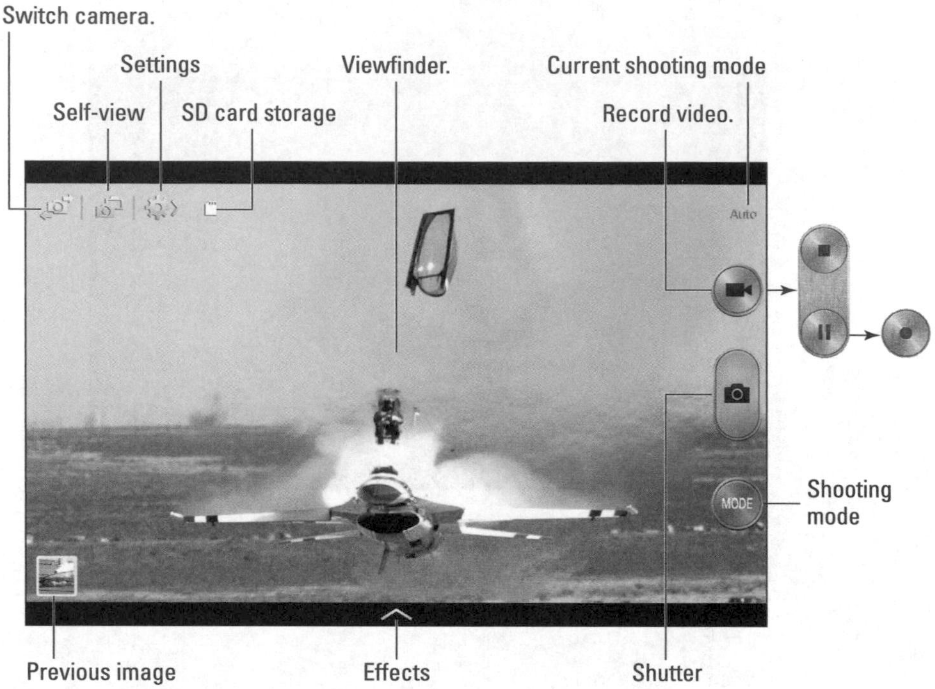

Switch camera.

Settings

Viewfinder.

Current shooting mode

Self-view

SD card storage

Record video.

Previous image

Effects

Shutter

Shooting mode

Figure 11-3: The Samsung Camera app.

While the tablet is recording, the Stop icon appears. A time indicator appears in the corner of the screen, telling you the video shot duration.

To stop recording, touch the Stop icon.

To preview the image or video in the stock Android Camera app, swipe the screen from right to left. Other Camera apps may feature the Previous Image icon, such as the one shown in Figure 11-3. Touch that icon to see the image. After viewing the preview, touch the Back icon to return to the Camera app, or swipe the screen from left to right.

✓ The camera focuses automatically, though you may be able to drag a focus ring around the touchscreen to specifically adjust the focus. Not every Camera app features a focus ring, and in some cases the "ring" may be square.

✓ Hold steady! The camera still works when you whip the tablet around, but wild gyrations render still images blurry and video unwatchable.

✓ Camera settings are reflected by icons on the screen. Figure 11-3 shows several examples in the upper left corner. For the stock Android Camera app, the Shutter icon changes to reflect the shooting mode.

✔ The tablet can take pictures in either landscape or portrait orientation. No matter how you take the picture, the image is stored upright. Even so, you can reorient images later, which is covered in Chapter 12.

✔ Spread your fingers on the touchscreen to zoom in to the stock Android camera app; pinch your fingers to zoom out. Other Camera apps may feature the zoom control: Slide the control up or down (or left or right) to zoom in or out. You may also be able to use the tablet's Volume key to zoom in and out.

✔ Be careful using the Volume key to zoom! Some tablets may use the Volume key as an alternative shutter button.

✔ You can take as many pictures and shoot as many videos with your Android tablet as you like — as long as the tablet's doesn't run out of storage space.

✔ Some versions of the Camera app may allow you to grab a still image while the tablet is recording: Touch the screen. The image is snapped and saved.

✔ If your pictures appear blurry, ensure that the camera lens on the back of the tablet isn't dirty.

✔ Use the Gallery app to manage the tablet's pictures and videos. See Chapter 12 for more information about the Gallery.

✔ The Android tablet not only takes a picture but also keeps track of where you were located on planet Earth when you took it. See the section "Setting the image's location," later in this chapter, for details. Also refer to Chapter 12 for information on reviewing a photograph's location.

✔ The tablet stores both pictures and videos in the DCIM/Camera folder. Pictures are stored in either the JPEG or PNG file format, they and have either the `jpg` or `png` filename extension. Videos are saved in the MPEG-4 video file format and feature the `mp4` filename extension.

✔ Tablets with removable storage feature a Settings option in the Camera app to control whether images are saved in internal or removable storage.

✔ Visual effects (the cheap kind, not the Hollywood CGI kind) can be applied to the video. The Effects icon may be on the screen, or you can access that item through the Control icon or another Settings icon on the screen. See the later section "Exploring special modes and effects."

Shooting yourself

Who needs to pay all that money for a mirror when you have an Android tablet? Well, forget the mirror. Instead, think about taking all those self-shots without having to second-guess whether the camera is pointed at your face.

To take your own mug shot, start the Camera app and switch to the front camera. For the stock Android Camera app, touch the Action Overflow icon (refer to Figure 11-1) and then touch the Switch Camera icon, shown in the margin. Other variations of the Camera app have a similar control, either directly on the Camera app screen or on a menu or an icon. For example, in Figure 11-3, the Switch Camera icon is found in the upper left corner of the screen.

As soon as you see your punum on the touchscreen, you've done things properly. Smile. Click.

Follow the same procedure to switch back to the rear camera. The icon may change its appearance, but you should find it in the same location in the Camera app.

Exploring shooting modes

All variations of the Camera app feature two shooting modes: Camera and Video. Additional shooting modes are available, including the popular Panorama and Photo Sphere. These modes let you capture the world around you in a unique way.

- ✓ The *panorama* is a wide shot — it works by panning the tablet across a scene. The Camera app then stitches together several images to build the panorama.

- ✓ The *photo sphere* is a wrap-around panorama, covering left, right, up, down, and all around. The result is an interactive image that you can pan and tilt to see everything around you.

To shoot a panoramic shot, follow these steps in the Camera app:

1. Choose the Camera app's Panorama mode.

For the stock Android Camera app, swipe your finger inward from the left side of the screen. The modes appear, as illustrated earlier in Figure 11-2. Touch the Panorama icon to switch the app into Panorama mode.

2. Hold the tablet steady, and then touch the Shutter icon.

3. Pivot in one direction as shown on the screen, following along with the animation.

Watch as the image is rendered and saved to the Gallery.

To create a photo sphere, obey these steps in the Camera app:

1. From the Camera app's Photo Sphere mode.

2. **Position the tablet so that the dot on the screen lines up with the circle.**

   Use the artificial horizon that appears on the touchscreen to help you orient the camera.

3. **Systematically turn in every direction, lining up the camera with the dots that appear on the screen.**

   You're not done until you've lined up the camera with every dot.

When the photo sphere image is complete, the Camera app renders the final result. You can peruse it in the Gallery, or immediately by swiping the screen to the left. Touch the Photo Sphere icon to interact (pan and tilt) with the image preview.

TIP

Photo sphere shots work best with static surroundings, such as landscapes and still-life images. Trying to take a photo sphere image of people or other lively objects, such as a zombie stampede, yields disappointing results.

REMEMBER

✔ To exit any special camera shooting mode, choose Camera, Video, or another shooting mode.

✔ The Android tablet camera automatically captures the panoramic shot. You touch the Shutter icon only when you're done.

Camera Settings and Options

Your tablet's camera is much more than just a hole in the case. Taking a picture or shooting a video can involve more than simply touching an icon. To help you get the most from the tablet's camera, various settings, options, and effects eagerly lurk beneath the Camera app's interface. This section describes some of the common features, the handy ones, and even some oddballs.

Deleting an image immediately after you take it

Sometimes, you just can't wait to delete an image. Either an irritated person is standing next to you, begging that the photo be deleted, or you're simply not happy and you feel the urge to smash into digital shards the picture you just took. Hastily follow these steps:

1. **Summon the previous image.**

   In the stock Android Camera app, swipe the screen from right to left. If your tablet's Camera app features the Preview icon, touch that icon to see the image that you just snapped or shot.

2. **Touch the Trash icon on the screen.**

You may see the Delete command instead of the Trash icon. If so, touch it. If you can't see either, tap the screen and the icons should appear. If not, try touching the Action Overflow or Menu icon to find the Delete command.

3. **Touch the OK button to confirm and erase the image.**

The image has been banished to bit-hell.

If necessary, touch the Back icon to return to the Camera app. If the Back icon has disappeared, tap the screen to see it.

You can always remove the image by using the Gallery app. See Chapter 12.

Setting the flash

Not all Android tablets feature a flash on the rear camera. If your tablet does, you can set the flash's behavior, as described in Table 11-1.

Table 11-1		Android Tablet Camera Flash Settings
Setting	*Icon*	*Description*
Auto	⚡A	The flash activates during low-light situations but not when it's bright out.
On	⚡	The flash always activates.
Off	⚡	The flash never activates, even in low-light situations.

To change or check the flash setting in the stock Android Camera app, touch the Action Overflow icon on the app's main screen (shown earlier, in Figure 11-1). The current flash setting is represented by an icon on the screen, as shown in Table 11-1. Choose that icon to switch to a different flash setting. Sometimes, you may have to tap the icon more than once.

On some Samsung tablets, touch the onscreen Settings icon, shown in the margin, to find the Flash setting. An example of this setting is shown in Figure 11-4.

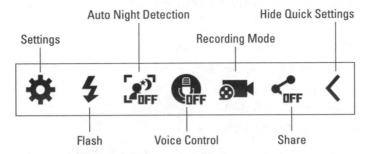

Figure 11-4: The flash control is found on this toolbar.

Most Camera apps display the current flash setting as an icon on the screen. For the stock Android Camera app, the Control icon changes to reflect the current flash setting.

✔ The Flash setting might also be found on a sliding control drawer or by first touching the Settings icon to see the Camera app's settings.

✔ A good time to turn on the flash is when taking pictures of people or objects in front of something bright, such as Aunt Ellen showing off her prized peach cobbler in front of a burning munitions factory.

✔ Some Android tablets lack flash hardware for the rear camera. On those devices, you cannot set the flash in the Camera app.

✔ A "flash" setting is also available for shooting video in low-light situations. In that case, the flash LED is on the entire time the video is being shot. This setting is made similarly to setting the flash, although the options are only On and Off. It must be set before you shoot video, and, yes, it devours a lot of battery power.

Changing the resolution

A useful Camera app setting that most people ignore is the image resolution. This setting is routinely ignored on digital cameras as well, mostly because people don't understand resolution. I'll be blunt:

You don't always need to use the highest resolution.

High-resolution images are great for printing photos. They're good for photo editing. They're not required for images you plan on sharing with Facebook or sending as e-mail attachments. Plus, the higher the resolution, the more storage space each image consumes.

Another problem with resolution is remembering to set it *before* you snap the photo or shoot the video. Here's how to set image resolution in the stock Android Camera app:

1. **Display the Camera app's shooting modes.**

2. **Touch the Settings icon.**

   The icon is shown in Figure 11-2.

3. **Choose Resolution & Quality.**

   The Resolution & Quality screen is organized by shooting mode and then by back or front camera.

4. **Choose a mode and a camera.**

   For example, choose the item Back Camera Photo to set the still-image resolution for the tablet's rear camera.

5. **Choose a resolution or video quality setting from the list.**

Not every Camera app follows these exact same steps. For example, in the Samsung Camera app, you choose Settings and then the Settings icon again, and then, finally, you choose Photo Size from a menu similar to the one shown in Figure 11-5.

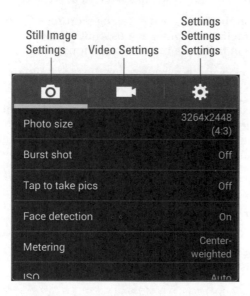

Figure 11-5: Setting the picture size.

To set the front camera's resolution, first switch to it as described earlier in this chapter. After the front camera is active, set its resolution. Unlike on the rear camera, only a handful or resolutions are available for the tablet's front-facing camera.

- Set the resolution or video quality *before* you shoot!

- Yes, low resolutions are just fine for uploading to Facebook. The resolution of the output device (a computer monitor or tablet screen) is low; therefore, you don't need to waste storage and upload time sending high-resolution images or videos to Facebook.

- A picture's *resolution* describes how many pixels, or dots, are in the image. The more dots, the better the image looks and prints.

- *Megapixel* is a measurement of the amount of information stored in an image. One megapixel is approximately 1 million pixels, or individual dots that compose an image. It's often abbreviated *MP*.

Setting the image's location

Your Android tablet not only takes pictures but also keeps track of where you're located when you take the picture — if you've turned on that option. The feature is called *geotag*, *GPS-tag*, or even *location tag*. Here's how to ensure that this option is set:

1. **In the stock Android Camera app, view the Camera modes.**

   Swipe the screen inward from the left edge toward the center to view the shooting modes.

2. **Touch the Settings icon.**

3. **Confirm that the master control icon by the Save Location item is in the On position.**

   If the master control icon isn't in the On position, slide it to the right.

On the Samsung variation of the Camera app, touch the Action Overflow or Menu icon to access the Settings command. Choose Location Tag or GPS Tag, and then set that option to either On or Off. When the Location Tag item is on, you see its icon on the touchscreen, as shown in the margin.

- Oftentimes, touching the Geotag icon on the Camera app's screen is a shortcut to enabling or disabling that feature.

- See Chapter 12 for information on reviewing a photograph's location.

- The geotag information is stored in the picture itself. That means that other devices, apps, and computer programs can read the GPS information to determine where the image was taken.

Exploring special modes and effects

Camera apps on Android tablets often sport a rich variety of features. Some apps go way beyond the basics and offer custom shooting modes, special effects, filters, animations, and more. At the basic level, however, the two features available in many Camera apps are shooting modes and visual effects.

A *shooting mode* sets the camera's behavior. It provides handy shortcuts to solve some typical photo-taking problems, such as the modes shown in Figure 11-6.

Reset to Auto mode.   Swipe through the modes.

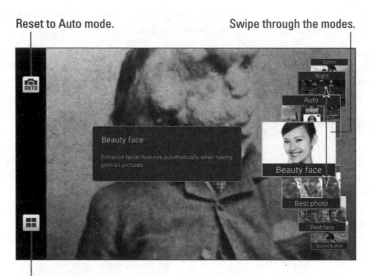

Display all modes in a grid.

Figure 11-6: Shooting modes.

To access shooting modes in the Samsung variation of the Camera app, touch the Mode button. You can swipe through the modes, as shown in Figure 11-6, or touch the Grid icon to see them all at one time.

As an example of a shooting mode, if you're taking a picture of something very close, choose the Macro shooting mode. That mode adjusts the camera so that tiny objects appear in focus.

Choose Auto mode to return to the standard, unmodified shooting mode.

Effects are a series of filters you can apply to the image before you shoot, such as those shown in Figure 11-7. These effects are summoned by choosing an Effects icon or swiping an Effects tool from the side of the screen.

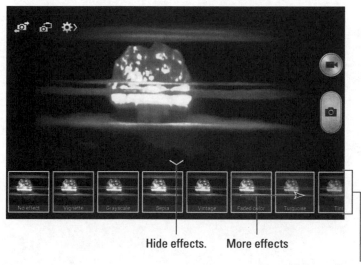

Hide effects.   More effects

Various effects

Figure 11-7: Various interesting visual effects.

Each effect has its own, wee preview window, as shown in Figure 11-7. Choose an effect before you shoot, and then take the picture. For example, to capture a *grayscale* ("black-and-white") shot, choose that effect and then touch the shutter button. The effects also apply to shooting video.

To cancel an effect, choose the No Effect option.

12

Image Management and Madness

*W*hat's the point of an Android tablet having a camera unless you can eventually review, peruse, browse, and chortle at those various images and videos? To solve that problem, your tablet features a digital photo album. You use it to view, manage, and manipulate the images stored in the tablet. Further, you can import other images, including photos stored on your computer or found on the Internet. It sounds easy, and I wish I could promise you that, but I've written this chapter anyway.

Where Your Pictures Lurk

Some people hang their pictures on the wall. Some put pictures on a piano or maybe on a mantle. In the digital realm, pictures are stored electronically, compressed and squeezed into a series of ones and zeroes that mean nothing unless you have an app that lets you view those images. On your Android tablet, that app is the *Gallery*.

Visiting the Gallery

Start the Gallery app by choosing its icon from the Apps drawer. Or you might find a Gallery app shortcut icon on the Home screen.

When the Gallery app opens, you see your visual media (pictures and videos) organized into piles, or *albums*. Figure 12-1 displays how the stock Android version of Gallery appears; what you see may look subtly different, but the organization is the same: Images are organized into albums.

Go to Main.　　　　　Go to album.　Google Drive

View menu　　　Camera app　　　Album name　　　　　Share icon

　　Main　　　　　　　　　Album　　　　　　　　Picture

Figure 12-1: Image organization in the Gallery's app.

If you see the Camera app when you start the Gallery, touch the Back icon to return to the Gallery. (The Camera and Gallery apps are linked, and sometimes one starts instead of the other.)

The number and variety of albums (refer to Figure 12-1) depend on how you synchronize your tablet with a computer, which apps you use for collecting media, or which photo-sharing services you use on the Internet and have synchronized with the tablet.

Touch an album to display that album's contents; the pictures appear in a grid of thumbnail previews. Swipe the screen left and right to peruse them all. Touch the App icon in the upper left corner of the screen to return to the main screen.

Touching an album in the Gallery app displays that album's contents in a grid of thumbnail previews. Peruse the images and videos in an album by swiping the screen left and right.

To view an image or play a video, touch a thumbnail image. Images appear full size on the screen, similar to what's shown on the right in Figure 12-1. You can rotate the tablet horizontally or vertically to see the image in another orientation. Later sections describe in more detail what you can do when viewing an image.

Videos stored in an album appear with the Play icon. Touch that icon to play the video. As the video is playing, touch the screen again to see the controls to pause.

You back up from an image or a video to an album by touching the Back icon. Touch the Back icon again to return to the main Gallery screen.

✔ The albums in the Gallery app feature names related to the image's source. The Camera album contains video you've shot using the tablet, the Download album contains images downloaded from the Internet, and so on.

✔ Albums labeled with the Picasa Web icon have been synchronized between Picasa Web on the Internet and your Android tablet. See the section "Using your Picasa Web account," later in this chapter.

✔ Various apps may also create their own albums in the Gallery app.

✔ Images synchronized with a computer may appear in their own albums.

✔ Some versions of the Gallery app let you create albums and organize your images; some versions do not.

✔ Your tablet's Gallery app may feature a View menu. Use that menu to control how the images and videos are displayed in the gallery. For example, images can be displayed by album or date.

✔ Use the View menu to choose how images appear in the Gallery. Albums view is shown earlier, in Figure 12-1.

✔ To view all images in an album, touch the Action Overflow or Menu icon and choose the Slideshow command. Playing a slide show turns your expensive tablet into a less-expensive digital picture frame.

Finding a picture's location

Your Android tablet can save location information when it takes a picture. The information is often called a geotag. To use that information in the Gallery app, heed these steps:

1. **View the image.**

2. **Touch the Action Overflow or Menu icon.**

3. Choose the Show on Map command.

The Maps app starts, showing the approximate location where the picture was taken, as illustrated in Figure 12-2.

Image viewed in the Gallery app

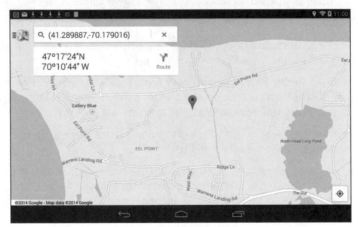

Image location on the map

Figure 12-2: Finding where an image was taken.

When the Show on Map command is unavailable, either your tablet lacks the geotag feature or the image wasn't saved with a geotag. See Chapter 11 for information on turning on this feature.

✔ Some tablets offer the Get Directions command instead of Show on Map. When this command is chosen, the Maps app starts and displays a route from your current location to the spot where the picture was taken. This command isn't really useful for finding a location on the map — especially when the location is in France and you're in the United States.

✔ Videos shot with an Android tablet can also store location information, though this information may not be accessible by using the steps outlined in this section.

Setting an image as wallpaper

To assign pictures from the Gallery for use as the tablet's Home screen wallpaper, follow these steps:

1. **View an image in the Gallery.**

2. **Touch the Action Overflow or Menu icon and choose the Set Picture As command.**

   The command might also be titled Set As. If you don't see that command or a similar one, you cannot use that image; not every album allows its images to be set as wallpaper.

3. **Choose Wallpaper.**

4. **Touch the Set Wallpaper button.**

   The wallpaper is set.

Some tablets let you set the lock screen image as well, or perhaps both Home and lock screen images. If so, you see a prompt asking you to choose Home Screen, Lock Screen, or Home and Lock Screens. By choosing the Home and Lock Screens command, you set both screen wallpapers at one time.

✔ You might also be prompted to crop the wallpaper image. Refer to the later section "Cropping an image" for details. When cropping wallpaper, you need to set the crop in two directions: vertically and horizontally.

✔ The *lock screen* is the background image you see when the tablet is locked; the *wallpaper* is the background that's displayed behind icons and widgets on the Home screen.

✔ You can also change the wallpaper by long-pressing the Home screen and choosing a Wallpapers category. See Chapter 19 for details.

Edit and Manage the Gallery

The best tool for image editing is a computer amply equipped with photo editing software, such as Photoshop or a similar program that's also referred to as "Photoshop" because the term is pretty much generic. Regardless, you can use the Gallery app to perform some minor photo surgery. This section covers that topic, as well as general image management.

✔ Some versions of the Gallery app offer more photo editing features than others. I've seen commands to remove red-eye, add special effects, and even make homely people look pretty. This section covers the most common commands.

✔ The Gallery app may restrict editing on images imported from Internet photo sharing sites. It's best to edit and manage those images on the hosting service's website directly.

Cropping an image

One of the few true image-editing commands available in the Gallery app is Crop. You use the Crop tool to slice out portions of an image, such as when removing ex-spouses and convicts from a family portrait. To crop an image, obey these directions:

1. **Summon the image you want to crop.**

2. **Touch the Action Overflow or Menu icon.**

   If you can't see the icon, touch the screen and the icon reappears.

3. **Choose Crop.**

   Sometimes, you must choose an Edit command before you can find the Crop command.

   If the Crop command is unavailable, you have to choose another image. (Not every album lets you modify images.)

4. **Work the crop-thing.**

   You can drag the rectangle around to choose which part of the image to crop. Drag an edge of the rectangle to resize the left and right or top and bottom sides. Or drag a corner of the rectangle to change the rectangle's size proportionally. Use Figure 12-3 as your guide.

   Some versions of the Gallery app may display a tool palette when you're prompted to crop an image. Don't mess with the palette! Just crop the image.

   If you screw up cropping, cancel the operation and start over: Touch the Cancel button or the Back icon.

Discard   Move rectangle.

Crop   Keep   Resize rectangle.

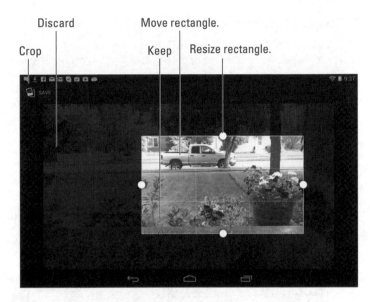

Figure 12-3: Working the crop-thing.

5. Touch the Done or Save button when you're done cropping.

Only the portion of the image within the colored rectangle is saved; the rest is discarded.

The cropped image is saved in the Gallery.

✔ On some tablets, the crop procedure is irreversible; you cannot undo the crop. Other tablets may save the cropped photo as a new photo, keeping the original.

✔ Also look for the Crop icon in some Gallery apps. Such an icon is shown in the margin.

✔ Some variations of the Gallery app feature the Edit icon. Touch that icon to review all the different tools for manipulating and mangling an image.

Trimming a video

Though you can't crop a video in the sense that you can't change its resolution, you can snip off the head or tail from the recording. This process is known as *trimming* the video. It works like this:

1. Display the video in the Gallery.

Do not play the video; just have it loitering on the screen.

Videos in an album are flagged with the Play icon.

2. Choose the Trim command.

Touch the Action Overflow or Menu icon to find the Trim command. In some versions of the Gallery app, the Trim icon appears on the screen, similar to the one shown in the margin. If you can't see the icon, touch the screen. If it still doesn't show up, the video is being shared from another source and cannot be edited.

3. Adjust the video's start and end points.

Figure 12-4 illustrates how to trim a typical video: Adjust the Start and End markers to trim the video's length. Touch the Play button on the screen to preview how the shortened video looks. Adjust the Start and End markers further, if needed.

You cannot trim a video so tiny that it's less than one second in duration.

4. Touch the Save or Done button to save the edited video.

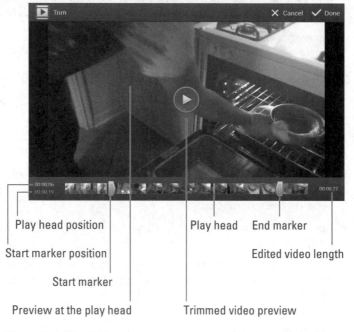

Play head position

Start marker position

Start marker

Preview at the play head

Play head   End marker

Edited video length

Trimmed video preview

Figure 12-4: Film Editing 101.

On some tablets, you may be prompted to give the trimmed video a new name. Otherwise, your shortened video is automatically saved under a new name and presented as its own item in the Gallery.

Rotating pictures

Showing someone else an image on your Android tablet can be frustrating, especially when the image is a vertical picture that refuses to fill the screen when the tablet is in a vertical orientation. You can fix that issue by rotating the picture. Heed these steps in the Gallery app:

1. **Choose an image to rotate.**

2. **Touch the Action Overflow or Menu icon.**

   Or if you see the Edit icon on the screen, touch it to view a buncha editing commands in one place.

3. **Choose Rotate Left to rotate the image counterclockwise; choose Rotate Right to rotate the image clockwise.**

You can rotate a whole slew of images at one time: Select all the images as described in the later section "Selecting multiple pictures and videos." Touch the Action Overflow or Menu icon and choose Rotate Left or Rotate Right. All the images are rotated at one time.

- You cannot rotate videos.

- You cannot rotate certain images, such as images shared from your Picasa Web albums.

- To undo an image rotation, just use the opposite Rotate command.

Deleting images and videos

It's entirely possible, and often desirable, to remove unwanted, embarrassing, or questionably legal images from the Gallery.

So how do you know what you can delete? Simple: If you see the Trash icon atop the screen when viewing an image, you can delete that image. Touch the Trash icon, and then touch the OK or Confirm Delete button. The image is gone.

If you don't see the Trash icon, touch the Action Overflow or Menu icon and then choose the Delete command.

The procedure for deleting a video might work the same as for deleting an image. When it doesn't, you have to select the video in its album and then delete it. See the next section.

- You can't undelete an image you've deleted. There's no way to recover a deleted image using available tools on the Android tablet.

- Some images can't be deleted, such as images brought in from social networking sites or from online photo sharing albums.

✔ To delete images from Picasa, visit Picasa Web on the Internet at

```
http://picasaweb.google.com
```

✔ You can delete a whole swath of images by selecting them as a group. See the next section.

Selecting multiple pictures and videos

You can apply certain commands, such as Delete and Rotate, to an entire swath of items in the Gallery at one time. To do so, you must select a group of images or videos. Here's how:

1. **Open the album you want to mess with.**

2. **Long-press an image or video to select it.**

   Instantly, you activate image selection mode. (That's my name for it.) The thumbnail you long-pressed might appear highlighted, or it may grow a check mark box, as shown in Figure 12-5.

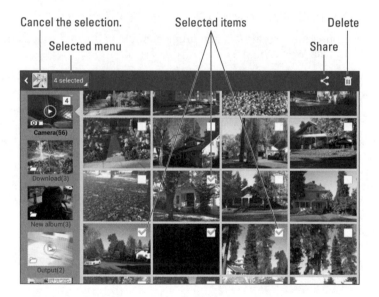

Figure 12-5: Choosing images to mess with.

3. **Continue touching images and videos to select them.**

   Or you can choose the Select All command to mark them all.

4. **Perform an action on the group of images or videos.**

   Other sections describe specifically what you can do, though your options generally are limited to sharing, deleting, and rotating.

To deselect items, touch them again. To deselect everything, touch the Back icon.

Set Your Pictures and Videos Free

Keeping your precious moments and memories in your tablet is an elegant solution to the problem of lugging around photo albums. But when you want to show your pictures to the widest possible audience, you need a much larger stage. That stage is the Internet, and you have many ways to send and save your pictures, as covered in this section.

Refer to Chapter 17 for information on synchronizing and sharing information between the tablet and a computer.

Using your Picasa Web account

Part of your Google account includes access to the online photo sharing website Picasa Web. If you haven't yet been to the Picasa Web site on the Internet, use a computer to visit it:

```
http://picasaweb.google.com
```

Configure things by logging in to your Google account on that website.

Your Picasa account is automatically synchronized with your Android tablet. Any pictures you put on Picasa are echoed to your tablet, accessed through the Gallery app. If not, follow these steps to ensure that Picasa is being property synced:

1. **On the Home screen, touch the Apps icon.**

2. **Open the Settings app.**

3. **Access your Google account.**

   Choose your Google account below the Accounts heading. If there is no Accounts heading, choose Accounts & Sync and then choose your Google account from the list under Manage Accounts.

   On some Samsung tablets, touch the General tab and choose the Accounts item from the left side of the screen. Choose Google and then touch your Google account (your Gmail address).

4. **Ensure that there's a check mark by the Sync Picasa Web Albums item, although it might be titled Google Photos.**

    That's pretty much it.

Any images you have on Picasa Web are automatically copied to your Android tablet from now on.

If you prefer not to have Picasa synchronize your images, repeat the steps in this section but remove the check mark in Step 4.

 ✔ Picasa albums feature the Picasa logo, as shown in the margin.

 ✔ Images stored on Picasa can be viewed on your tablet, but not edited. To edit or otherwise manage the images, go to the Picasa Web website on the Internet.

Uploading to the cloud

Another way to share images on the Internet is to use *cloud storage.* That's just a fancy term for online storage, such as that offered by Google Drive or the popular Dropbox service.

To instantly upload an image to your Google Drive, view the image in the Gallery and touch the Google Drive icon atop the screen, shown in the margin. Optionally, type a new name for the file and choose a folder or create a new folder. Touch the OK button to send a copy of the image to your Google Drive.

Another popular cloud storage service is Dropbox. In fact, quite a few Android tablets come supplied with the Dropbox app, which allows for the quick coordination of files across several devices and the Internet.

To send images to your Dropbox storage, touch the Share icon when viewing the image. Choose the Add to Dropbox command.

Dropbox also features an automatic photo upload service. Once active, all pictures and videos you take with your tablet are instantly shared and saved in your Dropbox account. Follow these steps to enable this service:

1. **Open the Dropbox app.**

    If your tablet doesn't come with the Dropbox app, you can obtain a free copy at the Google Play Store. (See Chapter 15.) You also need a Dropbox account, which is free; run the Dropbox app to sign up.

2. **Touch the Action Overflow or Menu icon and choose the Settings command.**

3. **Touch the text *Turn On Camera Upload.***

   The text is found beneath the Camera Upload heading. If it instead reads *Turn Off Camera Upload,* you're all set — unless you have a cellular tablet, in which case I recommend that you:

4. **Choose the Upload Using item.**

5. **Select Wi-Fi Only.**

   By setting this item, you ensure that the tablet uploads images only when connected to a Wi-Fi network. That means you won't use precious megabytes from your monthly mobile data allocation.

With the Camera Upload setting activated, any image you snap is instantly copied to your Dropbox account. It's saved in the Camera Uploads folder. If you use Dropbox on a computer, you can immediately access those pictures and videos. That's handy.

✔ Having cloud storage on Google Drive is yet another perk that comes with your Google account.

✔ You can access your Google Drive files from any computer by visiting this website:

```
https://drive.google.com
```

✔ Google Drive software can be obtained for Windows or the Macintosh so that you can also access your Google Drive files on your computer.

Printing pictures

Don't fret! To print items from your Android tablet, you don't need to lug around a computer printer. Such a burden goes completely against the wireless nature of a mobile device. That wireless freedom doesn't mean you have to sacrifice the ability to print out a photo or two.

Of the many printing options available to an Android tablet, the two most common are Bluetooth and Google Cloud print. Both are wireless printing methods, and both work quite well no matter which tablet you use.

Bluetooth

To print an image to a Bluetooth printer, follow these steps:

1. **Ensure that the Bluetooth printer has been paired with the computer and is on and ready to print.**

   The pairing process is discussed in Chapter 16.

2. **Locate the image you want to print in the Gallery.**

   Show the image by itself, not in an album.

3. **Touch the Share icon and choose Bluetooth.**

Some versions of the Gallery app may even sport the Bluetooth icon right on the screen. If not, tap the Share icon and you'll find the Bluetooth command.

4. **Select the Bluetooth printer from the list.**

5. **If prompted by the printer, confirm that the image upload is approved.**

Not every Bluetooth printer has such a prompt; some just go ahead and print the image.

Google Cloud Print

The Google Cloud Print option is perhaps the easiest way to print from your Android tablet. The problem is that you need these four things to make it work:

- A desktop computer, or access to one
- A printer connected to that computer, either directly or over a network
- The Google Chrome web browser on that computer
- The Google Cloud Print app on your tablet

If you can wrangle those four items, Google Cloud Print works by first configuring the computer and then your Android tablet. Computer configuration works like this:

1. **Log in to the Chrome browser on the computer.**

Use the same Google account that you use for your tablet. You can't forget this step, because Google insists that you log in when you first obtain the Chrome program for your computer.

2. **In the Chrome web browser on your computer, click the Menu icon in the upper right corner of the window.**

3. **Choose the Settings command.**

A new browser tab opens, listing Chrome Settings.

4. **Click the Show Advanced Settings link.**

It's found at the bottom of the page. After you click the link, the page grows longer with more options and settings.

5. **In the Google Cloud Print section, click the button Sign In to Google Cloud Print.**

That's it.

With the computer set up for Google Cloud Print, the next step is to download the Google Cloud Print app from the Play Store. General app-downloading directions are found in Chapter 15.

After the app is installed on your tablet, you can print from any app (not just the Gallery) by following these steps:

1. **Touch the Share icon.**

2. **Choose the Cloud Print item.**

3. **Select a local printer or device from the list.**

    The document prints.

The unusual thing about Google Cloud Print is that you don't need to be in the same place as the printer. I've printed from the library and from other states. I could even print a document on my home computer while flying cross-country, although I'm too cheap to pay $20 for in-flight Wi-Fi.

Posting a video to YouTube

The best way to share a video is to upload it to YouTube. As a Google account holder, you also have a YouTube account. You can use the YouTube app on your tablet along with your account to upload your videos to the Internet, where everyone can see them and make rude comments about them. Here's how:

1. **Ensure that the Wi-Fi connection is activated.**

    The best way to upload a video is to turn on the Wi-Fi connection, which doesn't incur data surcharges, like the digital cellular network does. In fact, if you opt to use the 4G LTE network for uploading a YouTube video, you see a suitable reminder about the data surcharges.

2. **Start the Gallery app.**

3. **Open the video you want to upload.**

    You do not need to play the video. Just have it on the screen.

4. **Touch the Share icon.**

    If you don't see the Share icon, tap the screen.

5. **Choose YouTube.**

    The Upload Video window appears, listing all sorts of options and settings for sending the video to YouTube.

6. **Type the video's title.**

    Feel free to replace the timestamp title with something more descriptive.

7. **Set other options.**

   Type a description, set the privacy level, add tags, and so on.

8. **Touch the Upload button.**

   You return to the Gallery, and the video is uploaded. It continues to upload even if the tablet falls asleep.

The uploading notification appears while the video is being sent to YouTube. Feel free to do other things with your tablet while the video uploads. When the upload has completed, the notification stops animating and becomes the Uploads Finished icon.

To view your video, open the YouTube app. It's found in the Apps drawer and discussed in detail in Chapter 14.

- ✔ YouTube often takes a while to process a video after it's uploaded. Allow a few minutes to pass (longer for larger videos) before the video becomes available for viewing.

- ✔ *Upload* is the official term to describe sending a file from your Android tablet to the Internet.

Sharing images with other apps

Just about every app wants to get in on the sharing bit, especially when it comes to pictures and videos. The key is to view something in the Gallery and then touch the Share icon atop the screen, as shown in the margin. From the Share menu, choose an app, and that image or video is instantly sent to that app.

What happens next?

That depends on the app. For Facebook, Twitter, and other social networking apps, the image is attached to a new post. For Email or Gmail, the image or video becomes an attachment. Other apps treat the image in a similar manner: It's made available to the app for sharing, posting, sending, or what-have-you. The key is to look for that Share icon.

13

Music, Music, Music

Your Android tablet's amazing arsenal of features includes its capability to play music. So it effectively replaces any gramophone that you've been lugging around, which is the whole idea behind such an all-in-one gizmo like an Android tablet. You can cheerfully and adeptly transfer all your old Edison cylinders and 78 LP's to the tablet for your listening enjoyment. More specifically, this chapter explains how to listen to music, get more music, and manage that music on your tablet.

Listen Here

Your Android tablet is ready to entertain you with music whenever you want to hear it. Simply plug in the headphones, summon the music-playing app, and choose tunes to match your mood.

✔ The stock Android music-playing app is Google's own Play Music app. Your tablet may feature another music-playing app. I've seen names such as Music and My Music. All music-playing apps offer similar features.

✔ Be wary of music subscription services offered through your tablet's manufacturer or cellular provider. I've subscribed to such services only to find them canceled for various reasons. To avoid that disappointment, stick with the services described in this chapter until you feel comfortable enough to buy into another service.

Browsing your music library

The Play Music app is your source of musical delight on your Android tablet. You can find it on the Apps screen, or perhaps you'll see a shortcut icon plastered on the Home screen.

After you start the Play Music app, you see a screen similar to the one shown in Figure 13-1. If you're displeased with the quantity of music available, refer to the later section "Add Some Music to Your Life." It explains how to get more tunes.

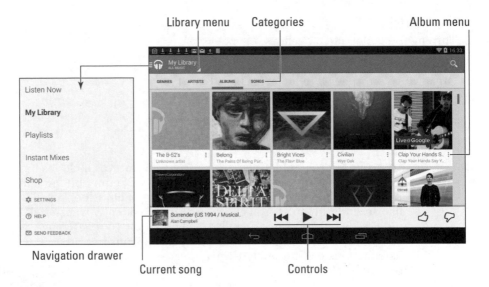

Figure 13-1: The Play Music app; Album category.

To view your music library, choose My Library from the navigation drawer, as shown in Figure 13-1. Your music library appears on the main Play Music screen. Touch a tab to view your music by category, such as Artists, Albums, or Songs.

Touch an album to see songs listed in that album. Likewise, choose an artist to view all songs associated with that artist.

You can choose the Listen Now category from the navigation drawer to see songs you frequently listen to or tunes that the tablet guesses you will like. The more you use the Play Music app, the more you'll appreciate the results that are displayed.

✔ Songs and albums feature the Action Overflow icon, similar to the one shown in the margin. Use that icon to view a list of commands associated with the album or artist.

✔ Music is stored on the tablet's internal memory and on the removable MicroSD card. It's also possible to keep music on the Internet at

```
play.google.com/music
```

✔ Use the Library menu, shown in Figure 13-1, to choose whether to view music that's available only on the tablet (On Device) or all your music (All Music), which includes music stored on the Internet in Google's Play music library.

✔ See the later section "Add Some Music to Your Life" for information on adding more music to the Play Music app.

✔ Your tablet's storage capacity limits the total amount of music that can be stored. Also, consider that storing pictures and videos horns in on some of the space that can be used to store music.

✔ The Pin icon is used to store on the tablet the music you purchase online. Otherwise, the Play Music app accesses your music over the Internet connection. See the later section "Pinning your music."

✔ Album artwork generally appears on imported music and on music you purchase online. If an album has no artwork, it cannot be manually added or updated (at least, not by using the Play Music app).

✔ When the tablet is unable to recognize an artist, it uses the title Unknown Artist. This happens with music you copy manually to the tablet. Music that you purchase, or import or synchronize with a computer, generally retains the artist and album information. (Well, the information is retained as long as it was supplied on the original source.)

Playing a tune

To listen to music on your tablet, you first find a song in your music library, as described in the preceding section. After you find the song, you touch its title. The song plays on another screen, similar to what's shown in Figure 13-2.

While the song plays, you're free to do anything else on the tablet. In fact, the song continues to play even when the tablet is locked or goes to sleep; a short-cut to the song, along with control icons, appears right on the lock screen, along with information about the song.

After the song is done playing, the next song in the list plays. The order depends on how you start the song. For example, if you start a song from Album view, all songs in that album play in the order listed.

The next song doesn't play if you have the Shuffle button activated (refer to Figure 13-2). In that case, the Play Music app randomly chooses another song from the same list. Who knows which one is next?

Album cover artwork

Show song queue.

Repeat Shuffle Slider Rewind Fast Forward Song length

Play/Pause

Figure 13-2: A song is playing.

The next song also might not play when you have the Repeat option on: The three repeat settings are illustrated in Table 13-1, along with the Shuffle settings. To change settings, simply touch either the Shuffle or Repeat icon. If those icons disappear from the screen, touch the screen briefly and they'll show up again.

Table 13-1		Shuffle and Repeat Icons
Icon	*Setting*	*What Happens When You Touch the Icon*
	Shuffle Is Off	Songs play one after the other.
	Shuffle Is On	Songs are played in random order.
	Repeat Is Off	Songs don't repeat.
	Repeat Current Song	The same song plays over and over.
	Repeat All Songs	All songs in the list play over and over.

To stop the song from playing, touch the Pause icon (labeled in Figure 13-2).

A notification icon (shown in the margin) appears while music is playing on your tablet. To quickly summon the Play Music app, touch that notification. The notification itself shows controls to pause the song or to skip forward or backward.

✔ The volume is set by using the Volume key on the side of the tablet.

✔ While you browse the Play Music app's library, the currently playing song is displayed at the bottom of the screen (refer to Figure 13-1).

✔ Some of the music on your Android tablet is Google music, originating from the Internet. It's not available to play unless the tablet has an Internet connection. See the next section for a tip on how to remedy this situation.

✔ To choose which songs play after each other, create a playlist. See the section "Organize Your Music," later in this chapter.

✔ After the last song in the list plays, the Play Music app stops playing songs — unless you have set the List Repeat option, in which case the list plays again.

✔ You can use the Android tablet's search capabilities to help locate tunes in your music library. You can search by artist name, song title, or album. The key is to touch the Search icon when you're using the Play Music app. Type all or part of the text you're searching for, and then touch the Search icon on the onscreen keyboard. Choose the song you want to hear from the list that's displayed.

Pinning your music

Most of the music you have in your Google Play music library, especially music obtained from the Play Store, is actually stored on the Internet, not on the tablet. As long as you have an Internet connection, your tablet can play the music; but when you don't have an Internet connection . . . silence.

To make your music available offline, you need to download it from the Internet to the tablet's storage. Here's how it works:

1. **Display the Play Music app's navigation drawer.**

2. **Choose My Library.**

   Behold your music library.

3. **Locate the song, artist, or album that you want to store on the tablet.**

4. **Touch the Action Overflow icon by the song, artist, or album.**

5. **Choose the Keep on Device command.**

   Or, if it's visible, you can touch the Pushpin icon next to the album or song.

"What's this song?"

You might consider getting the handy, music-oriented widget Sound Search for Google Play. You can obtain this widget from the Google Play Store and then add it to the Home screen. From the Home screen, you can use the widget to identify music playing within earshot of your tablet.

To use the widget, touch it on the Home screen. The widget immediately starts listening to your surroundings, as shown in the middle of the sidebar figure. After a few seconds, the song is recognized and displayed. You can choose to either buy the song at the Google Play Store or touch the Cancel button and start over.

The Sound Search widget works best (exclusively, I would argue) with recorded music. Try as you might, you cannot sing into the thing and have it recognize a song. Humming doesn't

work, either. I've tried playing the guitar and piano and — nope — that doesn't work either. But for listening to ambient music, it's a good tool for discovering what you're listening to.

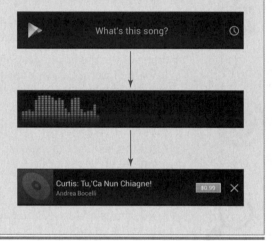

The music is downloaded to the tablet, after which it's available to play all the time, Internet connection or no.

✔ Pinned music (stored on the tablet) features the Pin icon, similar to the one shown in the margin. That icon can also be used when viewing an album; touch it to keep the entire album on the device.

✔ When you copy music to the tablet from a computer, it's always kept on the device. See the later section "Borrowing music from a computer."

✔ To review the music already on the tablet, go to the main Play Music app screen. Touch the Library menu and choose the On Device command.

Being the life of the party

You need to do four things to make your Android tablet the soul of your next shindig or soirée:

✔ Connect it to external speakers.

✔ Use the Shuffle command.

✔ Set the Repeat command.

✔ Provide plenty of drinks and snacks.

The external speakers can be provided by anything from a custom media dock or a stereo to the sound system on the Times Square Jumbotron. As long as the device has a standard line input, you're good.

Oh, and you need an audio cable. Get one with a mini-headphone connector for the tablet's headphone jack and an audio jack that matches the output device. Look for such a cable at Radio Shack or any other store where the employees wear name tags.

After you connect your tablet to the speakers, start the Play Music app. Choose the party playlist you've created, per the directions elsewhere in this chapter. If you want the songs to play in random order, touch the Shuffle button.

You might also consider choosing the List Repeat command (see Table 13-1) so that all songs in the list repeat.

 ✔ To play all songs saved on your Android tablet, choose the Songs category and touch the first song in the list.

 ✔ See the later section "Organize Your Music" for information on creating playlists. Build one playlist for your book club and another one for your theater friends.

 ✔ Enjoy your party, and please drink responsibly.

Add Some Music to Your Life

Consider yourself fortunate if your Android tablet comes with some tunes pre-installed. That may happen, courtesy of Google Play on the Internet. Otherwise, none of my favorites was in there! What to do? Why, add more music! This section goes over a few ways to get music into your tablet.

Borrowing music from a computer

The computer is the equivalent of the 20th century stereo system — a combination tuner-amplifier-turntable — plus, all your records and CDs. If you've already copied your music collection to your computer, or if you use your computer as your main music-storage system, you can share that music with your Android tablet.

On Windows, the most common music-playing (or *jukebox*) program is Windows Media Player. You can use this program to synchronize music between your PC and the Android tablet. Before you get dirty, however, a warning:

The Play Music app does not recognize music copied to the tablet from Windows Media Player. Yes, it's disappointing, but I can only guess that the restriction is to motivate you to purchase music from the Google Play Store (covered in the next section). Who would have thought?

The good news: If your tablet comes with another music playing app, you *can* copy music from your computer and enjoy it on the tablet. Here's how it works:

1. **Connect the Android tablet to your PC.**

   Use the USB cable that comes with the tablet.

   Over on the PC, the AutoPlay dialog box appears in Windows, prompting you to choose how best to add the Android tablet to the Windows storage system.

   Ensure that the tablet is connected as a media player or uses something called MTP. See Chapter 17 if you have difficulty making the connection.

2. **On the PC, choose Windows Media Player from the AutoPlay dialog box.**

   If the AutoPlay dialog box doesn't appear, start the Windows Media Player program.

3. **On the PC, ensure that the Sync list appears, as shown in Figure 13-3.**

   The Android tablet appears in the Sync list on the right side of the Windows Media Player, as shown in Figure 13-3. If not, click the Next Device link or button until it shows up.

Click to sync. Sync tab

Your tablet

Sync list

Music to sync

Drag music to here.

Figure 13-3: Windows Media Player meets Android tablet.

4. **Drag to the Sync area the music you want to transfer to your tablet.**

   In Figure 13-3, you see a list of songs that appear in the Sync list. To add more, drag an album or individual song into the Sync list. Dragging an album sets up all its songs for transfer.

5. **Click the Start Sync button to transfer the music from the PC to your tablet.**

   The Start Sync button may be located atop the list, as shown in Figure 13-3, or it might be found on the bottom.

6. **Close the Windows Media Player when the transfer is complete.**

   Or keep it open — whatever.

7. **Unplug the tablet from the USB cable.**

   You can unplug the USB cable from the computer as well. Chapter 17 specifically covers the tablet-to-computer connection, if you need more information.

The next time you start the Play Music app, you'll find your music right there in the library. Now you can enjoy your computer's music anywhere you take the Android tablet.

- ✔ You cannot use iTunes to synchronize music with Android devices.

- ✔ The Android tablet can store only so much music! Don't be overzealous when copying your tunes. In Windows Media Player (refer to Figure 13-3), a capacity-thermometer thing shows you how much storage space is used and how much is available on your tablet. Pay heed to the indicator!

Buying music at the Google Play Store

It's possible to get music for your Android tablet from the same source where you get apps for your Android tablet — the Google Play Store. Getting apps is covered in Chapter 15. Getting music is covered right here:

1. **Open the Play Store app.**

   You can find the app on the Home screen or, like all apps, in the Apps drawer. You can also get to the Google Play Store by choosing the Shop item on the Play Music app's navigation drawer (labeled in Figure 13-1).

2. **Choose the Music category.**

   The Music category is shown at the main screen. If you visited the Google Play Music store from the Play Music app, you're already viewing the Music category.

3. **Use the Search command to locate music you want, or just browse the categories.**

   Keep an eye out for free music offers at the Play Store. It's a great way to pick up some tunes.

Eventually, you see a page showing details about the song or album. Choose a song from the list to hear a preview. The button next to the song or album indicates the purchase price, or it says *Free,* for free music.

4. **Touch the FREE button to get a free song, or touch the BUY or price button to purchase a song or album.**

   Don't worry — you're not buying anything yet.

5. **Choose your credit card or payment source.**

   If a credit card or payment source doesn't appear, choose the Add Card option to add a payment method. Sign up with Google Checkout and submit your credit card or other payment information.

   You may be prompted to type your Google password.

6. **Touch the Buy button or Confirm button.**

   The song or album is added to your music library.

The music you buy at the Play Store isn't downloaded to your tablet. It shows up, but it plays only over an Internet connection. To ensure that the music is always available, see the earlier section "Pinning your music."

✔ You eventually receive a Gmail message listing a summary of your purchase.

✔ All music sales are final. Don't blame me — I'm merely relating Google's current policy for music purchases.

✔ When you see a song or album you kind of want, or you just can't make up your mind, touch the Wishlist icon. This action saves the song or album on your Google Play Store wish list, which you can review later. To access your current wish list, choose the Wishlist item from the navigation drawer (refer to Figure 13-1).

✔ If you plan to download, or *pin,* an album or multiple songs, connect to a Wi-Fi network. That way, you don't run the risk of encountering a data surcharge on your cellular plan. See Chapter 16 for information on activating Wi-Fi.

✔ For more information on the Google Play Store, see Chapter 15.

Accessing your tunes on the Internet

Music you purchase from the Google Play music store is available on any mobile Android device with the Play Music app installed, providing you use the same Google account on that device. You can also listen to your tunes by visiting the music.google.com site on any computer connected to the Internet.

As long as you log in to your Google account on a computer connected to the Internet, you can use Google Play on the Internet to buy music, listen to music, and even upload music from your computer to your Google Play music library.

Organize Your Music

The Play Music app categorizes your music by album, artist, song, and so forth, but unless you have only one album and enjoy all the songs on it, that configuration probably won't do. To better organize your music, you can create *playlists*. That way, you can hear the music you want to hear, in the order you want, for whatever mood hits you.

Reviewing your playlists

To view any playlists that you've already created, or that have been preset on the tablet, choose Playlists from the Play Music app's navigation drawer (refer to Figure 13-1). Playlists you've created are displayed on the screen, as shown in Figure 13-4.

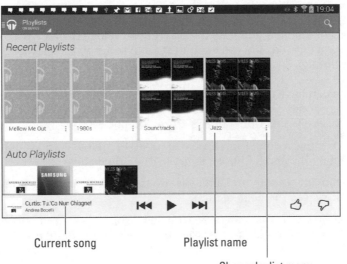

Figure 13-4: Playlists in the Play Music app.

To see which songs are in a playlist, touch the playlist's Album icon. To play the songs in the playlist, touch the first song in the list.

A playlist is a helpful way to organize music when a song's information may not have been completely imported into your Android tablet. For example, if you're like me, you probably have a lot of songs labeled Unknown. A quick way to remedy this situation is to name a playlist after the artist and then add those unknown songs to the playlist. The next section describes how it's done.

Creating your own playlists

The Play Music app features two "auto" playlists — one for the last songs you've added and another for free and purchased songs. Beyond that, the playlists you see are those you create. Here's how it works:

1. **Locate some music you want to add to a playlist.**
2. **Touch the Action Overflow icon by the album or song.**
3. **Choose the Add to Playlist command.**

   Ensure that you're viewing a song or an album; otherwise, the Add to Playlist command doesn't show up.

4. **Choose an existing playlist or, to create a new playlist, choose New Playlist.**

   If you choose to create a new playlist, type a name for the playlist and touch the OK button.

The song or album is added to the playlist you selected, or it's placed into a new playlist you created. You can continue to add songs to the playlist by repeating Steps 1 through 3.

- ✔ You can have as many playlists as you like on the tablet and stick as many songs as you like in them. Adding songs to a playlist doesn't noticeably affect the tablet's storage capacity.

- ✔ To remove a song from a playlist, open the playlist and touch the Menu icon by the song. Choose Remove from Playlist.

- ✔ Removing a song from a playlist doesn't delete the song from the music library; see the next section.

- ✔ Songs in a playlist can be rearranged: While viewing the playlist, use the tab on the far left end of a song title to drag that song up or down in the list.

- ✔ To delete a playlist, touch the Action Overflow icon in the Playlist icon's lower right corner (refer to Figure 13-4). Choose the Delete command. Touch OK to confirm.

Removing unwanted music

Depending on the source, you have two ways to deal with unwanted music in the Play Music app's library. The different ways depend upon whether or not the song is stored directly on the Android tablet.

For music stored on the device, locate the song or album and touch the Action Overflow icon. Choose the Delete command. Touch the OK button to remove the song.

If you don't see a Delete command on the menu, the song is available only through Google Play Music. To remove the song, visit Google Play on the Internet at `music.google.com`. View your library to locate the song. Click the Menu icon by a song and choose the Delete command. Click the Delete Song button to confirm.

Music from the Stream

Although they're not broadcast radio stations, some sources on the Internet — *Internet radio* sites — play music. If you're lucky, your tablet comes with some Internet radio apps. If you're not so lucky, or if you want to expand your options, you can look into obtaining these two apps:

- TuneIn Radio
- Pandora Radio

The TuneIn Radio app gives you access to hundreds of Internet radio stations broadcasting around the world. They're organized by category, so you can find just about whatever you want. Many of these radio stations are also broadcast radio stations, so the odds are good that you can find a local station or two, which you can listen to on your Android tablet.

Pandora Radio lets you select music based on your mood, and it customizes, according to your feedback, the tunes you listen to. The app works like the Internet site `www.pandora.com`, in case you're familiar with it. The nifty thing about Pandora is that the more you listen, the better the app becomes at finding music you like.

All these apps are available at the Google Play Store. They're free, though paid versions might also be available.

- It's best to listen to Internet radio when your tablet is connected to the Internet via a Wi-Fi connection. Streaming music can use a lot of your cellular data plan's data allotment.

- See Chapter 15 for more information about the Google Play Store.

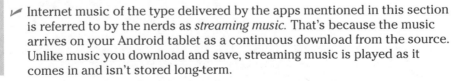

- Internet music of the type delivered by the apps mentioned in this section is referred to by the nerds as *streaming music.* That's because the music arrives on your Android tablet as a continuous download from the source. Unlike music you download and save, streaming music is played as it comes in and isn't stored long-term.

14

Amazing Tablet Feats

*Y*our Android tablet is bursting with potential, limited only by the apps installed on it. Despite the variety of things your tablet can do, you will find some limitations. For example, you cannot use an Android tablet as a yoga block. It makes a poor kitchen cutting board. And despite efforts by European physicists, the Android tablet simply cannot compete with the Large Hadron Collider. Still, for more everyday purposes, I believe you'll find your tablet more than up to the task.

This chapter corrals many (but not all) of the things you can do on your Android tablet. Among the devices it replaces are your alarm clock, calculator, day planner, game machine, e-book reader, and even your TV set. That's not even the full list, but rather everything I could legally cram into this chapter without violating the *For Dummies* chapter length regulations.

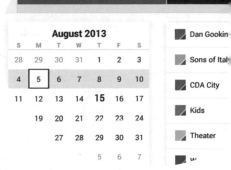

Clock

Your Android tablet keeps constant, accurate track of the time, which is displayed at the top of the Home screen as well as on the lock screen. That's handy, but it just isn't enough, so the tablet ships with an app that tells the time and also may double as an alarm clock.

The app may be called Clock or Alarm, but either way, the app does similar timey-type things: Display the time, act as a stopwatch, work as a timer, and set alarms. Of these activities, setting an alarm is pretty useful: In that mode, your tablet becomes your nightstand companion.

Here's how to set a wake-up alarm in the stock Android Clock app:

1. **Touch the Alarm icon on the Clock app's screen.**

   The icon may be a tab, or you may have to swipe the Clock app's screen left or right to view the Alarm screen.

2. **Touch the Add icon.**

   The Set Alarm screen appears.

3. **Fill in details about the alarm.**

   Set the alarm's time, decide whether it repeats daily or only on certain days, choose a ringtone, set the Vibration mode, and make any other settings displayed on the screen, including giving the alarm a name. For example, Wake Up, Get to the Airport, or Annoy My Spouse.

4. **Touch the OK button or Done button to create the alarm.**

   You see your alarm in the list in the Alarms window.

5. **Ensure that the alarm is set.**

   Alarms in the Clock app must be set to activate. If not, the alarm exists, but no alert is triggered.

When the alarm goes off, touch the Dismiss icon to tell the tablet, "Okay! I'm up!" Or you can touch the Snooze icon to be annoyed again after a few minutes.

- ✏ Your tablet keeps the clock accurate by using the Internet connection. You never have to set the time.

- ✏ Information about a set alarm appears on the Clock app's screen and on the tablet's lock screen.

- ✏ When an alarm is set, the Alarm notification appears in the status area atop the screen, similar to what's shown in the margin. That notification is your clue that an alarm is set and ready to trigger.

- ✏ Turning off an alarm doesn't delete the alarm. To remove an alarm, long-press it and choose the Delete Alarm option from the menu. Touch the OK button to confirm.

- ✏ The alarm doesn't work when you turn off the Android tablet. However, the alarm does go off when the tablet is locked or sleeping.

Calculator

Why are you still lugging around a calculator? Even one of those teensy, solar-powered calculators that banks used to give away. Remember when banks actually gave stuff away? Man, I am dating myself.

The next time you crave a calculator, start the Calculator app by choosing its icon from the Apps drawer. Each tablet's Calculator app looks subtly different. In Figure 14-1, you see the stock Android version of the Calculator app.

Clear/Delete button

Scary calculator buttons   Typical calculator buttons

Figure 14-1: The Calculator app.

Type your equations using the various keys on the screen. Parenthesis keys can help you determine which part of a long equation gets calculated first. Use the Clr or C key to clear input.

- Long-press the calculator's text (or results) to cut or copy the results.

- The Clr (Clear) key changes to the Delete key when you type a number. That way, you can delete your input without clearing the entire calculation.

- I use the Calculator app most often to determine my tip at a restaurant. In Figure 14-1, a calculation is being made for an 18 percent tip on an $89.56 tab.

Calendar

Feel free to take any date book you have and throw it away. You never need to buy another one again. That's because your Android tablet is the ideal date book and appointment calendar. Thanks to the Calendar app and the Google Calendar service on the Internet, you can manage all your scheduling right on your Android tablet. It's almost cinchy.

- ✐ Google Calendar works with your Google account to keep track of your schedule and appointments. You can visit Google Calendar on the web at

  ```
  http://calendar.google.com
  ```

- ✐ You automatically have a Google Calendar; it comes with your Google account.

- ✐ I recommend that you use the Calendar app on your Android tablet to access Google Calendar. It's a better way to access your schedule than using the web browser app to reach Google Calendar on the web.

- ✐ Before you throw away your datebook, copy into the Calendar app any future appointments and recurring info, such as birthdays and anniversaries.

Browsing your schedule

To see what's happening next, to peruse upcoming important events, or simply to know which day of the month it is, summon the Calendar app. It's located on the Apps screen, along with all the other apps that dwell on your Android tablet. You may also find a shortcut to the Calendar app on the Home screen — and maybe even a Calendar widget.

Figure 14-2 shows the Calendar app's three views: Month, Week, and Day. There's also Agenda view, which displays only upcoming events. Some Calendar apps feature 4-day view as well.

Be sure to note how the current day is highlighted on the calendar. In Figure 14-2, the current day is shown as August 15.

- ✐ Use Month view to see an overview of what's going on, and use Week view or Day view to see your appointments.

- ✐ I check Week view at the start of the week to remind me of what's coming up.

- ✐ To scroll from month to month, swipe the screen up or down. In Week and Day views, scroll from left to right. To return to the current day, touch the Today button, though that may also be a menu item. In Figure 14-2, it's a button.

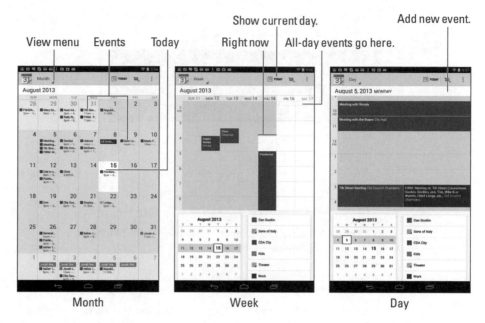

Figure 14-2: The Calendar app.

- A black bar appears across the current day, indicating the current time.

- Different colors flag your events, as shown in Figure 14-2. The colors represent a calendar category to which events are assigned. See the later section "Creating an event" for information on calendar categories.

Reviewing appointments

To see more detail about an event, touch it. When you're using Month view, touch the date with the event on it to see Week view. Then choose an event to see its details, similar to what's shown in Figure 14-3.

The details you see depend on how much information was recorded when the event was created. Some events have only a minimum of information; others may have details, such as a location for the event. When the event's location is listed, you can touch that location, and the Maps app pops up to show you where the event is being held.

Event details   Edit event.

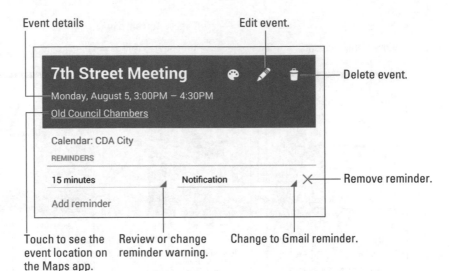

7th Street Meeting ——————— Delete event.

Monday, August 5, 3:00PM — 4:30PM

Old Council Chambers

Calendar: CDA City

REMINDERS

15 minutes   Notification   X ——— Remove reminder.

Add reminder

Touch to see the   Review or change   Change to Gmail reminder.
event location on   reminder warning.
the Maps app.

Figure 14-3: Event details.

Touch the Back icon to dismiss the event's details.

> ✓ Birthdays and a few other events on the calendar may be pulled in from the tablet's address book or from social networking apps. That probably explains why some events can be listed twice — they're pulled in from two sources.

> ✓ The best way to review upcoming appointments is to choose the Agenda item from the View menu.

> ✓ The Calendar app comes with a companion widget that you can apply to the Home screen. As in Agenda view, the widget displays only a list of your upcoming appointments. See Chapter 19 for information on applying widgets to the tablet's Home screen.

> ✓ The Google Now feature lists any immediate appointments or events. See the later section "Google Now."

Creating an event

The key to making the calendar work is to add events: appointments, things to do, meetings, or full-day events such as birthdays or colonoscopies. To create an event, follow these steps in the Calendar app:

1. **Select the day for the event.**

   Or, if you like, you can switch to Day view, where you can touch the starting time for the new event.

2. **Touch the Add New Event icon (refer to Figure 14-2).**

   The New Event screen or Add Event screen appears. Your job now is to fill in the blanks to create the new event.

3. **Add information about the event.**

   The more information you supply, the more detailed the event, and the more you can do with it on your Android tablet and on Google Calendar on the Internet. Here are some of the many items you can set when creating an event:

   - **Time/Duration:** If you followed Step 1 in this section, you don't have to set a starting time. Otherwise, specify the time the meeting starts and stops, or choose to set an all-day event such as a birthday or your mother-in-law's visit that was supposed to last for an hour.

   - **Event Name or Title:** This item can be a meeting name, a flight number, or perhaps the person you're meeting.

   - **Location:** Adding an event location not only tells you where the event will be located but also hooks that information into the Maps app. My advice is to type information in the event's Where field, just as though you're typing information to search for in the Maps app. When the event is displayed, the location is a link; touch the link to see where it is on a map.

   - **Repeat:** Use this item to configure a recurring schedule. For example, if your meeting is every month on the third Wednesday, touch the Menu icon by the Repetition item and choose that option.

   When you have events that repeat twice a month — say, on the first and third Mondays — you need to create two separate events: one for the first Monday and another for the third. Then have each event repeat monthly.

   - **Reminder:** Some versions of the Calendar app allow you to set a reminder before an event begins. If you prefer not to have a reminder, touch the X button by the Reminders item to remove the reminder. Otherwise, specify how long before the meeting you want to be notified and whether you want a tablet notification or a Gmail message reminder — or both.

   - **Calendar Category:** Touch the colored calendar text atop the screen to choose a calendar category.

   Calendar categories are handy because they let you organize and color-code your events. They're confusing because Google calls them calendars. I think of them more as categories. So I have different calendars (categories) for my personal schedule, work, government duties, clubs, and so on.

4. **Touch the Done button or Save button to create the new event.**

The new event appears on the calendar, reminding you that you need to do something on such-and-such a day with what's-his-face.

✔ You can change an event at any time: Simply touch the event to bring up more information, and then touch the Edit icon to modify the event, similar to what's shown in Figure 14-3.

✔ To remove an event, touch the event to bring up more information, and touch the Delete icon. Touch the OK button to confirm.

✔ Setting an event's time zone is necessary only when the event takes place in another time zone or spans time zones, such as an airline flight. In that case, the Calendar app automatically adjusts the starting and stopping times for events depending on where you are.

✔ If you forget to set the time zone and you end up hopping around the world, your events are set according to the time zone in which they were created, not the local time.

✔ Reminders can be set so that the tablet alerts you before an event takes place. The alert can show up as a notification icon (shown in the margin), or it can come in the form of a new Gmail notice (which has its own notification icon). Pull down the notification shade and choose the calendar alert. You can then peruse pending events.

Game Machine

Nothing justifies your expensive, high-tech investment in electronics like playing games. Don't even sweat the thought that you have too much "business" or "work" or other important stuff you can do on an Android tablet. The more advanced the mind, the more the need for play, right? So indulge yourself.

Your Android tablet's manufacturer may have tossed in a few sample games to whet your appetite. The games are most likely teasers or samples of paid games. Don't fret! You can obtain an abundance of games, free or not, from the Google Play Store. Look for the "lite" versions of games, which are free. If you like the game, you can fork over the 99 cents or whatever the full version costs.

See Chapter 15 for details on shopping at the Google Play Store.

Google Now

Don't worry about your tablet controlling too much of your life: It harbors no insidious intelligence, and the Robot Revolution is still years away. Until then, you can use the tablet's listening abilities to enjoy the feature called Google Now. It's not quite like having your own personal Jeeves, but it's on its way.

The preferred method to summon Google Now is to swipe your finger upward from the bottom center of the touchscreen. This technique is supposed to work on the lock screen, the Home screen, or in any app, although your tablet may not support that technique. Otherwise, you can touch the Google Search widget to start Google Now or open the Google app in the Apps drawer.

The main Google Now screen is shown in Figure 14-4. Below the Search text box, you'll find cards. The variety and number of cards depend on how often you use Google Now. Though you can't manually add cards, the more the app learns about you, the more cards appear.

You can use Google Now to search the Internet, just as you would use Google's main web page. More interestingly than that, you can ask Google Now questions; see the nearby sidebar "Barking orders to Google Now."

Search for something.   Ask a question.

Cards

Figure 14-4: Google Now is ready for business. Or play.

Barking orders to Google Now

One way to have a lot of fun is to use Google Now app verbally: Say "Okay, Google." Say it out loud. Any time you see the Google Now app, the tablet is listening to you. Or, when the tablet is being stubborn, touch the Microphone icon.

You can speak simple search terms, such as "Find pictures of Megan Fox." Or you can give more complex orders, among them:

- Will it rain tomorrow?

- What time is it in Frankfurt, Germany?

- How many euros equals $25?

- What is 103 divided by 6?

- How can I get to Disneyland?

- Where is the nearest Canadian restaurant?

- What's the score of the Lakers–Celtics game?

- What is the answer to life, the universe, and everything?

When asked such questions, Google Now responds with a card and a verbal reply. When a verbal reply isn't available, you see Google search results.

You can also use Google Now to verbally control your tablet. To use the camera, say "Okay, Google, take a picture" or "Okay, Google, record a video." Future versions of Google Now may offer additional spoken commands.

E-Book Reader

Printed books are O so 14th century. These days, reading material is presented electronically in the form of an eBook. To read eBooks on your Android tablet, you need an eBook reader app.

The Amazon Kindle app is a popular eBook reader, available for your Android tablet from the Google Play Store. But Google secretly desires you to use the Play Books app, which is most likely already installed on your tablet.

Begin your digital reading experience by opening the Play Books app. If you're prompted to turn on synchronization, touch the Turn On Sync button.

The Play Books app organizes the books into a library and displays them for reading, similar to the way they're shown in Figure 14-5. The library lists any titles you've obtained for your Google Books account. Or when you're returning to the Play Books app after a break, you see the current page of the eBook you were last reading. You can choose either mode from the navigation drawer, as shown in the figure.

Scroll through the library by swiping the screen up or down.

Touch a book in the Play Books app library to open it. If you've opened the book previously, you're returned to the page you last read. Otherwise, the first page you see is the book's first page.

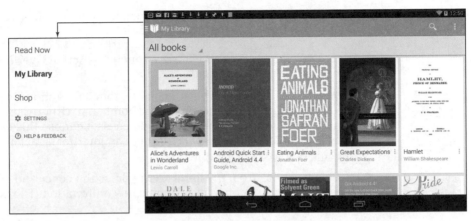

Navigation drawer

Figure 14-5: The Play Books library.

To begin reading, touch a book to open it. Figure 14-6 illustrates the basic book-reading operation in the Play Books app. You turn pages by swiping left or right, but probably mostly left. You can also turn pages by touching the far left or right side of the screen.

Touch here to turn the page backward.

Adjust the text display.

Display the library.

Search the book.

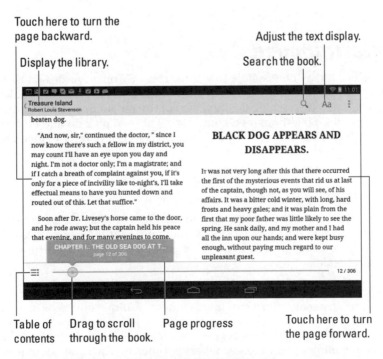

Table of contents

Drag to scroll through the book.

Page progress

Touch here to turn the page forward.

Figure 14-6: Reading an eBook in the Play Books app.

The Play Books app also works in the vertical orientation; when you turn the tablet that way, only one page is shown at a time.

- ✔ If you don't see a book in the library, touch the Action Overflow icon and choose the Refresh command.

- ✔ To ensure that a book is always available, touch its Action Overflow icon button and choose the Keep on Device command. Otherwise, you cannot read an eBook without Internet access. I choose this command specifically before I leave on a trip where an Internet signal may not be available (such as in an airplane).

- ✔ To remove a book from the library, long-press the cover and choose the Delete from Library command. There's no confirmation: The book is instantly removed.

- ✔ If the onscreen controls (refer to Figure 14-6) disappear, touch the screen to see them again.

- ✔ The Aa button is used to adjust the display. Touching this button displays a palette of options for adjusting the text on the screen and the brightness.

- ✔ To return to the library, touch the Play Books app icon in the upper left corner of the screen or touch the Back icon.

- ✔ Copies of all your Google Books are available on all your Android devices and on the `http://books.google.com` website.

Video Entertainment

Someday, it may be possible to watch "real" TV on an Android tablet, but why bother? You'll find plenty of video apps available on your tablet to sate your television-watching desires. Two of the most common are YouTube and Play Movies. So although you may not be able to pick up and enjoy the local Action News Team every day at 5 p.m., you're not bereft of video enjoyment on your tablet.

Enjoying YouTube

YouTube is the Internet phenomenon that proves that real life is indeed too boring and random for television. Or is that the other way around? Regardless, you can view the latest YouTube videos by using the YouTube app on your Android tablet.

Search for videos by touching the Search icon. Type the video's name, a topic, or any search terms to locate videos. Zillions of videos are available.

The YouTube app displays suggestions for any channels you're subscribed to, which allows you to follow favorite topics or YouTube content providers.

To view a video, touch its name or icon in the list.

- ✔ Refer to Chapter 12 for information on adding a video you've recorded on your Android tablet to your account on YouTube.

- ✔ To view the video in a larger size, tilt the tablet to the horizontal orientation.

- ✔ Use the YouTube app to view YouTube videos, rather than use the tablet's web browser app to visit the YouTube website.

- ✔ Because you have a Google account, you also have a YouTube account. I recommend that you log in to your YouTube account when using YouTube on your Android tablet: Touch the Action Overflow icon and choose the Sign In command. Log in if you haven't already. Otherwise, you see your account information, your videos, and any video subscriptions.

- ✔ Not all YouTube videos are available for viewing on mobile devices.

- ✔ If your Android tablet features NFC, you can use the Android Beam feature to instantly share YouTube videos with other Android users. Just touch the back of your Android tablet to the other mobile device. When prompted, touch the text on the screen to send your friend the video.

Buying and renting movies

The Google Play Store lets you not only buy apps and books for your Android tablet but also rent movies. Open the Play Movies app, found in the Apps drawer, to boost your tablet's video potential.

Renting or purchasing a movie is done at the Google Play Store. Choose a movie or TV show to rent or buy. Touch the price button, and then choose your method of payment. The process works just like getting an app for your tablet, which is described in Chapter 15.

Movies and shows rented at the Play Store are available for viewing for up to 30 days after you pay the rental fee. After you start the movie, you can pause and watch it again and again during a 24-hour period.

- ✔ Not every film or TV show is available for purchase. Some are rentals only.

- ✔ You can use the Personal Videos category in the Play Movies app to view any videos stored on your Android tablet.

- ✔ One of the best ways to view movies on your Android tablet is to connect it to an HDMI monitor or TV set. That way, you get the big-screen experience and can share the movie with several friends without having to crowd around the tablet. This trick works when your tablet features an HDMI connection and you've purchased the appropriate HDMI cable. If your tablet doesn't have an HDMI connection, you might be able to add one by plugging into a docking stand with HDMI output.

15

More Apps

Your Android tablet's capabilities aren't limited to the paltry assortment of preinstalled apps. No way! A digital cornucopia of apps is available — hundreds of thousands of them, from productivity apps to references to educational to finance to games. The variety is almost unlimited. Those apps can be found at a single location, the Google Play Store.

Not only does the Play Store offer apps, but it's also the place to go for eBooks, music, videos, and sometimes even magazines. Other chapters throughout this book discuss obtaining those items at the Play Store; this chapter offers more detailed descriptions of how the Play Store works, as well as app management in general.

Hello, Google Play Store

Your tablet most likely shipped with several dozen apps preinstalled. It's a pittance. You'll find zillions more apps at the Google Play Store. Each of them extends the abilities of what your tablet can do. Some cost money. Most are free. They're all waiting for you to try, and it starts by visiting the Play Store.

- ✔ Officially, the store is the *Google Play Store.* It may also be referenced as Google Play. The app, however, is named Play Store.

- ✔ The Google Play Store was once known as the Android Market, and you may still see it referred to as the Market.

- ✔ This section is about getting apps for your tablet. For information on getting music, see Chapter 13. Refer to Chapter 14 for information on books and video available at the Play Store.

- ✔ *App* is short for *app*lication. It's a program, or software, that you can add to your Android tablet to make it do new, wondrous, or useful things.

- ✔ Because your tablet uses the Android operating system, it can run nearly all apps written for Android.

- ✔ The Play Store is available only when the tablet has an Internet connection. Therefore:

- ✔ I highly recommend that you connect your tablet to a Wi-Fi network if you plan to obtain apps, books, or other digital goodies at the Play Store. Wi-Fi Not only gives you speed but also helps avoid data surcharges. See Chapter 16 for details on connecting your tablet to a Wi-Fi network.

- ✔ The Play Store app is frequently updated, so its look may change from what you see in this chapter. Updated information on the Google Play Store is available on my website, at

    www.wambooli.com/help/android/google-play

Browsing the Google Play Store

You access the Google Play Store by opening the Play Store app, found on the Apps screen and, possibly, also on the main Home screen.

After opening the Play Store app, you see the main screen, similar to the one shown on the far left in Figure 15-1. Categories appear that help you browse for apps, games, books, and so on. The rest of the screen highlights popular or recommended items.

Find apps by choosing the Apps category from the main screen, also known as Store Home (refer to Figure 15-1). The next screen lists popular and featured items, plus categories you can browse by swiping the screen from right to left. The category tabs appear toward the top of the screen.

When you have an idea of what you want, such as an app's name or even what it does, searching works fastest: Touch the Search icon at the top of the Play Store screen (refer to Figure 15-1). Type all or part of the app's name or perhaps a description.

To see more information about an item, touch it. Touching doesn't buy anything. Instead, you see a more detailed description, screen shots, or perhaps a video preview, as shown in Figure 15-2.

Figure 15-1: The Google Play Store.

Return to the main Google Play Store screen at any time by touching the Google Play app icon in the upper left corner of the screen.

- ✔ The first time you enter the Google Play Store, or after the Play Store app is updated, you have to accept the terms of service. To do so, touch the Accept button.

- ✔ You can be assured that all apps that appear in the Google Play Store can be used with your Android tablet. There's no way to download or buy something that's incompatible.

- ✔ Pay attention to an app's ratings. Ratings are added by people who use the apps — people like you and me. Having more stars is better. You can see additional information, including individual user reviews, by choosing the app.

- ✔ Another good indicator of an app's success is how many times it's been downloaded. Some apps have been downloaded more than 10 million times. That's a good sign.

App icon   Scroll categories.   Share app.

Search

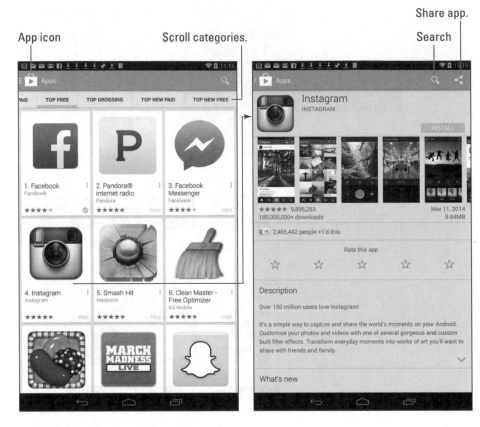

Figure 15-2: App details.

Obtaining an app

After you locate the app you've always dreamed of, the next step is to download it, by copying it from the Google Play Store on the Internet into your Android tablet. The app is then installed automatically, building up your collection of apps and expanding what your Android tablet can do.

Good news: Most apps are available for free. Better news: Even the apps you pay for don't cost dearly. In fact, it seems odd to sit and stew over whether paying 99 cents for a game is "worth it."

I recommend that you download a free app first, to familiarize yourself with the process. Then try your hand at a paid app.

Free or not, the process of obtaining an app works pretty much the same. Follow these steps:

1. **If possible, activate the Wi-Fi connection to avoid incurring data overages.**

   See Chapter 16 for information on connecting your Android tablet to a Wi-Fi network.

2. **Open the Play Store app.**

3. **Find the app you want, and open its description.**

   The app's description screen looks similar to the one shown on the right side in Figure 15-2.

   The difference between a free app and a paid app is found on the button used to obtain the app. For a free app, the button says Install. For a paid app, the button shows the price.

   You may find three other buttons next to an app: Open, Update, and Uninstall. The Open button opens an app that's already installed on your Android tablet; the Update button updates an already installed app; and the Uninstall button removes an already installed app. See the later sections "Updating an app" and "Removing an app" for more information on using the Update button and Uninstall button, respectively.

4. **Touch the Install button to get a free app; for a paid app, touch the button with the price on it.**

   Don't fret if you touched a price button! You're not buying anything yet. Instead, you see a screen describing the app's permissions.

5. **Touch the Accept button.**

   The App Permissions list isn't a warning, and it doesn't mean anything bad. The Play Store is simply telling you which of your tablet's features the app has access to.

6. **For a paid app, touch the Buy button.**

   The purchase summary lists any credit cards you've registered with Google Play. If not, you have to configure a payment method. After the method is configured, touching the Buy button makes the purchase.

   If you have any Google Credit, choose your Google Play balance from the credit card list.

7. **Touch the Open button to run the app.**

   Or, if you were doing something else while the app was downloading and installing, choose the Successfully Installed notification, shown in the margin. The notification features the app's name with the text *Successfully Installed* beneath it.

At this point, what happens next depends on the app you've downloaded. For example, you may have to agree to a license agreement. If so, touch the I Agree button. Additional setup may involve setting your location, signing in to an account, or creating a profile.

After you complete initial app setup, or if no setup is necessary, you can start using the app.

✔ Apps you download are added to the Apps drawer, made available like any other app on your tablet.

✔ Some apps may install shortcut icons on the Home screen after they're installed. See Chapter 19 for information on removing the icon from the Home screen, if that is your desire.

✔ When you dither over getting a paid app, consider adding it to your wish list. Touch the Wishlist icon when viewing the app. (The icon is shown in the margin.) You can review your wish list by choosing the My Wishlist item from the Play Store app's navigation drawer, shown earlier, in Figure 15-1.

✔ Payment information, as well as your purchase history, can be accessed through the Google Wallet. On the web, visit

    wallet.google.com

✔ For a paid app, you receive a Gmail message from the Google Play Store, confirming your purchase. The message contains a link you can click to review the refund policy, in case you change your mind on the purchase.

✔ Be quick on that refund: Some apps allow you only 15 minutes to get your money back. You know when the time is up because the Refund button on the app's description screen changes its name to Uninstall.

Never buy an app twice

Any apps you've already purchased from the Google Play Store — say, for another mobile device — are available for download on your Android tablet at no charge. Simply find the app. You see it flagged as *Purchased* in the Play Store. Touch the Install button to install it as described in this chapter.

You can review any already purchased apps in the Play Store: Choose the My Apps item from the navigation drawer (shown in Figure 15-1). Choose the All tab from the top of the screen. You see all the apps you've ever obtained at the Google Play Store, including apps you've previously paid for. Those apps are flagged as *Purchased*. Choose that item to reinstall the paid app on your tablet.

Installing apps from a computer

You don't need to use an Android tablet to install apps. Using a computer, you can visit the Google Play website, choose software, and have that app installed remotely. It's kind of cool yet kind of scary at the same time. Here's how it works:

1. **Use a computer's web browser to visit the Google Play store on the Internet at**

   https://play.google.com/store

   Bookmark that site!

2. **If necessary, click the Sign In button to log in to your Google account.**

   Use the same Google account you used when setting up your Android tablet. You need to have access to that account so that Google can remotely update your various Android devices.

3. **Browse for something.**

   You can hunt down apps, books, music — the whole gamut. It works just like browsing the Play Store on your tablet.

4. **Click the Install button or Buy button.**

5. **Choose your Android tablet.**

   The Choose a Device menu lists all your Android devices, or at least those that are compatible with what you're getting.

   Your Android tablet may be listed using its technical name, not the brand name you're used to.

6. **For a free app, click the Install button. For a paid app, click the Continue button, choose your payment source, and then click the Buy button.**

   Installation proceeds.

As if by magic, the app is installed on your Android tablet — even though you used a computer to do it. Heck, the tablet need not even be within sight of you, and the app still remotely installs.

App Management

The Play Store app is not only where you buy apps — it's also used for performing app management. This task includes reviewing apps you've downloaded, updating apps, organizing apps, and removing apps you no longer want or that you severely hate.

Reviewing your apps

To peruse the apps you've downloaded from the Google Play Store, follow these steps:

1. **Start the Play Store app.**

2. **Choose My Apps from the navigation drawer.**

   Touch the Play Store app icon, illustrated in Figure 15-1, to view the navigation drawer.

3. **Peruse your apps.**

Your apps are presented in two categories: Installed and All, as shown in Figure 15-3. Installed apps are found on your tablet; the All category includes apps you have downloaded but that may not currently be installed.

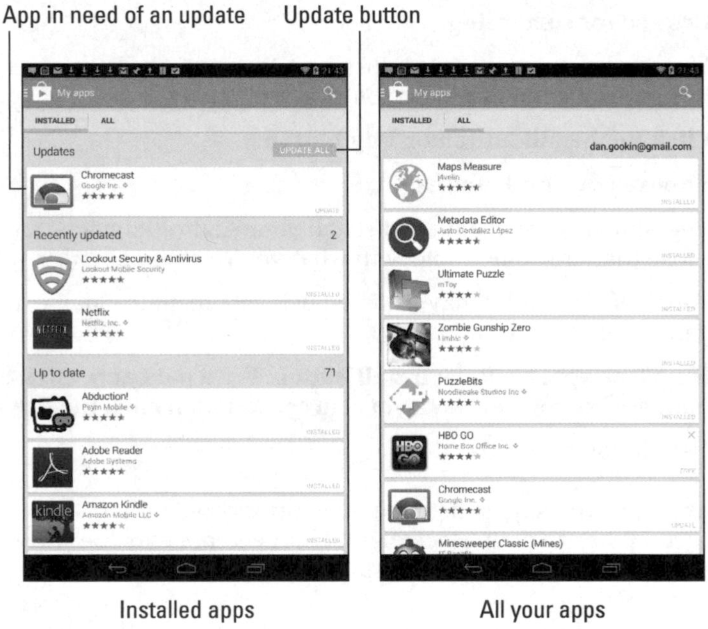

App in need of an update   Update button

Installed apps   All your apps

Figure 15-3: The My Apps list.

Touch an app to see details. Touch the Open button to run the app; the Update button to update to the latest version; or the Uninstall button to remove the app. Later sections in this chapter describe the details on updating and uninstalling apps.

✔ While viewing an app's details, you can activate automatic updating: Touch the Action Overflow or Menu icon and choose the Auto-Update item. When a check mark is by that item, the Auto-Update feature has been activated. Not every app features automatic updating.

✔ Uninstalled apps remain on the All list because you did, at one time, download the app. To reinstall them (and without paying a second time for paid apps), choose the app from the All list and touch the Install button.

Sharing an app

When you love an app so much that you just can't contain your glee, feel free to share that app with your friends. You can easily share a link to the app in the Google Play Store by obeying these steps:

1. **In the Google Play Store, choose the app to share.**

   You can choose any app, but you need to be at the app's Details screen, the one with the Free or price button or the Details screen on an app you've installed (refer to Figure 15-2).

2. **Touch the Share icon.**

   A menu appears, listing various apps and methods for sharing the app's Play Store link with your pals.

3. **Choose a sharing method.**

   For example, choose Gmail to send a link to the app in an e-mail message.

4. **Use the chosen app to send the link.**

   What happens next depends on which sharing method you've chosen.

The end result of completing these steps is that your friends receive a link. They can touch that link on their Android device and be whisked instantly to the Google Play Store, where they can easily install the app.

Updating an app

Whenever a new version of an app is available, you see it flagged for updating, as shown in Figure 15-3. Don't worry if it's been a while since you've been to the My Apps screen; apps in need of an update also display the App Update notification, shown in the margin.

To update an individual app, view its Information screen: Choose the app from the My Apps screen (refer to Figure 15-3). Touch the Update button, and then touch Accept to download the new version. Or, from the list of installed apps, touch the Update All button to update a slew of apps at one time. That step still involves touching the Accept button for each app.

The updating process often involves downloading and installing a new version of the app. That's perfectly fine; your settings and options aren't changed by the update process.

✔ Look for the App Update notification to remind yourself that apps are in need of an update. You can choose that notification to be taken instantly to the app's screen, where the Update button eagerly awaits your touch.

✔ I highly recommend checking for updates when a Wi-Fi connection is handy. Apps aren't really huge in size, but there's no point in using the mobile data network when you don't have to.

Removing an app

I can think of a few reasons to remove an app. It's with eager relish that I remove apps that don't work or that somehow annoy me. It's also perfectly okay to remove redundant apps, such as when you're trying to find a decent music-listening app and you end up with a dozen or so that you never use.

Whatever the reason, remove an app by following these directions:

1. **Start the Play Store app.**

2. **Choose My Apps from the navigation drawer.**

   Figure 15-1 illustrates the navigation drawer; touch the app button to view it.

3. **In the Installed list, touch the app that offends you.**

4. **Touch the Uninstall button.**

5. **Touch the OK button to confirm.**

   The app is removed.

The app continues to appear on the All list even after it's been removed. That's because you downloaded it once. That doesn't mean, however, that the app is still installed.

✔ In most cases, if you uninstall a paid app right away, your credit card or account is fully refunded. The definition of *right away* depends on the app and is stated on the app's Description screen. It can be anywhere from 15 minutes to 24 hours.

✔ Removing an app frees a modicum of storage inside the tablet — just a modicum.

✔ You can always reinstall paid apps that you've uninstalled. You aren't charged twice for doing so.

✔ Some apps are preinstalled on your tablet, or they're part of the Android operating system. They cannot be removed. I'm sure there's probably a technical way to uninstall those apps, but seriously: Just don't use the apps if you can't remove them.

WARNING!

Avoiding Android viruses

How can you tell which apps are legitimate and which might be viruses or evil apps that do odd things to your Android tablet? Well, you can't. In fact, most people can't, because most evil apps don't advertise themselves as such.

The key to knowing whether an app is evil is to look at what it does, as described in this chapter. If a simple grocery-list app uses the tablet's microphone and the app doesn't need to use the microphone, it's suspect.

In the history of the Android operating system, only a handful of malicious apps have been

distributed, and most of them were found on devices used in Asia. Google routinely removes malicious apps from the Play Store, and a feature of the Android operating system even lets Google remotely wipe such apps from all Android devices. So you're pretty safe.

Generally speaking, avoid "hacker" apps, porn apps, and apps that use social engineering to make you do things on your tablet that you wouldn't otherwise do, such as visit an unknown website to see racy pictures of politicians or celebrities.

Stopping an app run amok

Sometimes, an app goofs up or crashes. You may see a warning message on the touchscreen, informing you that the app has been shut down. That's good. What's better is that you too can shut down apps that misbehave or those you cannot otherwise stop. Follow these steps:

1. **Touch the Apps icon on the Home screen.**

2. **Open the Settings app.**

3. **Choose the Apps item.**

   This item might also be called Applications or Applications Manager. On Samsung tablets, it might be found by first choosing the General tab.

4. **Touch the Running tab.**

   Or you can swipe the screen left or right until the list of running apps appears.

5. **Choose the errant app from the list.**

   Touch the app. For example, if the Annoying Sound app is bothering you, choose it from the list.

6. **Touch the Stop or Force Stop button.**

   The app quits.

Using the Stop or Force Stop button is a drastic act. Don't kill off any app or service unless the app is annoying or you are otherwise unable to stop it. Avoid killing off Google Services, which can change the tablet's behavior or make the Android operating system unstable.

Keep reading in the next section for more ways you can manipulate apps on your Android tablet.

Controlling your apps

The Play Store app isn't your final destination for truly managing the apps installed on your tablet. To really get your hands dirty, you need to visit the Application Manager. Be forewarned: The Application Manager isn't the friendliest location on your Android tablet.

Follow these steps to find the Applications Manager:

1. **Open the Settings app.**

   It's found on the Apps drawer.

2. **Choose the Apps item on the Settings app screen.**

   On some Samsung tablets, first touch the General tab and then choose the Application Manager item.

All the apps installed on your tablet are displayed in four categories, each represented as a tab on the top of the screen:

Downloaded: This screen lists all the apps you've obtained from the Google Play Store.

SD Card: Apps listed here have been installed on, or transferred to, removable storage — the MicroSD card. If your tablet lacks removable storage, this item doesn't appear.

Running: Apps actively running on the tablet appear in this list, which includes services and other non-app items that are required for the tablet to function properly.

All: This screen lists all apps on the tablet, including services, Android functions, and lots of things you can look at but should never touch.

To view more information about an app, choose a category and then touch the app. For example, to witness the details of a running app, touch or swipe to the Running tab and choose an app from the list. You see details about the app, most of which are quite technical in nature.

Various buttons show up on the app's Details screen. The variety of buttons you see depends on which category is chosen. Here are some of the buttons and a description of what they do:

Stop/Force Stop: Touch this button to halt a program run amok. For example, I had to stop an older Android app that continually made noise and offered no other option to exit. Touching this button halted the app.

Report: This button allows you to inform Google of suspect software or other problems with the app.

Uninstall: Touch the Uninstall button to remove the app, which is another way to accomplish the same steps described in the preceding section.

Refund: Freshly purchased apps feature the Refund button rather than the Uninstall button. Touch the Refund button to uninstall the paid app *and* get your money back.

Move to SD Card: Touch this button to transfer the app from the tablet's internal storage to the MicroSD card.

Move to Storage Device: Touch this button to transfer an app from the MicroSD card to internal storage. (This button replaces the Move to SD Card button when an app already dwells on the MicroSD card.)

Clear Data: Touch this button to erase any information stored by the app. That information includes items you've created (text, pictures, and so on), settings, accounts, and other information stored by the app.

Clear Cache: I've used this button to fix an app that doesn't work or just sits all stubborn on the screen. This trick doesn't work every time, but it's worth a try when an app seems slow or suddenly stops working.

Clear Defaults: This button disassociates the app from certain file types. It's a reset switch for the Always/Just Once prompt, so when you've selected to have an app always open a certain type of file — music, picture, or whatever — touching this button removes that choice. See Chapter 21 for more details.

Controversy is brewing in the Android community about whether to store apps on the internal storage or MicroSD card. I prefer internal storage because the app stays with the tablet and is always available. Further, Home screen shortcuts to apps stored on the MicroSD card may disappear from time to time. That can be frustrating. My advice: Keep the apps on internal storage.

App drawer organization

Some tablets offer tools for arranging apps in the Apps drawer. These tools allow you to present the apps in an order other than alphabetical, rearrange the apps, or even collect apps and place them into folders.

The key to organizing the Apps drawer is to look for the Action Overflow or Menu icon. If it's available, touch that icon and look for the View command or View Type command. Choosing this command presents options for changing the Apps drawer presentation. For example, on some tablets, you can choose Customizable Grid view, which allows you to drag icons around to redecorate the Apps drawer.

The Apps drawer folder allows you to collect and organize similar apps in one location, just like the Home screen folder. To create an Apps drawer folder, touch the Action Overflow or Menu icon and choose the Create Folder command. Name the folder. To add apps to the folder, long-press their icons on the Apps Drawer screen and drag them into the folder. Also see Chapter 19 for information on Home screen folders, which operate in a similar manner.

Part IV
Nuts and Bolts

In this part . . .

✔ Learn how to seek out and find Wi-Fi networks, connect, and use the Internet.

✔ Discover how to exchange files between your Android tablet and a PC by using a USB cable.

✔ Find out how to connect your tablet to an HDTV or a monitor for viewing things on the Big Screen.

✔ Add security to an Android tablet by applying a password or providing lock screen information.

✔ Learn how to save battery life and discover which items on the tablet are using the most battery juice.

16

It's a Wireless Life

A long time ago, progress was judged by how many wires something had. Newsreels showcased telephone poles and power lines marching across the countryside like victorious troops. Truly, the more wires, the better.

Today, things are not quite as promising for wires. The new theme is to be entirely wireless. Tablets epitomize the wireless paradigm by operating a free and unbound existence; there is no wire for networking, no wire communicating with peripherals, and no decorative wires to make a fashion statement. Beyond a single cable to both charge the battery and communicate with a computer, your Android tablet truly is a wireless gizmo.

The Wonderful World of Wireless

You know that wireless networking has hit the big time when you see people asking Santa Claus for a wireless router at Christmastime. Such a thing would have been unheard of years ago because routers were used primarily for woodworking back then.

The primary reason for wireless networking is to connect your Android tablet to the Internet. For exchanging and synchronizing files, refer to Chapter 17.

Understanding the mobile data network

Not every Android tablet is designed to be used with the mobile data network. When your tablet is so blessed, it can use that network to connect to the Internet. The mobile data network signal is the same type used by cell phones and cellular modems to wirelessly connect to the Internet, and the signal is available almost everywhere.

Several types of mobile-data networks are available to your tablet. The current network being used sports a special icon that appears on the status bar. Here's a description of the variety of network types and their speed values:

4G LTE: The speed of this fourth generation of mobile-data network is comparable to standard Wi-Fi Internet access. It's fast. It also allows for both data and voice transmission at the same time.

4G / HSPA+: It isn't as fast as the full 4G LTE, but it's still faster than the 3G network. The speed is tolerable for surfing the web, watching YouTube videos, and downloading information from the Internet.

3G: The third generation of wide-area data networks is several times faster than the previous generation of data networks.

E / EDGE: The slowest data connection is the original. It's also known as 1X because it's the first generation.

Your Android tablet always uses the best network available. So, when the 4G LTE network is within reach, that network is used for Internet communications. Otherwise, a slower network is chosen and reflected on the status bar. Or, when no mobile data network is available, that part of the status bar is blank.

- The mobile-data signal may still appear when you're using Wi-Fi. That's because some apps use that signal exclusively. Or something.

- Accessing the digital cellular network isn't free. You likely signed up for some form of subscription plan for a certain quantity of data when you first received your Android tablet. When you exceed that quantity, the costs can become prohibitive.

- The data subscription is based on the *quantity* of data you send and receive. At 4G LTE speeds, the prepaid threshold can be crossed quickly.

- See Chapter 18 for information on how to avoid cellular data overcharges when taking your Android tablet out and about.

- A better way to connect your tablet to the Internet is to use the Wi-Fi signal, covered in the next section. The mobile-data network signal makes for a great fallback because it's available in more places than Wi-Fi is.

- If you opt out of the cellular data plan, you can always use a cellular Android tablet as a Wi-Fi tablet. You cannot, however, adapt a Wi-Fi tablet to access the digital cellular network.

Understanding Wi-Fi

Android tablets use the same Wi-Fi networking standards as other wireless Internet devices, such as a laptop computer. So, as long as Wi-Fi networking is set up in your home or office or in the lobby at your proctologist, it's the same.

To make Wi-Fi work on an Android tablet requires two steps. First, you must activate Wi-Fi, by turning on the tablet's wireless radio. The second step is connecting to a specific wireless network. That network gives the tablet access to the Internet.

✔ When your tablet is connected to a Wi-Fi network, it uses that network rather than the digital cellular network.

✔ Wi-Fi stands for *wi*reless *fi*delity. It's brought to you by the numbers 802.11 and the letter B, N, and G.

Activating Wi-Fi

Follow these steps to activate Wi-Fi on your Android tablet:

1. **At the Home screen, touch the Apps icon.**

2. **Open the Settings app.**

3. **Ensure that the Wi-Fi Master Control icon is on.**

   On some Samsung tablets, touch the Connections tab to locate the Wi-Fi Master Control icon.

If you've already configured the tablet to connect to an available wireless network, it's connected automatically. Otherwise, you have to connect to an available network, which is covered in the next section.

To turn off Wi-Fi, repeat the steps in this section, but in Step 3 slide the master control switch to the left, turning if off.

Turning off Wi-Fi disconnects the tablet from any wireless networks.

✔ You can quickly activate or deactivate the tablet's Wi-Fi radio by choosing the Wi-Fi Quick Action. See Chapter 3 for more information on the Quick Actions.

✔ It's perfectly okay to keep the tablet's Wi-Fi radio on all the time. It does drain the battery, but you really need that Internet access to get the most from your Android tablet.

✔ Using Wi-Fi to connect to the Internet doesn't incur data usage charges.

Connecting to a Wi-Fi network

After you've activated the Android tablet's Wi-Fi radio, you can connect to an available wireless network. Obey these steps:

1. **Open the Settings app.**

2. **Choose Wi-Fi.**

   On some Samsung tablets, you find the Wi-Fi item on the Connections tab. Choose Wi-Fi to view a list of available Wi-Fi networks on the right side of the screen. Otherwise, the list shows up full screen, as illustrated in Figure 16-1.

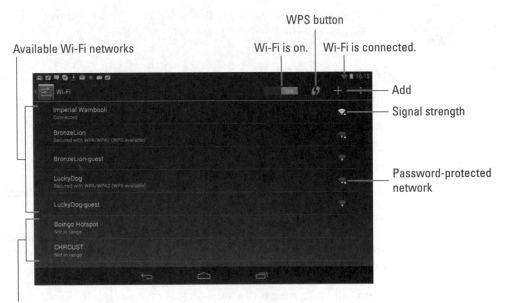

Available Wi-Fi networks   WPS button   Wi-Fi is on. | Wi-Fi is connected.

Add — Signal strength — Password-protected network

Memorized Wi-Fi networks

Figure 16-1: Hunting down a wireless network.

3. **Choose a wireless network from the list.**

   When no wireless networks are listed, you're sort of out of luck regarding Wi-Fi access from your current location.

4. **If prompted, type the network password.**

   Touch the Show Password check box so that you can see what you're typing; some of those network passwords can be *long*.

5. **Touch the Connect button.**

   The network is connected immediately. If not, try the password again.

When the tablet is connected to a wireless network, you see the Wi-Fi Connected status icon, similar to the one shown in the margin. This icon indicates that the tablet's Wi-Fi is on, connected, and communicating with a Wi-Fi network.

Some wireless networks don't broadcast their names, which adds security but also makes connecting more difficult. In those cases, touch the Add icon (refer to Figure 16-1). This icon might also be labeled Add Wi-Fi or Manually Connect. To make the connection, type the network name, or *SSID,* and choose the type of security. You also need the password, if one is used. You can obtain this information from the girl with the pink hair who sold you coffee or from whoever is in charge of the wireless network at your location.

✓ Not every wireless network has a password. Still:

✓ Be careful when connecting to a non-password-protected network. It's possible that the Bad Guys can monitor such a network, stealing passwords and other information.

✓ Some public networks are open to anyone, but you have to use the web browser app to find a login web page that lets you access the network: Simply browse to any page on the Internet, and the login web page shows up.

✓ The Android tablet automatically remembers every Wi-Fi network it has ever been connected to and automatically reconnects upon finding the same network again.

✓ To disconnect from a Wi-Fi network, simply turn off Wi-Fi. See the preceding section.

✓ Use Wi-Fi whenever you plan to remain in one location for a while. Unlike a mobile data network, a Wi-Fi network's broadcast signal has a limited range. If you wander too far away, your tablet loses the signal and is disconnected.

Connecting via WPS

 Many Wi-Fi routers feature WPS, which stands for Wi-Fi Protected Setup. It's a network authorization system that's really simple and quite secure. If the wireless router features WPS, you can use it to quickly connect your Android tablet to the network.

To make the WPS connection, follow these steps:

1. **Touch the WPS connection button on the router.**

   The button either is labeled WPS or uses the WPS icon, shown in the margin.

2. **On your tablet, visit the Wi-Fi screen in the Settings app.**

   Refer to Steps 1 and 2 in the preceding section.

3. **Touch the WPS icon, or touch the Action Overflow or Menu icon and choose the WPS Push Button command**.

   The Wi-Fi connection is made.

Some WPS Wi-Fi routers feature a PIN instead of a push button. In that case, touch the Action Overflow or Menu icon on the Wi-Fi screen and choose the command WPS Pin Entry.

Share the Cellular Connection

It's good to have a cellular tablet and be able to use the Internet wherever you roam. It's so good that people around you, those without a mobile-data connection, will seethe with jealousy. You'll even be able to hear the seething. It's maddening.

Rather than endure endless seething, you can take advantage of a technology called Internet connection sharing. As a gesture of goodwill, you can stifle the seething and share your Android tablet's cellular connection, as described in this section.

Creating a mobile hotspot

The best way to share a digital cellular connection with the most people is to set up your own wireless mobile hotspot on your Android tablet. Carefully heed these steps:

1. **Turn off the tablet's Wi-Fi radio.**

   There's no point in creating a Wi-Fi hotspot where one is already available.

2. **If possible, connect your Android tablet to a power source.**

   It's okay if you don't find a power outlet, but running a mobile hotspot draws a lot of power.

3. **Open the Settings app.**

   It's found in the Apps drawer. Some tablets may feature an app named Mobile Hotspot or 4G Hotspot. If so, open it instead.

4. **Touch the More item in the Wireless & Networks section, and then choose Tethering & Portable Hotspot.**

   The Tethering & Mobile Hotspot item might be found on the main Settings app screen. On some Samsung tablets, touch the Connections tab and then choose the command Tethering and Portable Hotspot.

   You may see text describing the process. If so, dismiss the text.

5. **Touch the box to place a check mark by the Portable Wi-Fi Hotspot item or Mobile Hotspot item, or if the Master Control icon is present, slide it to the right to turn on the hotspot.**

   The Hotspot is on and available, but you probably want to do some additional customization, such as give the hotspot a better name and set up a password.

6. **Choose the item Set Up Wi-Fi Hotspot or Portable Wi-Fi Hotspot.**

   You can give the hotspot a name, or SSID, and review, change, or assign a password. You may need to touch a Configure button to set up these items.

   Touch the Save button or OK button to set your changes.

 When the mobile hotspot is active, you see the Hotspot Active notification icon appear, similar to the one shown in the margin. You can then access the hotspot by using any computer or mobile device that has Wi-Fi capabilities.

To turn off the mobile hotspot, repeat the steps in this section but remove the check mark or slide the master control off in Step 5.

- ✔ You can continue to use the tablet while it's sharing the mobile data connection, but other devices can now use their Wi-Fi radio to access the shared connection.

- ✔ If the hotspot doesn't come on or the Portable Wi-Fi Hotspot item is disabled, your tablet is incapable of creating a Wi-Fi hotspot or is unavailable under your data subscription plan.

- ✔ The range for the mobile hotspot is about 30 feet. Items such as walls and tornadoes can interfere with the signal, rendering it much shorter.

- ✔ Data usage fees apply when you use the mobile hotspot, and they're on top of the fee your cellular provider may charge for the basic service. These fees can add up quickly.

 - ✔ Don't forget to turn off the mobile hotspot when you're done using it. Those data rates add up quickly!

Sharing the Internet via tethering

A personal way to share your Android tablet's digital cellular connection is to *tether.* This operation is carried out by connecting the tablet to another gizmo, such as a laptop computer, via its USB cable. Then you activate USB tethering, and the other gizmo is suddenly using the tablet like a modem.

Yes: I am fully aware that tethering goes against the wireless theme of this chapter. Still, it remains a solid way to provide Internet access to another gizmo, such as a laptop or desktop computer. Follow these steps to set up Internet tethering:

1. **Connect the tablet to a computer or laptop by using the USB cable.**

   I've had the best success with this operation when the computer is a PC running Windows.

2. **Open the Settings app.**

3. **Choose More and then Tethering & Mobile Hotspot.**

   On some Samsung tablets, touch the Connections tab and then choose Tethering and Portable Hotspot.

4. **Place a check mark by the USB Tethering item.**

   Internet tethering is activated.

The other device should instantly recognize the Android tablet as a "modem" with Internet access. Further configuration may be required, which depends on the computer using the tethered connection. For example, you may have to accept the installation of new software when prompted by Windows.

To end Internet tethering, repeat Steps 2 through 4 to remove the check mark. You can then disconnect the USB cable.

✔ When tethering is active the Tethering Active notification icon appears, similar to the one shown in the margin. Choose that notification to further configure tethering.

✔ Unlike creating a Wi-Fi hotspot, you don't need to disable the Wi-Fi radio to activate USB tethering.

✔ Sharing the digital network connection incurs data usage charges against your mobile data plan. Be careful with your data usage when you're sharing a connection.

The Bluetooth World

If the terms *Wi-Fi* and *mobile data connection* don't leave you completely befuddled, I have another term for you. It's *Bluetooth*, and it has nothing to do with the color blue or dental hygiene.

Bluetooth is a wireless protocol for communication between two or more Bluetooth-equipped devices. Your Android tablet just happens to be Bluetooth-equipped, so it too can chat it up with Bluetooth devices, such as headphones, keyboards, printers, and robotic mice armed with deadly lasers.

Understanding Bluetooth

If you're unfamiliar with how Bluetooth works, here's a five-step overview of the process:

1. **Turn on the Bluetooth wireless radio on both gizmos.**

2. **Make the gizmo you're trying to connect to discoverable.**

3. **On your tablet, choose the peripheral gizmo from the list of Bluetooth devices.**

4. **Optionally, confirm the connection on the peripheral device.**

   For example, you may be asked to input a code or press a button.

5. **Use the device.**

When you're done using the device, you simply turn it off. Because the Bluetooth gizmo is paired with your tablet, it's automatically reconnected the next time you turn it on (that is, if you have Bluetooth activated on the tablet).

- ✔ Bluetooth devices are marked with the Bluetooth logo, shown in the margin. It's your assurance that the gizmo can work with other Bluetooth devices.

- ✔ You'll most frequently use the Share icon to take advantage of Bluetooth peripherals. In an app, choose the Share icon to send whatever you're viewing to a Bluetooth peripheral.

- ✔ Bluetooth was developed as a wireless version of the old RS-232 standard, the serial port on early personal computers. Essentially, Bluetooth is wireless RS-232, and the variety of devices you can connect to and the things you can do with Bluetooth are similar to what you could do with the old serial-port standard.

Activating Bluetooth

You must turn on the tablet's Bluetooth radio before you can enjoy using any Bluetoothy peripherals. Here's how to activate Bluetooth on an Android tablet:

1. **Open the Settings app.**

2. **On some Samsung tablets, touch the Connections tab.**

3. **Ensure that the master control next to the Bluetooth item is set to On.**

   Slide the icon to the right to activate.

When Bluetooth is on, the Bluetooth status icon appears. It uses the Bluetooth logo, shown in the margin.

To turn off Bluetooth, repeat the steps in this section, but slide the master control to the left, to the Off position.

You'll also find a Bluetooth switch in the tablet's Quick Actions. See Chapter 3 for more information on Quick Actions.

Pairing with a Bluetooth peripheral

To make the Bluetooth connection between your tablet and some other gizmo, such as a Bluetooth keyboard, follow these steps:

1. **Ensure that Bluetooth is on.**

   Refer to the preceding section.

2. **Turn on the Bluetooth gizmo or ensure that its Bluetooth radio is on.**

   Some Bluetooth devices have separate power and Bluetooth switches. Your goal here is to make the Bluetooth device *discoverable*.

3. **On the Android tablet, touch the Apps icon on the Home screen and open the Settings app.**

4. **Choose Bluetooth.**

   On some Samsung tablets, the Bluetooth item is found on the Connections tab in the Settings app.

   You see the Bluetooth screen. It shows any devices already paired with the tablet, such as the printer shown in Figure 16-2. Also shown in the list are any other Bluetooth devices available for pairing.

5. **If the Bluetooth device has an option to become visible or discoverable, select it.**

   For example, some Bluetooth gizmos have a tiny button to press that makes the device visible to other Bluetooth gizmos.

   After you make the Bluetooth device visible, it should appear on the Bluetooth screen. If it doesn't, touch the Search for Devices button. On some tablets, the button may be labeled Scan.

6. **Choose the Bluetooth device from the list.**

7. **If necessary, type the device's passcode or otherwise acknowledge the connection.**

   Not every device has a passcode. If prompted, acknowledge the passcode on either the Android tablet or the other device.

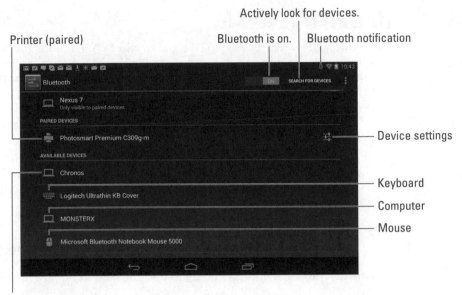

Figure 16-2: Finding Bluetooth gizmos (Jelly Bean).

After you acknowledge the passcode (or not), the Bluetooth gizmo and your Android tablet are connected and communicating. You can begin using the device.

Connected devices appear in the Bluetooth Settings window, under the heading Paired Devices.

To break the connection, you can either turn off the gizmo or turn off the Bluetooth radio on your Android tablet. Because the devices are paired, when you turn on Bluetooth and reactivate the device, the connection is instantly reestablished.

✔ How you use the device depends on what it does. For example, a Bluetooth keyboard can be used for text input; a computer using Bluetooth can be accessed for sharing files (although that process is slow and painful); and a printer can be used for printing documents or pictures.

✔ Refer to Chapter 12 for details on printing to a Bluetooth printer.

✔ You can unpair a device by touching its Settings icon, found on the far right, next to a paired device (refer to Figure 16-2). Choose the Unpair command to break the Bluetooth connection and stop using the device.

✔ You need to unpair devices that you don't plan to use again in the future. Otherwise, simply turn off the Bluetooth device when you're done.

Android, Beam It to Me

Many Android tablets feature an NFC radio, where *NFC* stands for Near Field Communications and *radio* is a type of vegetable. NFC allows your tablet to communicate with other NFC devices. That connection is used for the quick transfer of information. The technology is called Android Beam.

Turning on NFC

You can't play with the Android Beam feature unless the tablet's NFC radio has been activated. To confirm that it has, or to activate it, follow these steps:

1. **Open the Settings app.**

2. **Locate the NFC item.**

   On a stock Android device, you find the NFC item by choosing the More item beneath the Wireless & Networks heading. On some Samsung tablets, touch the Connections heading to find the NFC item.

3. **Ensure that a check mark is found by the NFC item or that its Master Control icon is on or green.**

With NFC activated, you can use your tablet to communicate with other NFC devices. These include other Android tablets, Android phones, and payment systems for various merchants.

Using Android Beam

The Android Beam feature works when you touch your tablet to another NFC device. As long as the two devices have an NFC radio and the Android Beam feature is active, they can share information. You can beam contacts, map locations, web pages, YouTube videos, or just about anything you're viewing on the tablet's touchscreen.

When two Android Beam devices touch — usually back-to-back — you see a prompt appear on the screen: Touch to Beam. Touch the screen, and the item you're viewing is immediately sent to the other device. That's pretty much it.

✔ Generally speaking, if an app features the Share icon, you can use Android Beam to share an item between two NFC gizmos.

✔ Both devices present the Touch to Beam prompt when they get close. If the other person touches his screen at the same time you do, information is swapped between the devices.

✔ The NFC field is most frequently found on the back of the device. The pitiful documentation that came with your Android tablet may illustrate the exact spot.

Using Jim Beam

Follow these steps to enjoy a bottle of Kentucky straight bourbon whiskey:

1. **Unscrew cap.**

2. **Pour.**

3. **Enjoy.**

It isn't truly necessary to pour the whiskey into another container for consumption, though many users find a glass, mug, or red Solo cup useful.

Alcohol and social networking do not mix.

Connect, Share, and Store

A s much as it tries, your Android tablet just can't be completely wireless. Unless you have a wireless charging pad for the tablet, you're going to need the USB cable to resupply the battery with juice. But the USB cable is more than a power cord: It's also a method of communications — specifically, file transfer between your tablet and a computer. This chapter carefully describes how that transfer works. Also discussed is the anxiety-laden issue of storage and sharing, which is presented in a deceptively cheerful manner.

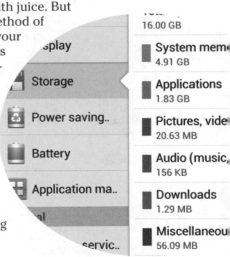

The USB Connection

The most direct way to connect an Android tablet to a computer is by using a wire — specifically, the wire nestled at the core of a USB cable. You can do lots of things after making the USB connection, but everything starts with connecting the cable.

Connecting the tablet to a computer

The USB cable that comes with your Android tablet can be used to physically connect both the tablet and a computer. It's cinchy, thanks to three-dimensional physics and the following two important pieces of advice:

- ✔ One end of the USB cable plugs into the computer.
- ✔ The other end plugs into the Android tablet.

The connectors on either end of the USB cable are shaped differently and cannot be plugged in incorrectly. If one end of the cable doesn't fit, try the other end. If it still doesn't fit, try plugging it in another way.

- ✔ After the USB connection has been made successfully, the USB notification appears, similar to the one shown in the margin. Don't freak if you don't see it; not every tablet displays this notification.

- ✔ The tablet-computer connection works best with a powered USB port. If possible, plug the USB cable into the computer itself or into a powered USB hub.

- ✔ Tablets with a USB 3.0 jack come with a USB 3.0 cable. You can still use the old-style, USB 2.0 micro-USB cables on such devices: Simply plug the micro-USB connector into the right side of the USB 3.0 jack on the bottom of the tablet.

- ✔ For data transfer to take place at top speeds over the USB 3.0 cable, you must connect the tablet's USB 3.0 cable into the USB 3.0 port on a computer. These ports are color-coded blue.

- ✔ The standard Android tablet USB cable is known as a USB-A-male-to-micro–USB cable. You can obtain this cable at any computer- or office-supply store.

- ✔ A flurry of activity takes place when you first connect an Android tablet to a Windows PC. Notifications pop up about new software that's installed. Don't fret if you see a message about software not being found. That's okay. If see the AutoPlay dialog box prompting you to install software, do so.

Configuring the USB connection

The USB connection is configured automatically whenever you connect your Android tablet to a computer. Everything should work peachy. When it doesn't, you can try manually configuring the USB connection: Swipe down the notifications panel and choose the USB notification.

The USB Computer Connection screen lists two options for configuring the USB connection:

Media Device (MTP): When that setting is chosen, the computer believes the tablet to be a portable media player, which it is, kinda. This option is the most common one.

Camera (PTP): In this setting, the computer is misled into thinking that the tablet is a digital camera. Select this option only when the MTP option fails to make the connection or when you desire to transfer images and video when using a media organization program on the computer.

See the later section "Files Back and Forth" to see how to use the basic, USB MTP connection.

✔ If you can't get the USB connection to work, check to see whether the tablet features a proprietary synchronization program, such as Samsung's Kies utility. See the later section "Connecting with Samsung Kies."

✔ No matter which USB connection option you've chosen, the tablet's battery charges whenever it's connected to a computer's USB port — as long as the computer is turned on, of course.

✔ If your Android tablet has a MicroSD card, its storage is also mounted to the computer, as well as to the tablet's internal storage. You do not need to configure that storage separately to make the USB connection.

✔ PTP stands for Picture Transfer Protocol. MTP stands for Media Transfer Protocol.

Connecting an Android tablet to a Mac

You need special software to deal with the Android-to-Macintosh connection. That's because the Mac doesn't natively recognize Android devices. Weird, huh? It's like Apple wants you to buy some other type of tablet. I just don't get it.

To help deal with the USB connection on a Mac, obtain the Android File Transfer program. On your Mac, download that program from this website:

```
www.android.com/filetransfer
```

Install the software. Run it. From that point on, whenever you connect your Android tablet to the Mac, you see a special window appear, similar to the one shown in Figure 17-1. It lists the tablet's folders and files. Use that window for file management, as covered later in this chapter.

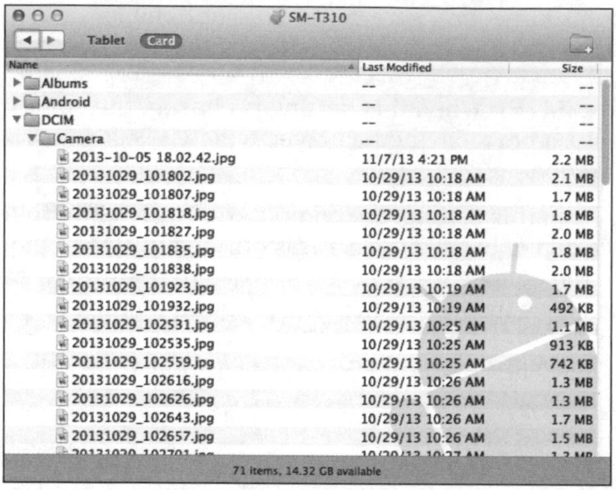

Figure 17-1: The Android File Transfer program.

- ✔ The Kies program can be used to transfer files between a Samsung tablet and a Mac. See the later section "Connecting with Samsung Kies."

- ✔ Cloud storage can also be used to transfer files between your tablet and a Macintosh (and a PC). See the later section "Sharing files with the cloud."

Disconnecting the tablet from a computer

The process is cinchy: When you're done transferring files, music, or other media between your PC and the tablet, close all programs and folders you have opened on your computer — specifically, those you've used to work with the tablet's storage. Then you can disconnect the USB cable. That's it.

- ✔ It's a Bad Idea to unplug the tablet while you're transferring information or while a folder window is open on your computer. Doing so can damage the tablet's internal storage, rendering unreadable some of the information that's kept there. To be safe, close those programs and folder windows you've opened before disconnecting.

- ✔ Unlike other external storage on the Macintosh, there's no need to eject the tablet's storage when you're done accessing it. Simply disconnect the tablet. The Mac doesn't get angry when you do so.

Files Back and Forth

The point of making the USB connection between an Android tablet and a computer is to exchange files. You can't just wish the files over. Instead, I recommend following the advice in this section.

File transfer works best when you have a good understanding of basic file operations. You need to be familiar with file operations such as copy, move, rename, and delete. It also helps to know what folders are and how they work. The good news is that you don't need to manually calculate a 64-bit cyclical redundancy check on the data, nor do you need to know what a parity bit is.

Transferring files

I can think of plenty of reasons why you would want to copy a file between a computer and an Android tablet, many of which are legal.

For example, you can copy pictures and videos, music and audio files, and even vCards that help you build contacts for the tablet's address book. And you can just copy random files when you're on a caffeine high and nothing is on TV.

Follow these steps to copy a file or two between a computer and an Android tablet:

1. **Connect the Android tablet to the computer by using the USB cable.**

   Specific directions are offered earlier in this chapter.

2. **On a PC, if the AutoPlay dialog box appears, choose the option Open Folder/Device to View Files.**

   When the AutoPlay dialog box doesn't appear, you can view files manually: Open the Computer window, and then open the tablet's icon, found at the bottom of that window. Open the Storage icon to view files.

   The tablet's folder window that you see looks like any other folder in Windows. The difference is that the files and folders in that window are on your Android tablet, not on the computer.

   On a Macintosh, the Android File Transfer program should start, appearing on the screen as shown earlier, in Figure 17-1.

3. **Open the source and destination folder windows.**

   Open the folder that contains the files you want to copy. The folder can be found on the computer or on the tablet. Then open the folder on the computer or tablet where you want the file copied. Have both folder windows, computer and phone, visible on the screen, similar to what's shown in Figure 17-2.

Specific folders on the tablet

Drag files to here to
copy to the "root."

Files on your computer

Files on your tablet

Figure 17-2: Copying files to the Android tablet.

4. **Drag the file icon(s) from one folder to another to copy.**

   Dragging the file copies it, either from tablet to computer or from computer to tablet.

   If you want to be specific, drag the file to the tablet's download folder or to the root folder, as shown in Figure 17-2.

   On the PC, drag icons from the phone's storage to the My Documents, My Pictures, or My Videos folder, as appropriate. You can also drag directly to the desktop and decide later where to store the file.

   The same file dragging technique can be used for transferring files from a Macintosh. You need to drag the icon(s) to the Android File Transfer window, which works just like any folder window in the Finder.

5. **Close the folder windows and disconnect the USB cable when you're done.**

Though this manual technique works, the best way to transfer media to the tablet is to use a media program, such as Windows Media Player. See Chapter 13 for information on synchronizing music. You can also synchronize pictures and videos in the same way, by using a media program on the computer.

✔ When your Android tablet has a MicroSD card installed, Windows displays two AutoPlay dialog boxes. Each dialog box represents a different storage source — internal storage as well as the MicroSD card.

- On a Macintosh using Android File Transfer, each storage device appears as a toolbar button, such as Tablet and Card, shown in Figure 17-1.

- Files you've downloaded on the tablet are stored in the Download folder.

- Pictures and videos on the tablet are stored in the DCIM/Camera folder, which is found on both internal storage and the MicroSD card.

- Music on the tablet is stored in the Music folder, organized by artist.

- The best way to synchronize music is to use a music jukebox program on your computer. See Chapter 13.

Connecting with Samsung Kies

The Samsung way to connect your phone to a computer is to use something called Samsung Kies. Don't bother asking: No one on the planet has any idea what Kies stands for, let alone how to pronounce it. I think it may be the name of Mr. Samsung's pet parakeet.

A Samsung tablet uses Kies in one of two ways to connect with a computer and swap files. The best way is the Kies Air app, which wirelessly connects your tablet to a computer when both devices are on the same Wi-Fi network.

When the Kies Air app isn't available, you must download a copy of the Kies program for your PC or Macintosh. The program is obtained from this website:

```
www.samsung.com/us/kies
```

Ensure that you download the proper version of Kies for your specific Samsung tablet.

The Media Card Transfer

If your Android tablet features removable storage, you can use it to transfer files: Remove the MicroSD from the tablet and insert it into a computer. From that point on, the files on the media card can be read by the computer just as they can be read from any media card.

See Chapter 1 for details on how to remove the MicroSD card from your phone. You can't just yank out the thing! You also need a MicroSD adapter to insert the card into a media reader on the computer. Or you can get a MicroSD card thumb-drive adapter, in which case you merely need a USB port for the computer to access the card's information.

Once started, Kies lets you back up and swap files between your Samsung tablet and the computer. Kies Air uses your computer's web browser to swap and send files; the Kies program acts as its own file synchronizing utility.

✔ When using Kies Air, follow the directions on the tablet's screen to configure your computer's web browser.

✔ To end the Kies Air connection, touch the Stop button on the tablet's touchscreen. You can then close the web browser window on your computer.

✔ Don't click the Back button on your computer's web browser screen when using the Kies Air website. Just use the controls on the web page itself to navigate.

✔ To copy files to the tablet from a computer using the Kies program (not Kies Air), use the File menu. Choose File⇨Add File to Galaxy Note 3⇨Internal (or External), and then choose the file to send over.

✔ Using Kies doesn't prevent you from transferring files as described in the preceding section, which I believe is a more effective way to move files back and forth between tablet and computer. In fact:

✔ If you don't like Kies, don't use it. However:

✔ Kies is required in order to install updates for some Samsung tablets. Even when the tablet notifies you of an update, and you attempt to install the update by obeying the tablet's directions, the update may fail. You're informed that you must use Kies to complete the update. Also see Chapter 20 for additional information on updating your Samsung tablet.

Sharing files with the cloud

A handy way to share files between a computer and your Android tablet is to use *cloud storage*. That's just fancy talk for storing files on the Internet.

Many choices are available for cloud storage, including Google's own Google Drive and Microsoft's SkyDrive. I'm fond of the Dropbox service.

All files saved to cloud storage are synchronized instantly with all devices that access the storage. Change a file on a computer and it's updated on your tablet. The files are also available directly on the Internet from a web page. Even so, I recommend that you use a specific cloud storage app on your tablet to access the files.

To make the file transfer from the computer to the tablet, save a file in the cloud storage folder. On your tablet, open the cloud storage app, such as Google Drive or Dropbox. Browse the folders to touch a file icon and view that file on your phone.

To transfer a file from your tablet to a computer, view the file or media and then touch the Share icon. Choose the Drive icon or Dropbox icon to share the item via Google Drive or Dropbox, respectively.

Because all devices that share the cloud storage are instantly synchronized, you don't need to worry about specific file transfers. All files saved to cloud storage are available to all devices that can access that storage.

✔ The Google Drive app is named Drive. It's part of the Google suite of apps on just about every Android phone. If not, you can obtain it for free from the Google Play Store. See Chapter 15.

✔ If you don't find the Dropbox app on your tablet, obtain a copy from the Play Store. You also need to sign up for a Dropbox account and, probably, get the Dropbox program for your computer. Visit www.dropbox.com to get started.

✔ These cloud storage services are free for a limited amount of storage. Beyond that, you need to pay a monthly fee.

Android Tablet Storage

Somewhere, deep in your Android tablet's bosom, lies a storage device or two. That storage works like the hard drive in a computer, and for the same purpose: to keep apps, music, videos, pictures, and a host of other information for the long term. This section describes what you can do to manage that storage.

✔ Android tablets come with 8GB, 16GB, or 32GB of internal storage. In the future, models with larger storage capacities might become available.

✔ Removable storage in the form of a MicroSD card is available on some Android tablets. The capacity of a MicroSD card can vary between 8GB and 64GB.

✔ A GB is a *gigabyte,* or 1 billion bytes (characters) of storage. A typical 2-hour movie occupies about 4GB of storage, but most things you store on the tablet — music and pictures, for example — take up only a sliver of storage. Those items do, however, occupy more storage space the more you use the tablet.

Reviewing storage stats

You can see how much storage space is available on your Android tablet's internal storage by following these steps:

1. **At the Home screen, touch the Apps icon.**

2. **Open the Settings app**

3. Choose the Storage item.

On some Samsung tablets, you'll find the Storage item on the General tab in the Settings app.

You see a screen similar to the one shown in Figure 17-3. It details information about storage space on the tablet's internal storage and, if available, the MicroSD card.

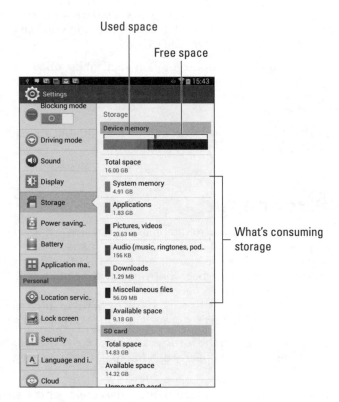

Figure 17-3: Android tablet storage information.

Touch a category on the Storage screen to view details on how the storage is used or to launch an associated app. For example, touching Applications (refer to Figure 17-3) displays a list of running apps. Choosing the Pictures, Videos item lets you view pictures and videos.

✔ Things that consume the most storage space are videos, music, and pictures, in that order.

✔ To see how much storage space is left, refer to the Available item.

✔ Don't complain if the Total Space value is far less than the stated capacity of your Android tablet. For example, your tablet may have 16GB of storage but the Storage screen reports on 11.94GB of total space. The missing space is considered overhead, as are several gigabytes taken by the government for tax purposes.

Managing files

You probably didn't get an Android tablet because you enjoy managing files on a computer and you wanted another gizmo to hone your skills. Even so, you can practice the same type of file manipulation on the Android tablet as you would on a computer. Is there a need to do so? Of course not! But if you want to get dirty with files, you can.

Some Android tablets come with a file management app. It's called File or My Files, and it's a traditional type of file manager, which means that if you detest managing files on your computer, you'll experience the same pain and frustration on your tablet

When your tablet lacks a file management app, you can swiftly obtain one. You'll find an abundance of file management apps available at the Google Play Store. One that I admire and use is the ASTRO file manager/browser from Metago. See Chapter 15 for more information on the Google Play Store.

If you simply want to peruse files you've downloaded from the Internet, open the Downloads app, found in the Apps drawer. Refer to Chapter 7.

Formatting MicroSD storage

Once installed, a MicroSD card's storage is available for use by your Android tablet. You can save pictures on the card, move apps, and use the external storage to keep more junk on the tablet. Before you can do all that, however, the MicroSD card must be formatted. Here are the steps that are necessary to accomplish this task:

1. **Open the Settings app.**

2. **Choose the Storage item.**

    On some Samsung tablets, you'll find the Storage item on the General tab.

3. **Touch the Format SD Card command.**

    The command is found at the bottom of the Storage screen.

4. **Touch the Format SD Card button.**

    All data on the MicroSD card is erased by the formatting process.

5. **Touch the Delete All button.**

The MicroSD card is unmounted, formatted, and then mounted again and made ready for use.

After the card is formatted, you can use it to store information, music, apps, photos, and stuff like that.

✔ The basic installation and removal of the MicroSD card are covered in Chapter 1.

✔ Some tablets may not let you format the MicroSD card when the device is connected to a computer. Disconnect the tablet (unplug the USB cable) and try again.

✔ The Camera app for most tablets automatically stores images on the MicroSD card. This setting can be changed; see Chapter 11.

✔ When copying music to the tablet, choose the device's "Card" storage when using programs such as Windows Media Player. Refer to Chapter 13.

✔ Apps can be relocated to the MicroSD card storage. See Chapter 15.

✔ The Unmount SD Card command is also found on the Storage screen in the Settings app. It allows you to remove the MicroSD card without turning off the tablet. This unmounting process is necessary to prevent data from being lost or the media card from being destroyed if it's removed while information is being accessed. If such a thing concerns you, turn off the tablet and then remove the MicroSD card. That way, you'll always be safe.

The HDMI Connection

You may think that having a 10-inch tablet really smokes those folks with the smaller, 8-inch tablets. Ha! You're in for a surprise. That's because any tablet with HDMI output — even those doinky 7-inch models — can hook up to an 80-inch plasma HDTV screen and really show who's boss.

When your Android tablet features an HDMI connection, whether it's a 7-inch model or a 10-inch behemoth, you too can enjoy the pleasures of a larger screen. It doesn't have to be an 80-inch plasma screen, either; any monitor or HDTV with HDMI input does the job.

To make the HDMI connection, plug your tablet into an HDMI-equipped monitor or HDTV. You need a special HDMI cable to make the connection; such an item can be found on the Internet or wherever you purchased your tablet.

Upon success, an HDMI notification or pop-up appears on the tablet's screen. Choose it and select how to display information on the external monitor. Depending on the tablet, you can choose to run a slideshow, present videos or music, or simply mirror the information displayed on the touchscreen. Among the options you'll find for using the larger screen are these:

Gallery: You can view pictures or a slideshow, according to the directions on the screen.

Music: Choose a playlist, an album, or an artist, and enjoy watching the Music app on the big screen. (The sound should play from the TV's speakers.)

Mirror On Display: The screen output on your Android tablet is duplicated on the HDMI TV or monitor. This option is the one you choose when you want to watch a rented movie on the big screen.

When you're finished using the HDMI connection, simply disconnect the tablet from the HDTV or monitor. The display returns to normal operation.

✔ If your tablet lacks an HDMI port, check to see whether a multimedia dock or HDMI USB dongle is available. Or:

✔ Any tablet, even one without an HDMI connection, can share its screen by using Google Chromecast. Attach the Chromecast dongle to an HDMI connector on your HDMI TV. Follow the onscreen directions to set up and configure your tablet or control the TV. In such a configuration, the HDMI connector on a tablet isn't necessary, though not every app features the ability to share its screen via Chromecast.

✔ HDMI stands for High Definition Multimedia Interface.

18

On the Road

In This Chapter

▶ Traveling with your Android tablet

▶ Using the tablet on an airplane

▶ Activating Airplane mode

▶ Taking an Android tablet overseas

▶ Avoiding data roaming charges

As a mobile device, your Android tablet is designed to go wherever you go. And if you throw the tablet, it can go beyond where you go, but that's not my point. Being wireless and having a generous battery, the tablet is built to go on the road. Where can you take it? How can it survive? What if it runs off by itself? These are the issues regarding taking your tablet elsewhere, all of which are covered in this chapter.

You Can Take It with You

How far can you go with an Android tablet? As far as you want. As long as you can carry the tablet with you, it goes where you go. How it functions may change depending on your environment, and you can do a few things to prepare before you go, which are all covered in this section.

Preparing to leave

Unless you're being unexpectedly abducted, you should prepare several things before leaving on a trip with your Android tablet.

First and most important, of course, is to charge the thing. I plug in my Android tablet overnight before I leave the next day. The tablet's battery is nice and robust, so it should last you your entire journey.

Second, consider loading up on some reading material, music, and a few new apps before you go.

For example, consider getting some eBooks for the road. I prefer to sit and stew over the Play Store's online library before I leave, as opposed to wandering aimlessly in some airport sundry store, trying hard to focus on the good books rather than on the salty snacks. Chapter 14 covers reading eBooks on your Android tablet.

Picking up some music might be a good idea as well. Visit Chapter 13.

I usually reward myself with a new game before I go on a trip with my tablet. Visit the Play Store and see what's hot or recommended. A good puzzle game can make a nice, long international flight go by a lot quicker. See Chapter 15 for information on obtaining games from the Google Play Store.

Going to the airport

I'm not a frequent flier, but I am a nerd. The most amount of junk I've carried with me on a flight is two laptop computers and three cell phones. I know that's not a record, but it's enough to warrant the following list of travel tips, all of which apply to taking an Android tablet with you on an extended journey:

- ✔ Take the Android tablet's AC adapter and USB cable with you. Put them in your carry-on luggage.

- ✔ Most airports feature USB chargers, so you can charge the tablet in an airport, if you need to. Even though you need only the cable to charge, bring along the AC adapter, anyway.

- ✔ At the security checkpoint, place your Android tablet in a bin by itself or with other electronics.

- ✔ Use the Calendar app to keep track of your flights. The event title serves as the airline and flight number. For the event time, use the take-off and landing schedules. For the location, list the origin and destination airport codes. And, in the Description field, put the flight reservation number. If you're using separate calendars (categories), specify the Travel calendar for your flight.

- ✔ See Chapter 14 for more information on the Calendar app.

- ✔ Most airlines offer apps you can use while traveling. Use the apps to not only keep track of flights but also check in. Eventually, printed tickets will disappear, and you'll merely show your "ticket" on the Android tablet screen, which is then scanned at the gate.

- ✔ Some apps you can use to organize your travel details are similar to, but more sophisticated than, the Calendar app. Visit the Google Play Store and search for *travel* or *airline* to find a host of apps.

Flying with an Android tablet

It truly is the most trendy of things to be aloft with the latest mobile gizmo. Like taking a cell phone on a plane, however, you have to follow some rules. Although your Android tablet isn't a cell phone, you still have to heed the flight crew's warnings regarding cell phones and other electronics — and those rules are changing.

Generally speaking, follow the flight crew's direction when it comes to using your Android tablet whilst in the air. They'll let you know when and how you can use the device — specifically, whether it needs to be turned off for take-off and landing and, once in the air, whether you can use it to access the mobile data network or to enable any wireless features, such as Wi-Fi and GPS.

First and foremost, turn off the Android tablet when instructed to do so. This direction is given before take-off and landing, so be prepared.

Before take-off, you'll most likely want to put the tablet into Airplane mode. Yep, it's the same Airplane mode you'd find on a cell phone: The various scary and dangerous wireless radios on the tablet are disabled in this mode. With Airplane mode active, you're free to use the tablet in-flight, facing little risk of causing the plane's navigational equipment to fail and the entire flight to end as a fireball over Wyoming.

The most convenient way to place the tablet in Airplane mode is to obey these quick steps, which don't even require that you unlock the device:

1. **Press and hold the Power/Lock key.**

   The Device Options menu appears.

2. **Choose Airplane Mode.**

3. **Touch the OK button to confirm.**

The most inconvenient way to put the tablet into Airplane mode is to use the Settings app, which I won't even go into here. That's because you'll probably find an Airplane mode Quick Action that's far easier to get to. See Chapter 3 for information on quick actions.

 When the Android tablet is in Airplane mode, a special icon appears in the status area, similar to the one shown in the margin.

To exit Airplane mode, repeat the steps mentioned in this section.

  ✏ Airplane mode might be called Flight mode on some tablets.

  ✏ You can compose e-mail while the tablet is in Airplane mode. Messages aren't sent until you disable Airplane mode and connect again with a data network.

🖝 Bluetooth wireless is disabled in Airplane mode. Even so:

   🖝 Many airlines feature onboard wireless networking. You can turn on wire-
      less networking for your Android tablet and use a wireless network in the
      air: Simply activate the Wi-Fi feature, per the directions in Chapter 16,
      after placing the tablet in Airplane mode — well, after the flight attendant
      tells you that it's okay to do so.

Getting to your destination

After you arrive at your destination, the tablet may update the date and time
according to your new location. One additional step you may want to take
is to set the tablet's time zone. By doing so, you ensure that your schedule
adapts properly to your new location.

To change the tablet's time zone, follow these steps:

   1. **Open the Settings app.**

   2. **Choose Date and Time.**

      On some Samsung tablets, the Date and Time item is found by first
      touching the General tab.

   3. **If you find an Automatic Time Zone setting, ensure that a check mark
      appears by that option.**

      If so, you're done; the tablet automatically updates its time references.
      Otherwise, continue with Step 4.

   4. **Choose Select Time Zone.**

   5. **Pluck the current time zone from the list.**

If you've set appointments for your new location, visit the Calendar app to
ensure that their start and end times have been properly adjusted. If you're
prompted to update appointment times based on the new zone, do so.

When you're done traveling or you change your time zone again, make sure
that the tablet is updated as well. When the Automatic Time Zone setting
isn't available, follow the steps in this section to reset the tablet's time zone.

The Android Tablet Goes Abroad

Yes, your Android tablet works overseas. The two resources you need to consider are a way to recharge the battery and a way to access Wi-Fi. As long as
you have both, you're pretty much set. You also must be careful about roaming surcharges when using a cellular tablet.

Using overseas power

You can easily attach a foreign AC power adapter to your tablet's AC power plug. You don't need a voltage converter — just an adapter. After it's attached, you can plug your tablet into those weirdo overseas power sockets without the risk of blowing up anything. I charged my Android tablet nightly while I spent time in France, and it worked like a charm.

Accessing Wi-Fi in foreign lands

Wi-Fi is pretty universal. They use the same protocols and standards in Wamboolistan as they do back home. So, as long as Wi-Fi is available, your Android tablet can use it.

- ✔ See Chapter 16 for details on using Wi-Fi with your Android tablet.

- ✔ Internet cafés are more popular overseas than in the United States. They are the best locations for connecting your tablet and catching up on life back home.

- ✔ Many overseas hotels offer free Wi-Fi service, although the signal may not reach into every room. Don't be surprised if you can use the Wi-Fi network only while you're in the lobby.

- ✔ Use your Android tablet to make phone calls overseas by getting some Skype Credit. Skype's international rates are quite reasonable. The calls are made over the Internet, so when the tablet has Wi-Fi access, you're good to go. See Chapter 8 for more information on making Skype calls.

Disabling data roaming

The word *roam* takes on an entirely new meaning when it's applied to an Android tablet with a cellular modem. Whenever you venture outside of your carrier's service area, the tablet may end up latching onto another mobile data network. When that happens, the tablet is *roaming*.

Roaming sounds handy, but there's a catch: It almost always involves a surcharge for using another mobile data network — an *unpleasant* surcharge.

Relax: Your cellular tablet alerts you whenever you're roaming. The Roaming icon appears in the status area, similar to the one shown in the margin. You may even see the word Roaming on the lock screen and witness the name of a cellular provider other than your usual provider adorning the lock screen.

If you'd like to avoid using the alien mobile network and, potentially, avoid any unpleasant charges, disable the tablet's Data Roaming option. Follow these steps:

1. **Open the Settings app.**

2. **In the Wireless & Networks section, touch the More item.**

3. **Choose Mobile Networks.**

   On some Samsung tablets, touch the Connections tab and then choose More Networks to find the Mobile Networks item.

4. **Ensure that the Data Roaming option isn't selected.**

   On some tablets, the option is titled Global Data Roaming Access. Choose it and then choose the option Deny Data Roaming Access.

Your tablet can still access the Internet over the Wi-Fi connection while it's roaming. Connecting to a Wi-Fi network doesn't make you incur extra charges on your cellular bill. See Chapter 16 for more information about Wi-Fi.

✔ If roaming concerns you, simply place the tablet into Airplane mode, as covered earlier in this chapter. In Airplane mode, your tablet can access Wi-Fi networks, but its cellular modem is definitely disabled.

✔ Contact your cellular provider when you're traveling abroad to ask about overseas data roaming. A subscription service or other options may be available, especially when you plan to stay overseas for an extended length of time.

19

Customize Your Android Tablet

In This Chapter

▶ Changing the background image

▶ Putting apps and widgets on the Home screen

▶ Rearranging things on the Home screen

▶ Removing the screen lock

▶ Adding a password, PIN, or pattern lock

▶ Creating owner info text

▶ Changing the notification sound

▶ Adjusting the brightness

t's entirely possible to own an Android tablet for decades and never once customize it. It's not that customization is impossible; it's that most people just don't bother. Maybe they don't know how to customize it; maybe they don't try; or maybe they're deathly afraid that the tablet will seek revenge.

Poppycock!

It's *your* tablet! Great potential exists to make the device truly your own. You can change the way it looks to the way it sounds. Revenge is not part of the equation.

Home Screen Decorating

Lots of interesting items can festoon an Android tablet's Home screen. Icons, widgets, and shortcuts adorn the Home screen like olives in a festive salad. All that stuff can change — even the background images. Directions and suggestions are offered in this section.

Modifying the Home screen

The key to Home screen decorating can be subtly different from tablet to tablet. Perhaps the most predictable method is to long-press a blank part of the Home screen; do not long-press a shortcut icon or widget. Upon success, you may see a Home screen menu, similar to those shown in Figure 19-1.

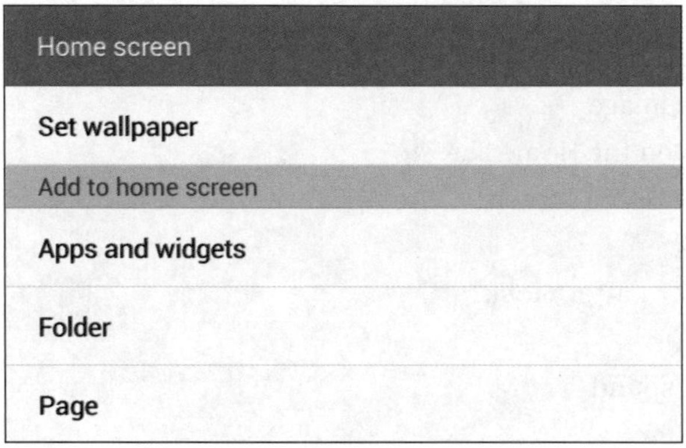

Home screen

Set wallpaper

Add to home screen

Apps and widgets

Folder

Page

Figure 19-1: The Home Screen menu.

On some Android tablets, you may see only a menu from which you can choose Wallpapers. Don't fret when that happens! You can still modify the Home screen by using the various techniques divulged in this chapter.

The standard items controlled by a Home screen menu include:

Wallpaper: Change the background image on the Home screen.

Apps and Widgets: Add shortcut icons (apps) and widgets to the Home screen.

Folders: Create folders for multiple apps on the Home screen.

Pages: Add, remove, or manage multiple Home screen pages.

Later sections in this chapter describe how to use each command.

✔ You cannot long-press the Home screen when it's full of launcher icons and widgets. Swipe to a screen that's all or partially empty. If that's not the case, remove an item from the screen; see the section "Rearranging and removing apps and widgets."

✔ Use folders to help organize apps on the Home screen, especially when the Home screen starts to overflow with launcher icons. See the later section "Building app folders."

✔ To customize the Home screen on certain Android tablets, touch the Menu icon and choose the Add or Add to Home Screen command. The menu may also list specific commands, such as those shown earlier, in Figure 19-1.

Hanging new wallpaper

The Home screen background can be draped with two types of wallpaper:

Traditional: The wallpaper is chosen from a selection of still images. These images may be preloaded on the tablet, or you can pluck an image from the tablet's Gallery, such as a photo you've taken.

Live: The wallpaper image is animated, either displaying changing images or reacting to your touch.

To set a new wallpaper for the Home screen, obey these steps:

1. Long-press the Home screen and choose either the Wallpaper or Set Wallpaper command or icon.

Refer to Figures 19-1, although not every tablet displays the Home screen menu.

2. Choose the wallpaper type.

For example, choose Gallery to use photos you've taken or choose Wallpapers to select some preset wallpaper designs. The Live Wallpapers item presents only animated or interactive options.

The variety of wallpaper types you see depends on the apps installed on your tablet.

3. Select the wallpaper you want from the list.

Depending on your choice for Step 2, you may be presented with a scrolling list of wallpaper selections, or you may see an app, such as the Gallery, from which you choose an image.

For certain live wallpapers, the Settings icon may appear so that you customize how the wallpaper interacts with you.

4. **Touch either the Done or Set Wallpaper button to confirm your selection.**

   The new wallpaper takes over the Home screen.

Live wallpaper features some form of animation, which can often be interactive. Otherwise, the wallpaper image scrolls slightly as you swipe from one Home screen page to another.

✔ You may also be able to change the lock screen wallpaper on some tablets, choosing a separate wallpaper or sharing the same Home screen wallpaper. If so, a prompt appears, asking which wallpaper to set: Home screen, lock screen, or both.

✔ Also see Chapter 21 for more information on changing the lock screen.

✔ The Settings apps may feature a Wallpaper command. Choose the Display item, and then look for a Wallpaper command. Likewise, you might find a Lock Screen command on the Settings app's main screen. Use it to set the lock screen's wallpaper.

✔ You may be prompted to crop the wallpaper image you've chosen. See Chapter 12 for details on how to crop images.

✔ The Zedge app has some interesting wallpaper features. Check it out at the Google Play Store; see Chapter 15.

Adding apps to the Home screen

The first thing I did on my Android tablet was to place my most favorite apps on the Home screen. Here's how that works:

1. **Visit the Home screen page on which you want to stick the app icon.**

   The screen must have room for the app icon.

2. **Touch the Apps icon to display the Apps drawer.**

3. **Long-press the app icon you want to add to the Home screen.**

4. **Drag the app to the Home screen page, lifting your finger to place the app.**

   A copy of the app's icon is placed on the Home screen, similar to what's illustrated in Figure 19-2.

Drag here to move one page left.

Drag here to uninstall the app.

Show the app's Info screen.

Drag here to move one page right.

Drag the icon to a position on the Home screen.

Figure 19-2: Placing an app icon on the Home screen.

The app hasn't moved: What you see is a copy or, officially, a *launcher.* You can still find the app in the Apps drawer, but now the app is available — more conveniently — on the Home screen.

 ✔ Don't worry if the app isn't in exactly the right spot. The later section "Rearranging and removing apps and widgets," describes how to rearrange icons on the Home screen. That section also covers removing apps from the Home screen.

 ✔ Keep your favorite apps, those you use most often, on the Home screen.

 ✔ The best apps to place on the Home screen are those that show updates, such as new messages, similar to the icon shown in the margin. These icons are also ideal to place on the Favorites tray, as covered in the next section.

✔ You can also add apps to the Home screen by choosing the Apps (or Apps and Widgets) command from the Home screen menu, shown earlier, in Figure 19-1. Often this command merely skips over Steps 1 and 2 in this section; you still have to long-press the icon and drag it to a Home screen page.

✔ Icons on the Home screen are aligned to a grid. You can't stuff more icons on the Home screen than will fit in the grid, so when a Home screen page is full of icons (or widgets), use another Home screen page.

Putting an app on the Favorites tray

The line of icons at the bottom of the Home screen is the *Favorites tray.* Icons are added to the Favorites tray in one of two ways:

✔ Drag an icon off the Favorites tray, either to the Home screen or to the Remove or Delete icon. That action makes room for a new icon to be placed on the Favorites tray.

✔ Drag an icon from the Home screen to the Favorites tray, in which case any existing icon swaps places with the icon that's already there.

Of these two methods, the second one may not work on all tablets. In fact, the second method may create an app folder on the Favorites tray, which is probably not what you want. (See the later section "Building app folders," for information.)

Slapping down widgets

The Home screen is the place where you can find *widgets,* or tiny, interactive information windows. A widget often provides a gateway into another app or displays information such as status updates, the name of the song that's playing, or the weather. To add a widget to the Home screen, heed these steps:

1. **Switch to a Home screen page that has room enough for the new widget.**

   Unlike app icons, widgets can occupy more than a postage-stamp-size piece of Home screen real estate.

2. **Touch the Apps icon to visit the Apps drawer.**

3. **Touch the Widgets tab.**

   If you don't see the Widgets tab, keep swiping the list of apps to the left until widgets are displayed.

   The widgets appear on the Apps screen in little preview windows. Swipe the list left or right to peruse the lot.

4. **Long-press the widget you desire and drag it to a Home screen page.**

   At this point, the operation works just like adding an app. One major difference, however, is that some widgets can be quite big. Room must be available on the Home screen page, or else you can't add the widget.

Some widgets may require additional setup after you add them, such as setting a few quick options. You might also see a resize rectangle around the widget, similar to the one shown in Figure 19-3. Drag the edges or corners of that rectangle to resize the widget.

Make widget taller.

Clock widget

Make widget wider.

Figure 19-3: Resizing a widget.

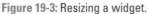 The variety of available widgets depends on the apps you have installed. Some apps come with widgets, some don't.

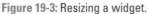 A great widget to add is the Power Control widget. It contains buttons for turning on or off various tablet features.

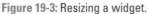 To remove, move, or rearrange a widget, see the later section "Rearranging and removing apps and widgets."

Building app folders

Each Home screen page sports a grid that holds only so many app icons. Though you can use math to calculate the maximum number of Home screen icons, a better choice is to use app folders to avoid any overflow.

An *app folder* is a collection of two or more apps, both in the same spot on the Home screen. Figure 19-4 illustrates an app folder on the Home screen, shown both closed and open.

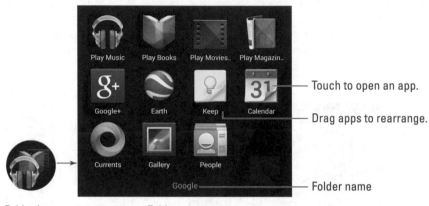

Figure 19-4: Anatomy of an app folder.

Folders are created in different ways, depending on the tablet. The stock Android method to create a folder is to long-press one icon and drag it right on top of the other icon. The folder is created. Both icon images show up inside a circle, similar to what's shown on the left in Figure 19-4.

When the stock Android method doesn't work, look for a Folder command, such as the one shown on the Home Screen menu (refer to Figure 19-1). Choose that command, which may also be called Create Folder. An empty folder is created, which you can then name. At that point, you can drag icons into the folder as described in this section.

Build the folder by dragging more icons into it. You can also drag an app into the folder directly from the Apps drawer.

Open a folder by touching it. You can then touch an icon in the folder to start an app. Or, if you don't find what you want, touch the Back icon to close the folder.

- Some tablets show the Create Folder icon when you long-press the Home screen. Drag an app icon onto the Create Folder icon to build the folder.

- Folders are managed just like other icons on the Home screen. You can long-press them to drag them around. They can also be deleted. See the next section.

- Change a folder's name by opening the folder and then touching the folder's name. Type the new name by using the onscreen keyboard.

- Add more apps to the folder by dragging them over the folder's icon.

✔ To remove an icon from a folder, open the folder and drag out the icon. When the second-to-last last icon is dragged out of a folder, the folder is removed. If not, drag the last icon out, and then remove the folder as you would any other icon on the Home screen; see the next section.

Rearranging and removing apps and widgets

Apps, folders, and widgets aren't fastened to the Home screen with anything stronger than masking tape. That's obvious because it's quite easy to pick up and move an icon, relocating it to a new position or removing it completely. It all starts by long-pressing the app, folder, or widget, as shown in Figure 19-5.

Delete icon or widget.

Long-press to "lift" icon.

Figure 19-5: Moving an icon.

You can drag a free icon to another position on the Home screen or to another Home screen page. You can also drag to the Remove icon that appears on the Home screen to banish that icon from the Home screen.

✔ The Remove icon may not always appear at the top of the Home screen, as shown in Figure 19-5. It might also appear as the Trash icon (shown in the margin).

- ✔ Removing an app or widget from the Home screen doesn't uninstall the app or widget. See Chapter 15 for information on uninstalling apps.

- ✔ When an icon hovers over the Remove or Trash icon, ready to be deleted, its color changes to red.

Managing Home screen pages

The number of pages on the Home screen isn't fixed. You can add pages. You can remove pages. You can even rearrange pages. This feature might not be available to all Android tablets and, sadly, it's not implemented in exactly the same way.

The stock Android method of adding a Home screen page is to drag an icon left or right, just as though you were positioning that icon on another Home screen page. When a page to the left or right doesn't exist, the tablet automatically adds a new, blank page.

Other tablets may be more specific in how pages are added. For example, you can choose a Page command from the Home screen menu, shown earlier, in Figure 19-1.

Samsung tablets feature a Home screen page overview, shown in Figure 19-6. To edit Home screen pages, pinch the Home screen: Touch the screen with two fingers and drag them together. You can then manage Home screen pages as illustrated in the figure.

Primary panel

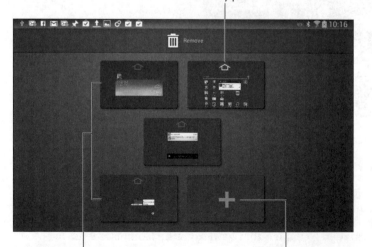

Drag thumbnails to rearrange.   Add a new, blank panel.

Figure 19-6: Manipulating Home screen pages.

Generally speaking, to rearrange the pages, long-press and drag it to a new spot. When you're done, touch the Back or Home icon.

- ✔ The maximum number of Home screen pages may be three, five, seven, or nine, depending on your tablet The minimum is one.

- ✔ On some tablets, the far right Home screen page is the Google Now app.

- ✔ Some tablets allow you to set the primary Home screen page, which doesn't necessarily have to be the center Home screen page. I've seen different ways to accomplish this task. The most common one is to touch the Home icon in a thumbnail's preview, which is what's illustrated in Figure 19-6.

- ✔ If you can't locate the Page command, if the Home screen lacks a long-press menu, and if pinching the screen doesn't work, touch the Menu icon. Choose the Edit Page command.

Android Tablet Security

Android tablets don't seem to have a secure lock. That screen-swipe thing is fancy, and it keeps the cat from unlocking the tablet, but it won't keep out the Bad Guys. A better form of protection is to employ a lock screen that's better than the standard sliding lock, as covered in this section.

Finding the locks

The keys to your Android tablet's screen locks are found within the Settings app. Here's how to get there:

1. **Open the Settings app.**

2. **Choose Security.**

   This item may have another name, such as Lock Screen. If you see both Security and Lock Screen items, choose Lock Screen.

   On some Samsung tablets, choose the Lock Screen item on the Device tab in the Settings app.

3. **Chose Screen Lock.**

   If you don't see a Screen Lock item, look for the item titled Set Up Screen Lock or Change Screen Lock.

If the screen lock is already set, you have to work the lock to proceed: Trace the pattern, or type the PIN or password. You then get access to the Choose Screen Lock screen, which shows several items. Among them you may find:

   Slide: Unlock the tablet by swiping your finger across the screen. This item might also be titled *Swipe*.

Pattern: Trace a pattern on the touchscreen to unlock the tablet.

PIN: Unlock the tablet by typing a personal identification number (PIN).

Password: Type a password to unlock the tablet.

Additional items might also appear, such as Face Unlock as well as any custom unlocking screens that were added by the tablet's manufacturer.

To set or remove a lock, refer to the following sections.

The Choose Screen Lock screen may also be called Select Screen Lock.

Removing the screen lock

You don't remove the screen lock on your Android tablet as much as you replace it. Therefore, to disable the pattern, PIN, or password screen lock, you visit the Choose Screen Lock screen (described in the preceding section) and choose the slide lock or swipe lock.

Another option available on some tablets is the None screen lock, which also disables all locks.

Setting a PIN

The PIN lock is second only to the password lock as the most secure for your Android tablet. To access the tablet, you must type a PIN, or personal identification number. This type of screen lock is also employed as a backup for less-secure screen unlocking methods, such as the pattern lock.

The *PIN lock* is a code between 4 and 16 numbers long. It contains only numbers, 0 through 9. To set the PIN lock for your Android tablet, follow the directions in the earlier section "Finding the locks" to reach the Choose Screen Lock screen. Choose PIN from the list of locks.

Use the onscreen keypad to type your PIN once. Touch the Continue button, and then type the same PIN again to confirm that you know it. Touch OK. The next time you unlock the tablet, you'll need to type the PIN to gain access.

To disable the PIN, reset the security level as described in the preceding section.

Assigning a password

The most secure way to lock an Android tablet is to apply a full-on password. Unlike a PIN, a *password* can contain numbers, symbols, and both upper- and lowercase letters.

Set a password by choosing Password from the Choose Screen Lock screen; refer to the earlier section "Finding the locks," for information on getting to that screen. The password you select must be at least four characters long. Longer passwords are more secure.

You're prompted to type the password whenever you unlock your Android tablet or whenever you try to change the screen lock. Touch the OK button to accept the password you've typed.

See the earlier section "Removing the screen lock," for information on resetting the password lock.

Creating an unlock pattern

One of the most common ways to lock an Android tablet is to apply an *unlock pattern*. The pattern must be traced exactly as it was created in order to unlock the device and get access to your apps and other features. To create an unlock pattern, follow along:

1. **Summon the Choose Screen Lock screen.**

   Refer to the earlier section "Finding the locks."

2. **Choose Pattern.**

   If you've not yet set a pattern lock, you may see a tutorial describing the process; touch the Next button to skip over the dreary directions.

3. **Trace an unlock pattern.**

   Use Figure 19-7 as your inspiration. You can trace over the dots in any order, but you can trace over a dot only once. The pattern must cover at least four dots.

4. **Touch the Continue button.**

5. **Redraw the pattern.**

   You need to prove to the doubtful tablet that you know the pattern.

6. **Touch the Confirm button.**

   Your tablet may require you to type a PIN or password as a backup to the pattern lock. If so, follow the onscreen directions to set that lock as well.

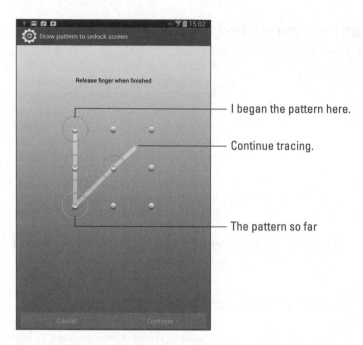

I began the pattern here.

Continue tracing.

The pattern so far

Figure 19-7: Set the unlock pattern.

Ensure that a check mark appears by the option Make Pattern Visible on the Screen or Screen Security screen. The check mark ensures that the pattern shows up. For even more security, you can disable the option, but you have to be sure to remember how — and where — the pattern goes.

✔ To remove the pattern lock, set the earlier section "Removing the screen lock."

✔ Wash your hands! Smudge marks on the display can betray your pattern.

Setting the owner info text

You can customize the lock screen by adding custom text that helps identify your Android tablet or simply displays a pithy saying for entertainment value. The feature is called Owner Info or Owner Information, so I suppose that the real reason is to type your name and contact info in case the tablet is lost or stolen.

TECHNICAL STUFF

Delaying the screen lock

Your tablet features a sleep time-out, a period of inactivity after which the tablet automatically locks. You can adjust that time-out, as described in this chapter's later section "Changing display settings," but you can also adjust how quickly the tablet locks after the time-out. The tablet can lock immediately, or you can set a delay during which the tablet can be unlocked by merely touching the screen.

To adjust the automatic lock, open the Settings app and choose the Security or Lock Screen item. Choose Automatically Lock to set how long the touchscreen waits to lock after the tablet's touchscreen display has a time-out. The Automatically Lock item appears only when a secure screen lock is set, so if you don't

see it, first set a secure lock. The value can be adjusted from Immediately to 30 minutes. The standard value is typically 5 seconds.

On some Samsung tablets, visit the Device tab in the Settings app and choose the Lock Screen item to find the Lock Automatically option. Use it to set the lock delay.

The Automatically Lock setting isn't enforced when you manually lock the tablet: Pressing the Power/Lock key always locks the tablet, applying whatever lock screen security you've set. But when the screen times out, the Automatically Lock delay value is used, which saves some time when the tablet tries to snooze on you.

To set the owner info for your Android tablet, follow these steps:

1. **Visit the Settings app.**

2. **Choose the Security or Lock Screen category.**

   On some Samsung tablets, Lock Screen category is found on the Device tab.

3. **Choose Owner Info or Owner Information.**

4. **Ensure that a check mark appears next to the Show Owner Info on Lock Screen option.**

 TIP

5. **Type text in the box.**

   You can type more than one line of text, though the information is displayed on the lock screen as a single line.

Whatever text you type in the box appears on the lock screen. Therefore, I recommend typing your name, address, phone number, e-mail, and so on. That way, should you lose your Android tablet and an honest person finds it, he or she can get it back to you.

The Owner Info doesn't show up on the lock screen when None is selected as a screen lock.

Various Adjustments

You'll find plenty of things to adjust, tune, and tweak on your Android tablet. The Settings app is the gateway to all those options, and I'm sure you could waste hours there, if you had hours to waste. My guess is that your time is precious; therefore, this section highlights some of the more worthy options and settings.

Singing a different tune

The Sound screen is where you control which sound the Android tablet plays for its notification alert, but it's also where you can set volume and vibration options.

To display the Sound screen, choose Sound from the Settings app screen. On some Samsung tablets, the Sound item is found by first touching the Device tab in the Settings app.

Some of the worthy options you'll find on the Sound screen include the following, although the specific names on your tablet may be slightly different from what's shown here:

Default Notification Sound: Choose which sound you want to hear for a notification alert. Choose a sound or choose Silent (at the top of the list) for no sound. This item may be titled Ringtone on some tablets.

Vibration: Choose the Vibration item to set whether the tablet vibrates during a notification and, potentially, how vigorously the tablet vibrates. Touch the OK button when you're done making adjustments. If you don't see this option, your Android tablet lacks the vibration feature.

Volumes: Though you can set the Android tablet volume using the Volume buttons on the side of the gizmo, the Volumes command on the Sound screen lets you set the volume for different types of sound events, such as music, video games, and notifications.

Touch Sounds: Put a check mark by this item so that you hear a faint click whenever you touch the screen. It's good for feedback.

Screen Lock Sound: I like having this item on because it lets me hear when the screen has locked.

You can put the Android tablet in Silent mode by pressing the Volume key all the way down until the sound is set to silence.

Changing display settings

The Settings app's Display item contains options and settings for adjusting the touchscreen. On some Samsung tablets, this item is found on the Settings app's Device tab.

Among the more popular items to set on the Display screen are these:

The Display item in the Settings app deals with touchscreen settings. Two popular settings worthy of your attention are the brightness and screen time-out options.

To access the Display screen, open the Settings app and choose Display.

Brightness: Use the slider to adjust the touchscreen's intensity. The Automatic Brightness setting sets the tablet's magical light sensor to determine how bright it is where you are.

Sleep or Screen Timeout: Select a time-out value from the list. This duration specifies when the tablet automatically locks the touchscreen.

A Brightness setting may also be in the Quick Actions drawer or in the notifications drawer.

20

Maintenance, Troubleshooting, and Help

Maintenance for your Android tablet is a lot easier than in the old days. Back in the 1970s, tablet computer owners were required to completely disassemble their devices and hand-clean every nut and sprocket with solvent and a wire brush. Special cloth was necessary to sop up all the electrical oil. It was a nightmare, which is why most people never did tablet maintenance back then.

Today, things are different. Android tablet maintenance is rather carefree, involving little more than cleaning the thing every so often. No disassembly is required. Beyond covering maintenance, this chapter offers suggestions for using the battery, gives you some helpful tips, and provides a Q&A section.

The Maintenance Chore

Relax. Maintenance of an Android tablet is simple and quick. Basically, I can summarize it in three words: Keep it clean. Beyond that, another maintenance task worthy of attention is backing up the information stored on your tablet.

Keeping it clean

You probably already keep your Android tablet clean. Perhaps you're one of those people who uses their sleeves to wipe the touchscreen. Of course, better than your sleeve is something called a *microfiber cloth.* This item can be found at any computer- or office-supply store.

✔ Never use any liquid to clean the touchscreen — especially ammonia or alcohol. Those harsh chemicals damage the touchscreen, rendering it unable to detect your input. Further, they can smudge the display, making it more difficult to see.

✔ Touchscreen-safe screen cleaners are available for those times when your sleeve or even a microfiber cloth won't cut it. Ensure that you get a screen cleaner designed for a touchscreen.

✔ If the screen keeps getting dirty, consider adding a *screen protector:* This specially designed cover prevents the screen from getting scratched or dirty but still allows you to use your finger on the touchscreen. Be sure that the screen protector is designed for use with the specific brand and model of your Android tablet.

Backing up your stuff

A *backup* is a safety copy of information. For your Android tablet, the backup copy includes contact information, music, photos, videos, and apps you've installed — plus, any settings you've made to customize your tablet. Copying that information to another source is one way to keep the information safe in case anything happens to your tablet.

Yes, a backup is a good thing. Lamentably, there's no universal method of backing up the stuff on your Android tablet.

Your Google account information is backed up automatically. That information includes the tablet's address book, Gmail inbox, and Calendar app appointments. Because that information automatically syncs with the Internet, a backup is always present.

To confirm that your Google account information is being backed up, heed these steps:

1. **At the Home screen, touch the Apps icon.**

2. **Choose Settings.**

3. **Display your Google account information.**

   On the stock Android version of the Settings app, swipe down the screen until you find the Accounts heading. Choose Google.

   On some Samsung tablets, choose the General tab to find the Accounts item. Choose Google from the right side of the screen.

4. **Touch the green Sync icon by your Gmail address.**

The Sync icon is shown in the margin, although it may appear slightly different on your tablet's screen.

5. **Ensure that check marks appear by every item in the list.**

Yeah, there are a lot of items. Each one needs a check mark if you want that item backed up.

6. **Touch the Back icon twice to return to the main Settings app screen.**

7. **Choose Backup & Reset.**

The command may also read as Back Up and Reset, or some such similar variation.

8. **Ensure that a check mark appears by the item Back Up My Data.**

You should see a blue check mark there. If not, touch the square to add one.

Beyond your Google account, which is automatically backed up, the rest of the information can be manually backed up. You can copy files from the tablet's internal storage to your computer as a form of backup. See Chapter 17 for information on manually copying files and folders between the Android tablet and your computer.

Yes, I agree: Manual backup isn't an example of technology making your life easier.

A backup of the data stored on an Android tablet would include all data, including photos, videos, and music. Specifically, the folders you should copy are DCIM, Download, and Music. Additional folders to copy include folders named after apps you've downloaded, such as Aldiko, Kindle, Kobo, Layar, and other folders named after the apps that created them.

Updating the system

Every so often, a new version of the Android tablet's operating system becomes available. It's an *Android* update because Android is the name of the operating system, not because the Android tablet thinks that it's some type of robot.

When an automatic update occurs, you see an alert or a message indicating that a system upgrade is available, similar to the one shown in Figure 20-1. My advice is to choose Restart & Install and — as long as the tablet has a good charge or is plugged in — proceed with the upgrade.

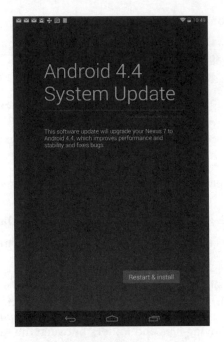

Figure 20-1: An Android update looms in your tablet's future.

✔ Yes, you can put off an update by simply dismissing the update notice (refer to Figure 20-1): Touch the Home icon. I do, however, strongly recommend that you upgrade.

✔ You can manually check for updates: In the Settings app, choose About Tablet or About Device. (On Samsung tablets, look on the General tab in the Settings app.) Choose System Updates or Software Update. When the system is up-to-date, the screen tells you so. Otherwise, you find directions for updating the Android operating system.

✔ Touching the Check Now button isn't magic. When an update is available, the tablet lets you know.

✔ Non-Android system updates might also be issued. For example, the tablet's manufacturer may send out an update to the Android tablet's guts. This type of update is often called a *firmware* update. As with Android updates, my advice is to accept all firmware updates.

Battery Care and Feeding

Perhaps the most important item you can monitor and maintain on your Android tablet is its battery. The battery supplies the necessary electrical juice by which the device operates. Without battery power, your tablet is basically an expensive trivet. Keep an eye on the battery.

Monitoring the battery

Android tablets display the current battery status at the top of the screen, in the status area, next to the time. The icons used to display battery status are similar to the icons shown in Figure 20-2. They can appear white-on-black or use a charming color scheme, as illustrated in the figure.

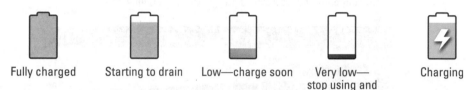

Fully charged   Starting to drain   Low—charge soon   Very low— stop using and charge at once!   Charging

Figure 20-2: Battery status icons.

You might also see an icon for a dead battery, but for some reason I can't get my Android tablet to turn on and display that icon.

- Heed those low-battery warnings! The tablet sounds a notification whenever the battery power gets low. Another notification sounds whenever the battery gets *very* low.

- When the battery level is too low, the Android tablet shuts itself off.

- The best way to deal with low battery power is to connect the tablet to a power source: Either plug it into a wall socket or connect it to a computer by using a USB cable. The tablet begins charging itself immediately; plus, you can use the device while it's charging.

- The tablet charges more efficiently when it's plugged into a wall socket rather than a computer.

- You don't have to fully charge the Android tablet to use it. When you have only 20 minutes to charge and you get only a 70 percent battery level, that's great. Well, it's not great, but it's far better than a lower battery level.

- Battery percentage values are best-guess estimates. Your Android tablet has a hearty battery that can last for hours. But when the battery meter gets low, the battery drains faster. So, if you get 8 hours of use from the tablet and the battery meter shows 20 percent remaining, those numbers don't imply that 20 percent equals 2 more hours of use. In practice, the amount of time you have left is much less than that. As a rule, when the battery percentage value gets low, the battery appears to drain faster.

Determining what is drawing power

An Android tablet is smart enough to know which of its features and apps use the most battery power. You can check it out for yourself on the Battery Usage screen, similar to what's shown in Figure 20-3.

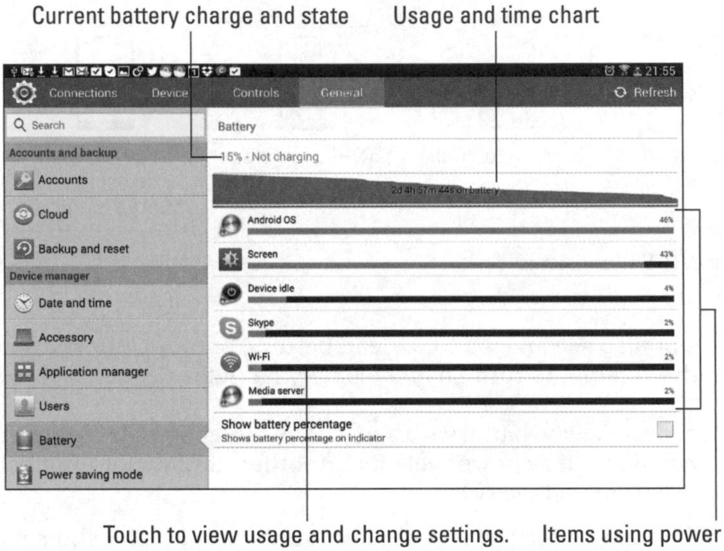

Current battery charge and state   Usage and time chart

Touch to view usage and change settings.   Items using power

Figure 20-3: Things that drain the battery.

To view the battery usage screen on your tablet, open the Settings app and choose the Battery item. On some Samsung tablets, touch the General tab in the Settings app to locate the Battery item (refer to Figure 20-3).

Touch an item in the list to view specific details. For some items, such as Wi-Fi (shown in Figure 20-3), the details screen contains a button that lets you adjust the setting — in this case, to turn off Wi-Fi.

The number and variety of items listed on the battery usage screen depend on what you've been doing with your tablet between charges and how many different apps you've been using. Don't be surprised if an item doesn't show up in the list, such as the Play Books app. Not every app uses a lot of battery power.

✔ Carefully note which applications consume the most battery power. You can curb your use of these apps to conserve juice — though, honestly, your savings are negligible. See the next section for battery-saving advice.

✔ Not everything you've done shows up on the battery usage screen. (Refer to Figure 20-4.) For example, even after I spent half an hour reading a Kindle book, Kindle didn't show up. Also, I've seen the Gallery app show up from time to time, even though I've not used it.

Extending battery life

A surefire way to make a battery last a good long time is to never turn on the device in the first place. That's kind of impractical, so rather than let you use your Android tablet as an expensive paperweight, I offer a smattering of suggestions you can follow to help prolong battery life in your tablet.

Dim the screen: Refer to Figure 20-4 and you can see that the display (labeled Screen) sucks down quite a lot of battery power. Although a dim screen can be more difficult to see, especially outdoors, it definitely saves on battery life.

Adjust the screen brightness from the Settings app, or you can choose the Brightness Quick Action from the Quick Actions drawer.

Lower the volume: Additionally, consider lowering the volume for the various noises the Android tablet makes, especially notifications. Information on setting volume options is also found in Chapter 19.

Disable the vibration options. The tablet's vibration is caused by a teensy motor. Though you don't see much battery savings by disabling the vibration options, it's better than no savings. To turn off vibration, see Chapter 19.

Turn off Bluetooth: When you're not using Bluetooth, turn it off. The fastest way to do that is to use the Bluetooth Quick Action. See Chapter 16 for information on Bluetooth.

Turn off Wi-Fi: Because I tend to use Wi-Fi in only one spot, I keep the tablet plugged in. Away from a single location, however, Wi-Fi "wanders" and isn't useful for an Internet connection, anyway. So why not turn it off? Refer to Chapter 16 for information on Wi-Fi.

Manage battery performance. Several Android tablets come with battery-saving software built in. You can access the software from a special app or from the Battery item in the Settings app. Similar to a computer, battery-performance management involves turning tablet features on or off during certain times of the day. Third-party battery-management apps are also available at the Google Play Store. See Chapter 15.

Help and Troubleshooting

Wouldn't it be great if you could have an avuncular Mr. Wizard type available at a moment's notice? He could just walk in and, with a happy smile on his face and a reassuring hand on your shoulder, let you know what the problem is and how to fix it. Then he'd give you a cookie. Never mind that such a thing would be creepy — getting helpful advice is worth it.

Fixing random and annoying problems

Here are some typical problems you may encounter on your Android tablet and my suggestions for a solution:

General trouble: For just about any problem or minor quirk, consider restarting the tablet by turning it off and then turning it on again. This procedure will most likely fix a majority of the annoying problems you encounter.

Some tablets feature the Restart command on the Device Options menu: Press and hold the Power/Lock key to see this menu. If a Restart command is there, use it to restart the tablet and fix whatever has gone awry.

Check the mobile data connection: As you move about, the mobile-data signal can change. In fact, you may observe the status bar icon change from 4G to 3G to even the dreaded 1X or — worse — nothing, depending on the strength and availability of the cellular data service.

My advice for random signal weirdness is to wait. Oftentimes, the signal comes back after a few minutes. If it doesn't, the mobile data network might be down, or you may just be in an area with lousy service. Consider changing your location.

Check the Wi-Fi connection: Ensure that the Wi-Fi network is set up properly and working. This process usually involves pestering the person who configured the Wi-Fi router or, in a coffee shop, bothering the cheerful person with the bad haircut who serves you coffee.

Reset the Wi-Fi connection: Perhaps the issue isn't with the tablet at all but rather with the Wi-Fi network. Some networks have a "lease time" after which your tablet might be disconnected. If so, follow the directions in Chapter 16 for turning off the tablet's Wi-Fi and then turn it on again. That often solves the issue.

For a home or small-office network, Wi-Fi connection problems might be resolved by restarting the router: Unplug the router, wait about a minute, and then plug the router back in. Especially for older routers, this trick solves many connection issues. (Getting a new router is the long-term solution.)

Music is playing and you want it to stop: It's awesome that your tablet continues to play music while you do other things. Getting the music to stop quickly, however, requires some skill. You can access the play controls for the Play Music app from a number of locations. They're found on the lock screen, for example. You can also find them in the notifications drawer.

An app has run amok: Sometimes, apps that misbehave let you know. You see a warning on the screen announcing the app's stubborn disposition, such as the warning shown in Figure 20-4. When that happens, touch the Force Close button to shut down the errant app.

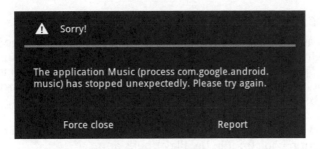

Figure 20-4: Halting an app run amok.

When you don't see a warning or when an app appears to be unduly obstinate, you can shut 'er down the manual way, as covered in Chapter 15.

Reset the Android tablet software: When all else fails, you can do the drastic thing and reset all tablet software, essentially returning it to the state it was in when it first popped out of the box. Obviously, do not perform this step lightly. In fact, consider finding support (see the later section "Getting support") before you start the following process:

1. **Open the Settings app.**

2. **Choose Backup and Reset.**

   On some Samsung tablets, the Backup and Reset item is found on the General tab.

3. **Choose Factory Data Reset.**

4. **Touch the Reset Tablet or Reset Device button.**

5. **Unlock the tablet.**

   If you've configured additional screen locks, you need to work the lock before you can proceed.

6. **Touch the Erase Everything button or Delete All button to confirm.**

   All the information you've set or stored on the Android tablet is purged. That includes apps you've downloaded, music, synchronized accounts — everything.

Again, do not follow these steps unless you're certain that they will fix the problem or you're under orders to do so from someone in tech support.

You can also choose to reset the tablet's software and erase everything should you ever return or sell your Android tablet. Of course, you probably love your tablet so much that the mere thought of selling it makes you blanch.

Finding help

Some tablet manufacturers, as well as cellular providers, offer more help than others. Though it's not part of stock Android, some tablets come supplied with the Help app. It may be called Help or Help Center or something similar, and it may not be the kind of avuncular, well-written help you get from this book, but it's better than nothing.

You may find the old, dratted manual lurking in eBook form, which doesn't make it any better. Look for it in the Play Books app.

A Guided Tour app or Tutorial app may also be available, which helps you understand how to work some of the tablet's interesting features.

Getting support

You can use several sources for support for your Android tablet. So no matter how isolated you feel, help is amply available.

For app issues, contact the developer in the Play Store app, which is covered in Chapter 15.

For issues with the Play Store, contact Google at

```
support.google.com/googleplay
```

If you have a cellular tablet and you're a current mobile-data subscriber, you can get help from the cellular provider. Table 20-1 lists contact information for U.S. cellular providers.

Table 20-1	U.S. Cellular Providers	
Provider	*Toll-free Number*	*Website*
AT&T	800-331-0500	`www.att.com/esupport`
Sprint Nextel	800-211-4727	`mysprint.sprint.com`
T-Mobile	800-866-2453	`www.t-mobile.com/Contact.aspx`
Verizon	800-922-0204	`http://support.vzw.com/clc`

Support might also be available from your tablet's manufacturer, such as Asus, Samsung, or LG. Information about support can be found in those random papers and pamphlets included in the box your Android tablet comes in. Remember how in Chapter 1 I tell you not to throw that stuff out? This is why.

When contacting support, it helps to know the device's ID and Android operating system version number:

1. **Open the Settings app.**

2. **On some Samsung tablets, touch the General tab.**

3. **Choose About Tablet or About Device.**

   The tablet's model number, as well as the Android version, is listed on the About screen.

Jot down the model number and Android version! Do it right here:

Model number: _____

Android version: _____

Valuable Tablet Q&A

I love Q&A! Not only is it an effective way to express certain problems and solutions, but some of the questions might also cover things I've been wanting to ask.

"I can't turn the tablet on (or off)!"

Yes, sometimes an Android tablet locks up. It's frustrating, but I've discovered that if you press and hold the Power/Lock key for about 8 seconds, the tablet turns either off or on, depending on which state it's in.

I've had a program lock my tablet tight when the 8-second Power/Lock key trick didn't work. In that case, I waited 12 minutes or so, just letting the tablet sit there and do nothing. Then I pressed and held the Power/Lock key for about 8 seconds, and it turned itself back on.

"The touchscreen doesn't work!"

A touchscreen, such as the one on the Android tablet, requires a human finger for proper interaction. The tablet interprets the static potential between the human finger and the device to determine where the touchscreen is being touched.

You can use the touchscreen while wearing special touchscreen gloves. Yes, they actually make such things. But for regular gloves? Nope.

The touchscreen might fail also when the battery power is low or when the Android tablet has been physically damaged.

I've been informed that there's an Android app for cats. This implies that the touchscreen can also interpret a feline paw for proper interaction. Either that or the cat can hold a human finger in its mouth and manipulate the app that way. Because I don't have the app, I can't tell for certain.

"The screen is too dark!"

Android tablets feature a teensy light sensor on the front. The sensor is used to adjust the touchscreen's brightness based on the amount of ambient light at your location. If the sensor is covered, the screen can get very, very dark.

Ensure that you don't unintentionally block the light sensor. Avoid buying a case or screen protector that obscures the sensor.

The automatic brightness setting might also be vexing you. See Chapter 19 for information on setting screen brightness.

"The battery doesn't charge!"

Start from the source: Is the wall socket providing power? Is the cord plugged in? The cable may be damaged, so try another cable.

When charging from a USB port on a computer, ensure that the computer is turned on. Most computers don't provide USB power when they're turned off.

Some tablets may charge from a special cord, not the USB cable. Check to confirm that your tablet is able to take a charge from the USB cable.

"The tablet gets so hot that it turns itself off!"

Yikes! An overheating gadget can be a nasty problem. Judge how hot the tablet is by seeing whether you can hold it in your hand: When it's too hot to hold, it's *too* hot. If you're using the tablet to cook an egg, it's too hot.

Turn off your Android tablet and let the battery cool.

If the overheating problem continues, have the Android tablet looked at for potential repair. The battery might need to be replaced. As far as I can tell, there's no way to remove and replace the Android tablet battery by yourself.

Do not continue to use any gizmo that's too hot! The heat damages the electronics. It can also start a fire.

"My tablet doesn't do Landscape mode!"

Not every app takes advantage of the tablet's capability to reorient itself when you rotate the device between Portrait and Landscape modes — or even Upside-Down mode. For example, many games set their orientations one way and refuse to change, no matter how you hold the tablet. So, just because the app doesn't go into Horizontal or Vertical mode doesn't mean that anything is broken.

Confirm that the orientation lock isn't on: Check the Quick Actions. Ensure that the Rotation Lock item isn't turned on; if so, the screen doesn't reorient itself.

Part V
The Part of Tens

Enjoy an additional *Android Tablets For Dummies* Part of Tens chapter online at www.dummies.com/extras/androidtablets.

In this part . . .

- ✔ Behold ten useful tips and tricks for getting the most from your Android tablet.

- ✔ Find out ten important things you shouldn't forget.

- ✔ Discover ten useful, free apps that help boost your tablet's capabilities.

Ten Tips, Tricks, and Shortcuts

A tip is a small suggestion, a word of advice often spoken from bruising experience or knowledge passed along from someone with bruising experience. A *trick,* which is something not many know about, usually causes amazement or surprise. A *shortcut* is a quick way to get home, even though it crosses the old graveyard and you never quite know whether Old Man Witherspoon is the groundskeeper or a zombie.

I'd like to think that just about everything in this book is a tip, trick, or shortcut for using an Android tablet. Even so, I've distilled a list of items in this chapter that are definitely worthy of note.

Quickly Switch Apps

Android apps don't quit. Sure, some of them have a Quit or Sign Out command, but most apps lurk inside the tablet's memory while you do other things. The Android operating system may eventually kill off a stale app. Before that happens, you can deftly and quickly switch between all running apps.

The key to making the switch is to use the Recent icon, found at the bottom of the touchscreen. On tablets that lack the Recent icon, long-press the Home icon. To switch to an app, choose it from the list. To dismiss the list, touch the Back icon or Home icon.

- ✔ To remove an app from the Recent list, swipe it left or right.

- ✔ Some tablets may feature a Task Manager, either in the form of an app or, often, as an icon found at the bottom of the Recent app list.

- ✔ The difference between a Task Manager and the Recent app list is that the Task Manager lets you kill off running apps. That brutal step isn't necessary, but some people take great satisfaction in the feature.

Add Lock Screen Widgets

Just as you can adorn the Home screen with widgets, you can also slap down a few right on the Lock screen. In fact, the time display on your tablet's lock screen is most like a widget. It's only one of several.

To add a lock screen widget, touch the large Plus icon on the lock screen. If you don't see that icon, swipe the lock screen left or right. Choose a widget to add from the list that's displayed, such as the Calendar, Gmail, Digital Clock, or another widget.

If you can't swipe the lock screen or see the large Plus icon, your tablet may not sport the lock-screen widget feature.

- ✔ Multiple widgets can be placed on the lock screen, though you can see only one at a time. Swipe the screen to see others.

- ✔ To remove a lock screen widget, long-press it. Drag the widget up to the Remove icon and it's gone. You can even remove the Clock widget, in which case only the large Plus icon appears on the lock screen.

Choose Default Apps

Every so often, you may see the Complete Action Using prompt, similar to the one shown in Figure 21-1.

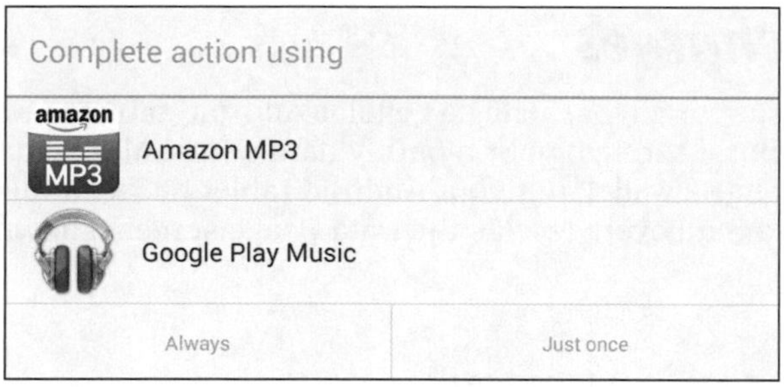

Figure 21-1: The Complete Action Using question is posed.

Multiple apps are available that can deal with your request. You pick one and then choose either Always or Just Once.

When you choose Always, the same app is always used for whatever action took place: listening to music, choosing a photo, or navigating, for example.

When you choose Just Once, you see the prompt again and again.

My advice is to choose Just Once until you get sick of seeing the Complete Action using prompt. At that point, after choosing the same app over and over, choose Always.

The fear, of course, is that you'll make a mistake. Fret not, gentle reader. The settings you choose can always be undone. For example, if you chose Google Play Music, shown in Figure 21-1, you can undo that setting by following these steps:

1. **Open the Settings app.**

2. **Choose Apps or Application Manager.**

   On some Samsung tablets, first choose the General tab in the Settings app to find the Application Manager item.

3. **Locate the app you chose to "always" use.**

   This is the tough step, in that you may not remember your choice. The way I can tell is when the same app opens and I don't really want it to.

4. **Touch the app to display its detailed information screen.**

5. **Touch the Clear Defaults button.**

   The tablet immediately forgets to always use that app.

After you clear the defaults for an app, you most likely will see the Complete Action Using prompt again. The next time you see it, however, make a better choice.

Avoid Data Surcharges

An important issue for anyone using a cellular Android tablet is whether you're about to burst through your monthly data quota. Mobile data surcharges can pinch the wallet, but your Android tablet has a handy tool to help you avoid data overages. It's the Data Usage screen, shown in Figure 21-2.

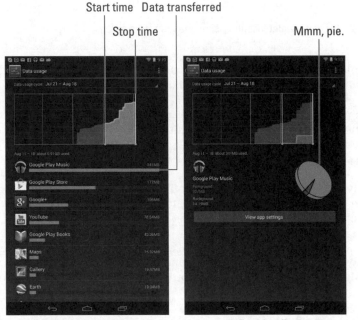

Start time   Data transferred

Stop time   Mmm, pie.

Data Usage screen   App details

Figure 21-2: Data usage (Wi-Fi tablet version).

To access the Data Usage screen, follow these steps:

1. **Open the Settings app.**

2. **Choose Data Usage.**

   On some Samsung tablets, you'll find the Data Usage item by choosing the Connections tab at the top of the Settings app screen.

The main screen is full of useful information and handy tools. The line chart (refer to Figure 21-2) informs you of your data usage over a specific period. You can touch the Data Usage Cycle action bar to set that timespan, for example, matching it up with your cellular provider's monthly billing cycle.

Figure 21-2 shows the Wi-Fi tablet's Data Usage screen. The cellular tablet's screen features additional options:

- Touch the Mobile Data item to monitor your cellular data usage.

- Touch the Limit Mobile Data Usage item to summon a red bar, which you can adjust based on your monthly data quota. When mobile data usage crosses that line, the tablet's mobile data access is restricted.

- Touch the Alert Me About Data Usage item to summon an orange bar. Adjust the orange bar to direct the tablet to display a warning message whenever usage crosses that threshold.

To review access for a specific app, scroll down and choose it from those shown on the Data Usage screen. Only apps that access the network appear. After choosing the app, detailed information shows up, similar to what's shown on the right in Figure 21-2. If you notice that the app is using more data than it should, touch the View App Settings button. You may be able to adjust some settings to curtail unintended Internet access.

Make the Tablet Dream

Does your tablet lock, or does it fall asleep? I prefer to think that the tablet sleeps. That begs the question of whether or not it dreams.

Of course it does! You can even see the dreams, providing you activate the Daydream feature — and you keep the tablet connected to a power source or in a docking station. Heed these steps:

1. **Start the Settings app.**

2. **Choose Display and then Daydream.**

   The Display item is found on the Device tab on some Samsung tablets.

3. **Ensure that the Daydream master control is in the On position.**

4. **Choose which type of daydream you want displayed.**

   Clock is a popular item, though I'm fond of Colors.

   Some daydreams feature the Settings icon, which can be used to customize how the daydream appears.

5. **Touch the When to Daydream button.**

6. **Choose the Either option.**

The daydreaming begins when the screen would normally time-out and lock. So if you've set the tablet to lock after 1 minute of inactivity, it daydreams instead — as long as it's plugged in or docked.

- To disrupt the dream, swipe the screen.

- The tablet doesn't lock when it daydreams. To lock the tablet, press the Power/Lock key.

Add Spice to Dictation

I feel that too few people use dictation, despite how handy it can be. Anyway, if you've used dictation, you might have noticed that it occasionally censors some of the words you utter. Perhaps you're the kind of person who doesn't put up with that kind of s***

Relax. You can lift the vocal censorship ban by following these steps:

1. **Start the Settings app.**

2. **Choose Language & Input.**

   On some Samsung tablets, you'll find the Language and Input item on the Controls tab in the Settings app.

3. **Touch the Settings icon by the item Google Voice Typing.**

4. **Remove the check mark by the option Block Offensive Words.**

And just what are offensive words? I would think that *censorship* is an offensive word. But no, apparently only a few choice words fall into this category. I won't print them here, because the tablet's censor retains the initial letter and generally makes the foul language easy to guess. D***.

Add a Word to the Dictionary

Betcha didn't know that your tablet sports a dictionary. The dictionary is used to keep track of words you type — words that may not be recognized as being spelled properly.

Words unknown to the tablet are highlighted on the screen. Sometimes the word is shown in a different color or on a different background, and sometimes it's underlined. To add that word to the tablet's dictionary, long-press it. You see the Add Word to Dictionary command, which sticks the word in the tablet's dictionary.

To review or edit the tablet's dictionary, follow these steps:

1. **Start the Settings app.**
2. **Choose Language & Input.**
3. **Choose Personal Dictionary.**

   The command may not be obvious on some tablets: Try choosing the keyboard first, and then choose either the Dictionary or User Dictionary command.

When the dictionary is visible, you can review words, edit them, remove them, or manually add new ones. To edit or delete a word, long-press it. To add a word, choose the Add icon.

The dictionary may not be accessible on all tablets.

Employ Some Useful Widgets

Your tablet features a wide assortment of widgets with which to festoon the Home screen. Of the lot, I prefer contact and navigation widgets.

For the folks you contact most frequently, consider slapping down some contact widgets. Here's how:

1. **Touch the Apps icon to visit the Apps drawer.**
2. **Touch the Widgets tab.**
3. **Choose the Contact widget: Long-press that widget and drag it to a position on the Home screen.**

   Specific directions for adding widgets are presented in Chapter 19.
4. **Select a contact.**

A widget representing the contact (with the contact's picture, if available) appears on the Home screen. Touching the widget displays information about the contact, similar to what's shown in Figure 21-3.

Another handy widget to add to the Home screen is the Directions widget. Follow Steps 1 through 3 in the preceding list, but choose the Directions widget in Step 3. Then type the location where you want to go. At this point, creating the widget works like getting directions in the Maps app. Touch the widget to summon the Maps app and get directions from your location.

See Chapter 10 for more information about using the Maps app.

Figure 21-3: A contact shortcut on the Home screen.

Add Another User

Computers have had the capability to allow multiple users for some time — even though I believe that people seldom use this feature. The whole motif of the personal computer is supposed to be one-computer-one-person, right? Your Android tablet should be the same, but just like your computer, your tablet can have more than one user account.

Over my objections, some tablets allow you to configure multiple users — several people who can have their own custom Home screens, widgets, and other options on a single tablet.

To add another user, follow these steps:

1. **Open the Settings app and choose Users.**

   On Samsung tablets, look on the General tab for the Users item.

   If you don't find the Users category, your tablet doesn't have this feature.

2. **Touch the Add User button.**

3. **Read the information (or not) and touch OK.**

4. **Configure the new user.**

   Touch the Set Up Now button to configure the user, or, better, hand the tablet to the other user and let that person configure it. The configuration process is basically the same setup procedure you suffered through when you first turned on the tablet.

All accounts on the tablet appear at the bottom of the lock screen, similar to what's shown in Figure 21-4.

User accounts

Figure 21-4: Choosing accounts on the lock screen.

To use the tablet as a specific user, touch the account circle on the lock screen (refer to Figure 21-4).

- I highly recommend that you apply a PIN or password to your account if you'll have multiple users on a single Android tablet.

- The tablet's first user (most likely, you) is the main user, the one who has primary administrative control.

- When you're done using the tablet, lock the screen. Other users can then access their own accounts.

- Remove an account by visiting the Users screen in the Settings app. Touch the Trash icon next to an account to remove it. Touch the Delete button to confirm.

- I don't like having separate users on my tablet. It makes a simple device complicated. With the tablet's low cost, it just makes more sense to have a second user get his own Android tablet — and, of course, his own copy of *Android Tablets For Dummies*.

Find Your Lost Tablet

Someday, you may lose your Android tablet — for a panic-filled few seconds or forever. The hardware solution is to weld a heavy object to the tablet, such as a bowling ball or furnace, yet that kind of defeats the entire mobile/wireless paradigm. The software solution is to use a cellular tablet locator service.

Tablet locator services employ apps that use a tablet's cellular signal as well as its GPS to help locate the missing gizmo. Even if you have a Wi-Fi–only tablet, the service still works, which is why I recommend it. These types of apps are available at the Google Play Store. One that I've tried and recommend is Lookout Mobile Security.

Lookout features two different apps. One is free, which you can try to see whether you like it. The paid app offers more features and better locating services. As with similar apps, you must register at a website to help you locate your tablet, should it go wandering.

Visit Chapter 15 for information about the Google Play Store, where you can obtain copies of the Lookout security app and search for other tablet-finding apps.

Ten Things to Remember

*H*ave you ever tried to tie a string around your finger to remember something? I've not attempted that technique just yet. The main reason is that I keep forgetting to buy string and I have no way to remind myself.

For your Android tablet, some things are definitely worth remembering. Out of the long, long list, I've come up with ten good ones.

Dictate Text

Dictation is such a handy feature — don't forget to use it! You can dictate most text instead of typing it. Just touch the Microphone key on the keyboard — or anywhere you see the Microphone icon — and begin speaking. Your utterances are translated to text. In most cases, the translation is instantaneous.

See Chapter 4 for more information on Android tablet dictation.

Change the Tablet's Orientation

Larger-format Android tablets have a natural horizontal orientation. Smaller tablets beg to be held vertically. You won't break any law by changing the tablet's orientation.

Apps such as Chrome and Email can look much better in the horizontal orientation, whereas apps such as Play Books and Play Music can look much better in the vertical orientation. The key to changing orientation is to rotate the tablet to view the app the way you like best. Rotate!

✔ Not every app changes its orientation. Some apps — specifically, games — appear in only one orientation: landscape or portrait.

✔ eBook reader apps have screen rotation settings that let you lock the orientation to the way you want, regardless of what the tablet is doing.

Work the Quick Actions

Many tablet controls are available at a single, handy location: the Quick Actions drawer. Pull it down to turn tablet features on or off, such as Wi-Fi, Bluetooth, screen orientation, and other On–Off settings. Using the Quick Actions drawer is far more expedient than visiting the Settings app.

✔ On some tablets, the Quick Actions appear in the notifications drawer.

✔ Some tablets feature a vast array of Quick Actions, only a handful of which appear at a time. Try swiping the Quick Actions left or right to see more.

✔ As a bonus, many Quick Actions drawers feature a shortcut to the Settings app.

Employ Keyboard Suggestions

Don't forget to take advantage of the suggestions that appear above the onscreen keyboard when you're typing text. In fact, you don't even need to touch a suggestion; to replace your text with the highlighted suggestion, simply touch the onscreen keyboard's Space key. Zap! The word appears.

To ensure that suggestions are enabled, follow these steps:

1. **Start the Settings app.**

2. **Choose Language & Input.**

   On some Samsung tablets, touch the Controls tab and then choose Language and Input.

3. **Touch the Settings icon by the Google Keyboard item.**

   Samsung tablets might refer to this item as Samsung Keyboard.

4. **Ensure that there's a check mark by the item Next-Word Suggestions.**

   This item might be titled Predictive Text.

Also refer to Chapter 4 for additional information on using the keyboard suggestions.

Avoid the Battery Hogs

Three items on an Android tablet suck down battery power faster than a massive alien fleet is defeated by a plucky antihero who just wants the girl:

- ✔ Navigation
- ✔ The display
- ✔ Wireless radios

Navigation is certainly handy, but the battery drains rapidly because the tablet's touchscreen is on the entire time and the speaker is dictating text to you. If possible, plug the tablet into the car's power socket when you're navigating.

The display is obviously a most necessary part of your Android tablet — but it's also a tremendous power hog. The Auto Brightness setting is your best friend for saving power with the display. If you shun Auto Brightness, avoid setting the screen to its maximum shine. That may make it easier to read outdoors, but the power will drain faster than your bank account at Christmas.

Wireless radios include Wi-Fi networking, Bluetooth, and GPS. Though they do require extra power, they aren't power hogs, like navigation and the display. Still, when power is getting low, consider disabling those items.

See Chapter 20 for more information on managing the tablet's battery.

Use a Docking Stand

When I'm not on the road, I tend to keep my tablet in one spot: in a multimedia stand designed to support my specific Android tablet. The stand is a helpful way to hold the tablet, to keep it propped up and easy to access. Because I use the stand as home base for my tablet, I always know where it is, and because I don't have the cleanest of desktops, I can always find the tablet despite ominous swells in seas of paper.

✔ Not every Android tablet has a companion docking stand. Sending the tablet's manufacturer an emotional letter begging them to produce such a stand doesn't seem to help.

✔ Given the choice of a multimedia stand or a keyboard dock, I prefer the multimedia stand. Though keyboard stands are nice, they occupy too much room for my desktop. The multimedia stand for my tablet also offers USB and HDMI output, which is nice to have.

Make Phone Calls

Yeah, I know: It's not a phone. Even Android tablets that use the cellular data system for Internet access cannot make phone calls. Why let that stop you?

Using the Skype app, you can place phone calls and video-chat with your friends. Skype even lets you dial into real phones, as long as you boost your account with some Skype Credit. See Chapter 9 for details.

Check Your Schedule

The Calendar app can certainly be handy to remind you of upcoming dates and generally keep you on schedule. A great way to augment the calendar is to employ the Calendar widget on the Home screen.

The Calendar widget lists the current date and then a long list of upcoming appointments. It's a great way to check your schedule, especially when you use your tablet all the time. I recommend sticking the Calendar widget right on the center Home screen panel.

✔ See Chapter 19 for information on adding widgets to the Home screen; Chapter 14 covers the Calendar app.

✔ As long as I'm handing out tips, remember to specify location information when you set up an appointment in the Calendar app. Type the information just as though you were using the Maps app to search. You can then quickly navigate to your next appointment by touching the location item when you review the event.

Snap a Pic of That Contact

Here's something I always forget: Whenever you're near one of your contacts, take the person's picture. Sure, some people are bashful, but most folks are flattered. The idea is to build up the tablet's address book so that all your contacts have photos.

When taking a picture, be sure to show it to the person before you assign it to the contact. Let them decide whether it's good enough. Or, if you just want to be rude, assign a crummy-looking picture. Heck, you don't even have to do that: Just assign to a contact a random picture of anything. A plant. A rock. Your cat. But seriously, keep in mind that your tablet can take a contact's picture the next time you meet up with that person.

Use Google Now

Google is known worldwide for its searching capabilities and its popular website. By gum, the word *Google* is synonymous with searching. So please don't forget that your Android tablet, which uses the Google Android operating system, has a powerful search, nay, *knowledge* command. It's called Google Now.

✔ On most Android tablets, you access Google Now by swiping the screen from bottom to top. This trick may even work on the lock screen.

✔ The Google Now app is titled Google.

✔ The Google Search widget provides a shortcut into Google Now.

✔ Review Chapter 14 for details on various Google Now commands.

✔ Beyond Google Now, you can take advantage of the various Search icons found in just about every app on an Android tablet. Use the Search icon to search for information, locations, people — you name it. It's handy.

Ten Great Free Apps

Hundreds of thousands of apps are available at the Google Play Store — so many that it would take you more than a relaxing evening to discover them all. Rather than list every single app, I've culled from the lot some that I find exceptional — that show the diversity of the Google Play Store but also how well your tablet can run Android apps.

Every app listed in this chapter is free; see Chapter 15 for directions on finding them using the Google Play Store.

ASTRO File Manager

Consider yourself fortunate when your Android tablet comes with a file manager app — even when you never plan on using the thing. Even if your tablet comes with a file manager, consider getting another one. The one I recommend is ASTRO, which does a lot more than get you dirty from exploring the bowels of your tablet's storage system.

For example, as a bonus, ASTRO can also be used to access files on your Wi-Fi network. It takes some configuration, which isn't the easiest thing, but after this feature is set up, you can use the app to access your computer over your Wi-Fi network.

Dropbox

One solid way to share files between your computer, laptop, and tablet is to use the file sharing and synchronizing utility Dropbox. You need to obtain an account at www.dropbox.com. Then install the Dropbox software on your computer to share files there. Finally, get the Dropbox app for your Android tablet to access and view those shared files.

With Dropbox, there's no need to synchronize files between your computer and your tablet. Any files stored in the Dropbox folders are synchronized automatically.

ESPN SportsCenter

I admit to not being a sports nut, so it's difficult for me to identify with the craving to have the latest scores, news, and schedules. Yet when I think of sports, I think of ESPN. Therefore, my recommendation for sports nuts is to obtain the ESPN SportsCenter app. It offers the latest in sports updates and helps you set up an account to better follow your favorite teams and athletes.

Fast Notepad

One program that most Android tablets are missing out of the box is a notepad. A good choice for an app to fill that void is Fast Notepad. Use it to type or dictate short messages and memos, which I find handy.

As an example, before a recent visit to the hardware store, I made (dictated) a list of items I needed by using Fast Notepad. I also keep some important items as notes — things that I often forget or don't care to remember, such as frequent flyer numbers, my dress shirt and suit size (like I ever need that info), and other important notes I might need handy but not cluttering my brain.

Google Finance

The Google Finance app is an excellent market-tracking tool for folks who are obsessed with the stock market or who want to keep an eye on their portfolios. The app offers you an overview of the market and updates to your stocks as well as links to financial news.

To get the most from this app, configure Google Finance on the web, using a computer. You can create a list of stocks to watch, which is then instantly synchronized with your Android tablet. You can visit Google Finance on the web at www.google.com/finance.

As with other Google services, Google Finance is provided to you for free, as part of your Google account.

Movies by Flixster

The Movies by Flixster app is your tablet's gateway to Hollywood. It lists currently running films and films that are opening, and it has links to your local theaters with showtimes and other information. The app is also tied into the popular Rotten Tomatoes website for reviews and feedback. If you enjoy going to the movies, you'll find the Movies app a valuable addition to your tablet's app library.

Sky Map

Ever look up into the night sky and say, "What the heck is that?" Unless it's a bird, an airplane, a satellite, or a UFO, the Sky Map can help you find what it is. You may discover that a particularly bright star in the sky is, in fact, the planet Jupiter.

The Sky Map app is elegant. It basically turns the tablet into a window you can look through to identify things in the night sky. Just start the app and point your Android tablet up to the sky. Pan the tablet to identify planets, stars, and constellations.

Sky Map promotes using the tablet without touching it. For this reason, the screen goes blank after a spell, which is merely the tablet's power-saving mode. If you plan extensive stargazing with the Sky Map, consider resetting the screen timeout. Refer to Chapter 19.

TuneIn Radio

I know I mention this app over in Chapter 13 also, but I really do recommend it. One of my favorite ways that my Android tablet entertains me is as a little radio I keep by my workstation. I use the TuneIn Radio app to find a favorite Internet radio station, and then I sit back and work.

While TuneIn Radio is playing, you can do other things with your tablet, such as check Facebook or answer e-mail. You can return to the TuneIn Radio app by choosing the triangle notification icon. Or just keep it going and enjoy the tunes.

Voice Recorder

All Android tablets can record your voice and other sounds, but few tablets come with a sound recording app. That's why I recommend Voice Recorder. It's a good, basic app for performing this task.

Voice Recorder features an elegant and simple interface: Touch the big Record icon to start recording. Make a note for yourself, or record a friend doing his Daffy Duck impression.

Previous recordings are stored in a list on the Voice Recorder's main screen. Each recording is shown with its title, the date and time of the recording, and the recording duration.

Zedge

The Zedge program is a helpful resource for finding wallpapers and ringtones — millions of them. It's a sharing app, so you can access wallpapers and ringtones created by other Android users as well as share your own. If you're looking for a specific sound or something special for Home screen wallpaper, Zedge is the best place to start your search.

Index

• H •

About the Author

Dan Gookin has been writing about technology for over 25 years. He combines his love of writing with his gizmo fascination to create books that are informative, entertaining, and not boring. Having written over 130 titles with 12 million copies in print translated into over 30 languages, Dan can attest that his method of crafting computer tomes seems to work.

Perhaps his most famous title is the original *DOS For Dummies,* published in 1991. It became the world's fastest-selling computer book, at one time moving more copies per week than the *New York Times* number-one bestseller (though, as a reference, it could not be listed on the *Times'* Best Sellers list). That book spawned the entire line of *For Dummies* books, which remains a publishing phenomenon to this day.

Dan's most popular titles include *PCs For Dummies, Word For Dummies, Laptops For Dummies*, and *Android Phones For Dummies.* He also maintains the vast and helpful website www.wambooli.com.

Dan holds a degree in Communications/Visual Arts from the University of California, San Diego. He lives in the Pacific Northwest, where he enjoys spending time with his sons playing video games indoors while they enjoy the gentle woods of Idaho.

Publisher's Acknowledgments

Acquisitions Editor: Katie Mohr

Senior Project Editor: Mark Enochs

Copy Editor: Rebecca Whitney

Editorial Assistant: Annie Sullivan

Sr. Editorial Assistant: Cherie Case

Project Coordinator: Sheree Montgomery

Cover Image: iStockphoto.com/Kirillm

Apple & Mac

iPad For Dummies,
5th Edition
978-1-118-72306-7

iPhone For Dummies,
7th Edition
978-1-118-69083-3

Macs All-in-One
For Dummies, 4th Edition
978-1-118-82210-4

OS X Mavericks
For Dummies
978-1-118-69188-5

Blogging & Social Media

Facebook For Dummies,
5th Edition
978-1-118-63312-0

Social Media Engagement
For Dummies
978-1-118-53019-1

WordPress For Dummies,
6th Edition
978-1-118-79161-5

Business

Stock Investing
For Dummies, 4th Edition
978-1-118-37678-2

Investing For Dummies,
6th Edition
978-0-470-90545-6

Personal Finance
For Dummies, 7th Edition
978-1-118-11785-9

QuickBooks 2014
For Dummies
978-1-118-72005-9

Small Business Marketing
Kit For Dummies,
3rd Edition
978-1-118-31183-7

Careers

Job Interviews
For Dummies, 4th Edition
978-1-118-11290-8

Job Searching with Social
Media For Dummies,
2nd Edition
978-1-118-67856-5

Personal Branding
For Dummies
978-1-118-11792-7

Resumes For Dummies,
6th Edition
978-0-470-87361-8

Starting an Etsy Business
For Dummies, 2nd Edition
978-1-118-59024-9

Diet & Nutrition

Belly Fat Diet For Dummies
978-1-118-34585-6

Mediterranean Diet
For Dummies
978-1-118-71525-3

Nutrition For Dummies,
5th Edition
978-0-470-93231-5

Digital Photography

Digital SLR Photography
All-in-One For Dummies,
2nd Edition
978-1-118-59082-9

Digital SLR Video &
Filmmaking For Dummies
978-1-118-36598-4

Photoshop Elements 12
For Dummies
978-1-118-72714-0

Gardening

Herb Gardening
For Dummies, 2nd Edition
978-0-470-61778-6

Gardening with Free-Range
Chickens For Dummies
978-1-118-54754-0

Health

Boosting Your Immunity
For Dummies
978-1-118-40200-9

Diabetes For Dummies,
4th Edition
978-1-118-29447-5

Living Paleo For Dummies
978-1-118-29405-5

Big Data

Big Data For Dummies
978-1-118-50422-2

Data Visualization
For Dummies
978-1-118-50289-1

Hadoop For Dummies
978-1-118-60755-8

Language &
Foreign Language

500 Spanish Verbs
For Dummies
978-1-118-02382-2

English Grammar
For Dummies, 2nd Edition
978-0-470-54664-2

French All-in-One
For Dummies
978-1-118-22815-9

German Essentials
For Dummies
978-1-118-18422-6

Italian For Dummies,
2nd Edition
978-1-118-00465-4

Available in print and e-book formats.

Available wherever books are sold. **For more information or to order direct visit www.dummies.com**

Math & Science

Algebra I For Dummies,
2nd Edition
978-0-470-55964-2

Anatomy and Physiology
For Dummies, 2nd Edition
978-0-470-92326-9

Astronomy For Dummies,
3rd Edition
978-1-118-37697-3

Biology For Dummies,
2nd Edition
978-0-470-59875-7

Chemistry For Dummies,
2nd Edition
978-1-118-00730-3

1001 Algebra II Practice
Problems For Dummies
978-1-118-44662-1

Microsoft Office

Excel 2013 For Dummies
978-1-118-51012-4

Office 2013 All-in-One
For Dummies
978-1-118-51636-2

PowerPoint 2013
For Dummies
978-1-118-50253-2

Word 2013 For Dummies
978-1-118-49123-2

Music

Blues Harmonica
For Dummies
978-1-118-25269-7

Guitar For Dummies,
3rd Edition
978-1-118-11554-1

iPod & iTunes
For Dummies, 10th Edition
978-1-118-50864-0

Programming

Beginning Programming
with C For Dummies
978-1-118-73763-7

Excel VBA Programming
For Dummies, 3rd Edition
978-1-118-49037-2

Java For Dummies,
6th Edition
978-1-118-40780-6

Religion & Inspiration

The Bible For Dummies
978-0-7645-5296-0

Buddhism For Dummies,
2nd Edition
978-1-118-02379-2

Catholicism For Dummies,
2nd Edition
978-1-118-07778-8

Self-Help & Relationships

Beating Sugar Addiction
For Dummies
978-1-118-54645-1

Meditation For Dummies,
3rd Edition
978-1-118-29144-3

Seniors

Laptops For Seniors
For Dummies, 3rd Edition
978-1-118-71105-7

Computers For Seniors
For Dummies, 3rd Edition
978-1-118-11553-4

iPad For Seniors
For Dummies, 6th Edition
978-1-118-72826-0

Social Security
For Dummies
978-1-118-20573-0

Smartphones & Tablets

Android Phones
For Dummies, 2nd Edition
978-1-118-72030-1

Nexus Tablets
For Dummies
978-1-118-77243-0

Samsung Galaxy S 4
For Dummies
978-1-118-64222-1

Samsung Galaxy Tabs
For Dummies
978-1-118-77294-2

Test Prep

ACT For Dummies,
5th Edition
978-1-118-01259-8

ASVAB For Dummies,
3rd Edition
978-0-470-63760-9

GRE For Dummies,
7th Edition
978-0-470-88921-3

Officer Candidate Tests
For Dummies
978-0-470-59876-4

Physician's Assistant Exam
For Dummies
978-1-118-11556-5

Series 7 Exam For Dummie
978-0-470-09932-2

Windows 8

Windows 8.1 All-in-One
For Dummies
978-1-118-82087-2

Windows 8.1 For Dummies
978-1-118-82121-3

Windows 8.1 For Dummies
Book + DVD Bundle
978-1-118-82107-7

 **Available in print and e-book formats.**

Take Dummies with you everywhere you go!

Whether you are excited about e-books, want more from the web, must have your mobile apps, or are swept up in social media, Dummies makes everything easier.

Leverage the Power

For Dummies is the global leader in the reference category and one of the most trusted and highly regarded brands in the world. No longer just focused on books, customers now have access to the For Dummies content they need in the format they want. Let us help you develop a solution that will fit your brand and help you connect with your customers.

Advertising & Sponsorships

Connect with an engaged audience on a powerful multimedia site, and position your message alongside expert how-to content.

Targeted ads • Video • Email marketing • Microsites • Sweepstakes sponsorship

21 Million Monthly Page Views & 13 Million Unique Visitors

# of For Dummies

Custom Publishing

Reach a global audience in any language by creating a solution that will
differentiate you from competitors, amplify your message,
and encourage customers to make a buying decision.

Apps • Books • eBooks • Video • Audio • Webinars

Brand Licensing & Content

Leverage the strength of the world's most popular reference brand to reach
new audiences and channels of distribution.

For more information, visit www.Dummies.com/biz

Dummies products make life easier!

- DIY
- Consumer Electronics
- Crafts
- Software
- Cookware
- Hobbies
- Videos
- Music
- Games
- and More!

For more information, go to **Dummies.com** and search the store by category.

FOR
DUMMIES

A Wiley Brar